BEING VULNERABLE

OUTSPOKEN

Series editor: Adrian Parr and Santiago Zabala

Pointed, engaging, and unafraid of controversy, books in this series articulate the intellectual stakes of pressing cultural, social, environmental, economic, and political issues that unsettle today's world. Outspoken books are disruptive: they shake things up, change how we think, and make a difference. The Outspoken series seeks above all originality of perspective, approach, and thought. It encourages the identification of novel and unexpected topics or new and transformative approaches to inescapable questions, whether written from within established disciplines or from viewpoints beyond disciplinary boundaries. Each book brings theoretical inquiry into a reciprocally revealing encounter with material realities and lived experience. This series tackles the complex challenges faced by societies the world over, rethinking politics, justice, and social change in the twenty-first century.

Being Vulnerable
Contemporary Political Thought
Arne De Boever

Ecoliberation
Reimagining Resistance and the Green Scare
Jennifer D. Grubbs

Revolutionary Routines
The Habits of Social Transformation
Carolyn Pedwell

Wish I Were Here
Boredom and the Interface
Mark Kingwell

Being Vulnerable

Contemporary Political Thought

ARNE DE BOEVER

McGill-Queen's University Press
Montreal & Kingston · London · Chicago

© McGill-Queen's University Press 2023

ISBN 978-0-2280-1627-4 (cloth)
ISBN 978-0-2280-1628-1 (paper)
ISBN 978-0-2280-1629-8 (ePDF)
ISBN 978-0-2280-1630-4 (ePUB)

Legal deposit first quarter 2023
Bibliothèque nationale du Québec

Printed in Canada on acid-free paper that is 100% ancient forest free (100% post-consumer recycled), processed chlorine free

We acknowledge the support of the Canada Council for the Arts.

Nous remercions le Conseil des arts du Canada de son soutien.

Library and Archives Canada Cataloguing in Publication

Title: Being vulnerable: contemporary political thought / Arne de Boever.

Names: De Boever, Arne, author.

Series: Outspoken (McGill-Queen's University Press)

Description: Series statement: Outspoken | Includes bibliographical references and index.

Identifiers: Canadiana (print) 20220420823 | Canadiana (ebook) 20220420858 | ISBN 9780228016274 (cloth) | ISBN 9780228016281 (paper) | ISBN 9780228016298 (ePDF) | ISBN 9780228016304 (ePUB)

Subjects: LCSH: Sovereignty—Political aspects.

Classification: LCC JC327 .D4 2023 | DDC 320.1/5—dc23

This book was typeset by Marquis Interscript in 10.5/13 Sabon.

To my pandemic friends – B, P, and J.

… since the same nations that insist upon their impermeability (and here the United States is foremost on my mind) are those that wage war in the name of defending against their own vulnerability. So they "know" that they are constituted by vulnerability, but think that they have the power to instate a radical invulnerability. It is this logic that any struggle against precarity must seek to undo.

Judith Butler, in conversation with Athena Athanasiou

That which does not kill us makes us more vulnerable.

Contents

Acknowledgments xi

A Backward Foreword xiii

PART ONE A CRITIQUE OF SOVEREIGNTY

1 Carl Schmitt Ups the Ante 3

2 Foucault with Schmitt 14

3 Giorgio Agamben's Civil War 28

4 Radical Benjamin 39

PART TWO FOUR PARADIGMS OF SOVEREIGNTY

5 The Camp 49

6 The Wall 65

7 The Police 75

8 The Drone 91

PART THREE SOVEREIGNTY AND VULNERABILITY

9 *Homo Vulnerabilis* 99

10 Democracy's Exceptions 112

11 Engage the Institution 130

12 Indigenous Sovereignties 147

Notes 163

Index 195

Acknowledgments

This book came about as a sequel to the work I present in *Plastic Sovereignties*, and it revisits and develops further issues that I approach there. It is based, roughly, on the "Contemporary Political Thought" graduate seminar that I taught in the MA Aesthetics and Politics Program at CalArts. I would like to include a special thanks to those students who took the seminar in fall 2017, when the first draft of this book was written. Claudia Grigg Edo, my spring 2018 research assistant, expertly dug up many of the secondary sources for this book. In 2019, I published a short polemic titled *Against Aesthetic Exceptionalism* (Minneapolis: University of Minnesota Press, 2019), which included the beginnings of the discussion of Schmitt that I pursue in chapter 1 and that influenced parts of chapter 10 as well. I submitted the manuscript to the press in fall 2020, where it was slowed down by Covid-19. One year later, when I received the reader reports, I had the opportunity to revisit the manuscript once more while teaching a course titled "Being Vulnerable" as a visiting professor in the Department of Comparative Literature at UCLA. I am grateful to Efraín Kristal and Michael Rothberg for the invitation. All final revisions were made in spring 2022.

This book owes much to the mentorship of Bruce Robbins. Stathis Gourgouris has had an anarchic hand in it as well. I owe a big thanks to Paul Bové and the editorial collective at *boundary 2* for supporting my writing, including a version of chapter 10 ("Art and Exceptionalism: A Critique," Rev. of Santiago Zabala, *Why Only Art Can Save Us: Aesthetics and the Absence of Emergency* [New York: Columbia University Press, 2017], *boundary 2* 45, no. 4 [2018]: 161–81). *Boundary 2 online* also ran a version of chapter 7 in a special issue edited by Ryan Bishop ("Futures of Sovereignty [Necropolitics in America]," *boundary 2 online* 5, no. 2 (2020), ed. Ryan Bishop, http://www.boundary2.org/2020/08/7529). Some parts of chapter 5 became part of an article on "Political Formalism" that is forthcoming in Spanish (translated by Martín Plot in a book edited by Juan José Martínez Olguín) and English (in a special issue of the journal *Distinktion* edited by Hannah Richter) at the time of writing. All of these materials appear here significantly revised.

At CalArts Martín Plot, Janet Sarbanes, Brian Evenson, Andrew Culp, Anthony McCann, and Ryan Jeffery have shaped some of my thoughts directly and indirectly – I always wish there were more time to talk. I am also grateful for my interactions with various speakers whom I have been able to invite to the MA Aesthetics and Politics Program at CalArts over the years, in particular Judith Butler, Bonnie Honig, Santiago Zabala, Martin Woessner, Sarah Brouillette, and Maggie Nelson. Finally, I am deeply grateful to two anonymous reviewers who read the entire manuscript and provided detailed comments on each chapter at a time when time was in short supply. It's increasingly rare to receive such generosity in our profession.

At home, Olivia Harrison brought her own work to bear on mine. Everybody knows she is the real scholar in our household.

The book is dedicated to my pandemic friends, B, P, and J – for the many heated conversations.

A Backward Foreword

Being Vulnerable's somewhat backward premise is that we live in a time when the political power called "sovereignty" is slowly but surely taking over again from what could be called "biopolitical liberalism" – a time when a concept of the political according to which one might die in the battle between friends and enemies is slowly but surely taking over from a concept of the political focused on reasoned debate that seeks to promote life.[1] To some in the West, this counterintuitive, history-in-reverse narrative may not be fully evident yet, but developments such as the frequency of terrorist attacks (in recent years not so much ISIS-related but motivated by ideologies of white supremacy), police violence against bodies of colour in the United States, or the death of protestors in the intensifying clashes between the left and the alt-right are all indicators of a sovereign reality that, outside of the West – or also within the West but outside of white, straight, male, and class privilege – is often quite simply the norm.

Such a premise invites one to reconsider the relation between sovereignty and biopolitics at some distance from how it has often been thought. If, supposedly following the work of Michel Foucault,[2] biopolitics is typically said to come after sovereignty as the power to make life (as opposed to the sovereign power to take it), my premise questions that chronology in view of how, today, sovereignty is eclipsing biopolitics. Other scholars – like Judith Butler, whose work in this context takes up an important role in this book – have already done this, most notably in relation to the terrorist attacks of 9/11 and the ways in which the US responded to them.[3] But, as Butler as well as others like Wendy Brown (another major interlocutor in what follows) have pointed out, the narrative in which biopolitics follows sovereignty – the so-called post-sovereignty thesis – may not have been Foucault's to begin with.[4]

xiv A Backward Foreword

Rather than insisting on the discontinuity between sovereignty and biopolitics, it may be necessary to consider their continuity – two positions that reflect divergent interpretations of Foucault's work on biopolitics, as Roberto Esposito has discussed.[5]

I suppose that if I had to make a sovereign decision on where *Being Vulnerable* comes down, it would be on the side of the continuity thesis (one may also call it a *monism*), but with an added emphasis – which I take from feminist scholars and scholars working in Black studies and Indigenous studies in particular – on sovereignty's take-over of biopolitics today. Let us consider these two forms of power as tendencies in a historically shifting relationship. The present is tending sovereign again. Politics is not just a matter of life but of life *and death*. I adopt this premise not so much in the wake of 9/11 and the return to a theological politics of sovereignty that it triggered, a phenomenon that is central to my earlier book *Plastic Sovereignties*.[6] Instead, I am now reconsidering the return to sovereignty some two decades into the twenty-first century, at a time when the 9/11 window has closed but the politics of sovereignty is still very much with us in the form of various new phenomena that I have already mentioned, ranging from clashes between the left and the alt-right to the ways in which nation-states have responded to the coronavirus pandemic. My question, however, is the following: After criticizing the return to sovereignty in the wake of 9/11, where does the left stand in relation to all of this today? Can a simple criticism of sovereignty still be the answer?

If the concept of *the political* that comes closest to the situation I have sketched out is that of "politics as war" (it is through this lens that I understand, for example, Bernard Harcourt's work on "the counterrevolution,"[7] or even Joshua Clover's theory of the riot,[8] even if it does not accept the language of sovereignty), it should be pointed out that, from another point of view – that of the subjects of capitalism – "death" was always a real consequence of the West's *economic* regime. The contemporary French writer Edouard Louis movingly documents this, including its close relation to sovereignty, in his book *Qui a tué mon père* (Who killed my father).[9] There, he records – following Ruth Wilson Gilmore's analyses of racism[10] – how life in the factory destroys his father's body in the context of the more general fact that to be born in the working class means to have a shorter life-expectancy than do those who are more privileged. Rather than tying this merely to economic conditions, however, Louis singles out the sovereign agents who, during his father's life-time, produced and worsened his situation: the French presidents Nicolas Sarkozy, François Hollande, and Emmanuel Macron – all of whom are mentioned by name in Louis's book.[11] This is part of Louis's pithy conclusion, excerpted on the back cover of the original French edition of his book, that the history of his father's body – and, by extension, if we trace this back to Gilmore, the history of black and brown bodies in the United States – "accuses" political history.[12] The overall takeaway is clear, whether from the perspective of class or race: *we have never been* biopolitical liberals. It has always been sovereignty and the politics of war throughout. As Louis puts it at the end of a long profile in the *New York Times Magazine*: "We forget it too often: Politics is a question of life and death."[13]

According to the more standard narrative, of course, biopolitical liberalism has overcome sovereignty, and the latter cannot provide the political lens needed to analyze our times. "The society of sovereignty," Byung-Chul Han writes in a sharp criticism of the work of the contemporary theorist of sovereignty Giorgio Agamben, "has long belonged to the past. Today, no one is politicized 'through an abandonment to an unconditional power of death.' There is no longer any exterior, no transcendence, no sovereignty of power to which one would be subjugated and exposed as an obedience-subject. Contemporary society is not a society of sovereignty. We now live in a society of achievement. The achievement-subject differs from the obedience-subject in that it is the *sovereign of itself*; as the entrepreneur of itself, it is *free*."[14] While the passage testifies to Han's perceptive analysis of the society of neoliberal achievement that he also presents elsewhere, for example in *The Burnout Society*, it also immediately strikes the reader as self-contradictory since it *both* claims sovereignty to be a thing of the past *and* turns the subject who is the sovereign of itself into the society of achievement's characteristic subject. Clearly, then, sovereignty is *not* a thing of the past.[15]

Moreover, while Han's description of the society of achievement and its subjects, who are the sovereigns of themselves, no doubt matches *some* people's experience – and perhaps all people's experience to a certain extent – it would be hard to argue that today, as Han puts it, "*no one*" is politicized through brute exposure to sovereign power. One need only consider the state of black lives in the US to see how narrow-minded Han's claim really is. Or just imagine Han proposing that sovereignty is a thing of the past to those who are exposed to drone violence.

Meanwhile, and in close relation to those examples of sovereign violence, sovereignty has reasserted itself in the West at the institutional level through political phenomena such as Brexit, the election of Donald J. Trump in the US, and the ongoing crisis in Spain regarding Catalonia's autonomy.

*

Being Vulnerable posits – and this is another reason it may seem backward – that, from a certain vantage point, some of the above developments have led or could lead to interesting changes: Trump's election, for example, triggered a repoliticization in the US in a time when neoliberalism's depoliticization of the country appeared to have been victorious. This has played itself out in various ways: within the electoral system, as increased support for Bernie Sanders, for example, and – after Sanders losing the democratic nomination for president – a push to radicalize presidential candidate (and, ultimately, president) Joe Biden's program; but also through a new civil rights movement and growing protests, both peaceful and violent. Given Europe's failing, it is not unthinkable – although, granted, highly doubtful – that the return to UK sovereignty would lead to a better political collectivity. At the very least, one needs to appreciate (in the sense of assess fully) the reluctance of so many to remain in the European Union. Finally, would the sovereignty of autonomous regions like Catalonia, for example, necessarily lead to bad politics? Couldn't this be part of the political path forward – with implications for Indigenous communities in the US and elsewhere, for example, or for the Israel/Palestine situation?

With the turn to sovereignty could come a revitalization of politics not only in the reactive sense (as a *reaction against* sovereignty, I mean) but also in what, after Esposito's work on biopolitics, one may call the "affirmative" sense (a popular, democratic *claim to* sovereignty). Indeed, one way to read this book is as a proposal for an affirmative politics of sovereignty on the left. With respect to the latter, however, there is one thing on which we ought to be able to agree: when it comes to that old power called sovereignty, and all of its by now well-known problems, it seems especially important to ask: Where is such a repoliticization going to go? How can the claim to sovereignty today not simply repeat all of sovereignty's old problems? If sovereignty is no longer withering, then whither sovereignty?

A Backward Foreword   xvii

It is as part of an attempt to answer these questions that vulnerability plays a central role in this book, as a concept that allows us both to mediate between sovereignty and biopolitics and to intervene in their relation. More precisely, in what follows vulnerability becomes the condition for the affirmative politics of sovereignty that I intend to lay out. As a condition that mediates not only between sovereignty and biopolitics, but between life and death itself, making it impossible to decide whether it falls on the side of life (and here it's worth noting, as artists ranging from Stephen Crane to J.G. Ballard and Francis Bacon to Paul McCarthy have shown, that a wound may at times make a body appear excessively alive) or death (the state of being wounded opens up a zone of undecidability between life and death, in which the very passageway between the two is being negotiated), vulnerability is a non-sovereign notion, more precisely it is a marker of death that is destabilized by the continued presence of life, or a marker of life that is destabilized by the potential presence of death. Sovereignty is typically motivated by guarding against such undecidability, in this particular case by warding off vulnerability and instating a radical invulnerability – even if it knows, as Judith Butler notes in a conversation with Athena Athanasiou from which I take the leading quotation for this book, that it is constituted by a vulnerability that then, due to the phantasm of invulnerability, will always inevitably come back to haunt it. *Life* for the *sovereign*; *death* – or in some contemporary variants also strategically inflicted injury (as Jasbir Puar's work has shown[16]) – to its *enemies*.

What if vulnerability were instead assumed as the foundation of sovereignty itself, in order to rid ourselves of invulnerability's phantasm, and construe another kind of political togetherness, even across friend/enemy lines, that is no less effective in or responsible for its actions? Might this also be, like other models of collectivity, a way of rethinking the individual starting from their vulnerability, outside of the phantasm of invulnerability, as the subject of a political anthropology that would start from the wound? *Who comes after the sovereign?* To answer this question, I start here from the vulnerable human being, *homo vulnerabilis*, not as a reality from which we need to be saved but as a touchstone.

I readily grant from the outset that one does not need to stay within the limits of sovereignty to discuss political possibilities today. Many would probably place contemporary political possibilities entirely elsewhere. This is certainly so at the level of terminology, where "sovereignty" has become a kind of boogeyman. In his important book *The Revenge of the Real: Politics for a Post-Pandemic World*, Benjamin Bratton criticizes the contemporary return to "sovereignty," a notion that he takes to refer to the theologico-political power of the king.[17] He *also* criticizes, however – and this is what makes him much more interesting than many other thinkers out there – negative biopolitics: the tendency in critical theory – which dubiously claims inspiration from Foucault – to reject everything biopolitical as "bad." Proposing instead a positive biopolitics that would practise a care for the population, Bratton embraces throughout his book what he calls "governance" – a governance that would take care of the people. Bratton argues that the pandemic has made clear the need for such governance, showing the rejection of biopolitics as well as the recourse to theologico-political sovereignty (rather than a positive biopolitics) to be ill-guided. (Giorgio Agamben, who plays a key role in this book, becomes Bratton's number one target on this count.)

At the level of terminology, Bratton and I thus seem to part ways: *he* rejects sovereignty to embrace a positive biopolitics, while *I* emphasize sovereignty's takeover from biopolitics and seek to lay out an affirmative politics of a sovereignty on the left. In my insistence, however, that this latter sovereignty would be *different* from the theologico-political power of the king, I come closer to Bratton again; sovereignty, after all, does not *only* refer to the theologico-political power of the king – that would imply that the history of sovereignty never moved beyond the French Revolution. And indeed, in Bratton's embrace of governance, there are many elements that surely can be associated with sovereignty: his provocative recuperation of "surveillance," for example, as an important practice of positive biopolitics that, in the case of the pandemic, for example, contributes to good governance;[18] his sharp criticisms of the "*further dismantling* of governance," "the imaginary escape from the state," and "anarchism"[19] – to name just a few of his targets. These are projects that, from my point of view, all fall under the header of construing an alternative sovereignty from the point of view of vulnerability; for Bratton, they come together in what he calls, with reference to his other work, "the biopolitical stack."[20]

In short, what Bratton refers to as governance, I see as the continued project of an alternative sovereignty today. "One of the things that the pandemic has revealed," Bratton writes, "is that the absence of control, authority, and competency in the West is very real and dangerous. Post-pandemic politics must revive its legitimacy, capacity,

A Backward Foreword

and effectiveness." I couldn't agree more, even if I think most of the nouns here – "authority," "competency," "legitimacy," "effectiveness,"[21] to be sure – are typically associated with "sovereignty" rather than with "biopolitics." This becomes perhaps most clear when Bratton positively discusses biopolitics' need to "see like a state" (a formulation he borrows from James C. Scott).[22] Can one really still avoid the term "sovereignty" at this point?

Bratton's focus on biopolitics rather than sovereignty is due not only to his narrow understanding of sovereignty (as the theologico-political power of the king only) but also to his focus on the pandemic. This becomes especially clear in the chapter titled "The Social Explosion," from which I quoted above: it's where Bratton seeks to expand his argument from the frame of Covid-19 to the demonstrations against the murder of George Floyd. One can read those demonstrations biopolitically of course, as sites where bodies risked intermingling again for the cause of social justice; however, ultimately the conversation they raise about social justice is not a biopolitical but a sovereign one, involving notions like "rights," "the law," "the people," and other concepts that are key to the (granted, biopolitical) history of the nation-state. I agree with Bratton that one should try to expand the frame and consider how an argument about the pandemic should be able to speak to "The Social Explosion" at the end of the summer of 2020 as well. And it is precisely for that reason that I think we need to mediate between sovereignty and biopolitics, to pursue both forms of power at the same time, in close relation to each other. My hypothesis is that the notion of vulnerability, which also appears in Bratton's book but is not developed as a concept, is crucial to such a project.

Much contemporary political theory has of course taken the path of the multitude (rather than of the people, which is associated with sovereignty) and proposed a politics of horizontalism (e.g., of the OccupyMovement or BlackLivesMatter) over and against the politics of verticality that is usually associated with sovereignty. While such theories have tended to emphasize, for example, structurelessness as a strategy, some of its leading voices have also come to realize the importance of working out strategies of assemblage if the goal of horizontal movements is to be politically effective.[23] (The difference between BlackLivesMatter politics and Black Panther Party politics can be instructive on this count.)[24] I read those realizations as reinsertions of a wizened verticality into a contemporary political practice that had, perhaps, swung too much in the direction of horizontalism.

Political inefficiency was hardly the only risk associated with that swing. Some have pointed out its resonances with the "flat" world of neo-liberalism, which,[25] while it may be populated by an elite of plutocratic, petty sovereigns, nevertheless rings the death knell – clang! – of popular sovereignty and the verticality of sovereignty at large.

My proposal for an affirmative politics of sovereignty takes into account that the history of sovereignty includes the modern, revolutionary shift from the sovereignty of the monarch to the sovereignty of the people – a horizontalizing but necessary, critical move that some conservative theorists of sovereignty find unbearable. Nevertheless, by still calling itself "sovereign," that popular, democratic power claimed for itself the highest authority when it came to taking a decision for the common good. It is that authority, and that collective power to take a decision, that in the overemphasis on horizontalism risks being lost.

Being Vulnerable thus holds on to the notion of sovereignty in view of its contemporary return, but I seek to rethink it from the point of view of vulnerability, a word that the Trump administration notably banned for officials of the Center of Disease Control and Prevention.[26] Whereas traditional theories of sovereignty define themselves against vulnerability, in the sense that sovereignty proposes to save those living under it from their capacity to be wounded, and, in turn, asks those whom it protects to protect it in a time of attack, *Being Vulnerable* pursues a sovereignty that would define itself as vulnerable and exercise its "power" – though the very notion of power would need to be rethought here – from that position. The goal is to get out of a political (but not just political) dynamic within which precarization can only be fought through fortification – through a phantasmatic *rendering-invulnerable*. My main allies for such a pursuit are contemporary scholars of sovereignty such as the political philosopher Bonnie Honig and the already mentioned Judith Butler and Wendy Brown, each of whom has mobilized the notions of sovereignty and vulnerability in their work – for example, to theorize contemporary political phenomena such as the OccupyMovement or BlackLivesMatter. Brown started her career with a book on injury; Honig writes very critically about a politics of vulnerability and arguably develops her notion of "counter-sovereignty" in response to such a politics; in Butler's work on public assemblies, theories of popular sovereignty and vulnerability merge to think new modes of political organization today. There is other work that can productively be brought into conversation with these

A Backward Foreword

positions: Chantal Mouffe's writings on hegemony and counter-hegemony, for example, and more recently on left populism, which is in dialogue with Honig's thought; Isabell Lorey's *State of Insecurity*, which takes the path of the multitude rather than the people but comes with a foreword by Butler; or Grégoire Chamayou's *Theory of the Drone*, which finds in what Chamayou calls "political vulnerabilization" (rather than our "ontological vulnerability") a possibility for the critical disidentification from sovereignty – a criticality that the drone, by making us forget about our vulnerability, arguably undoes. I discuss all of those thinkers in part 3 of this book, which starts from the anthropological notion of a *homo vulnerabilis*, a "vulnerable human," to lay out a new politics of sovereignty that would not operate within a phantasy of invulnerability (a phantasy that others have shown to be masculinist/sexist, white/racist, ablist, and overly technicized). One site of contemporary contestation where such a new politics of sovereignty becomes visible is in Indigenous politics, which I discuss in the final chapter. As a whole, part 3 shows how vulnerability is becoming the condition to rethink sovereignty today as an emancipatory notion for a left that seeks to be politically effective.

Such a take on sovereignty can of course not be developed naively, and in part 2 I provide a detailed analysis of what one might characterize as four "paradigms" of contemporary sovereign power that, while historical formations, all become particularly prominent after 9/11 and mark the return of theologico-political sovereignty à la Carl Schmitt (which I analyze elsewhere[27]): the camp, the wall, the police (I focus on the contemporary situation of black lives in the US), and the drone. Anticipating the final, affirmative part of the book, I work with theories by Chamayou, Brown, and Butler (among others) to consider some of sovereignty's most destructive realizations and operations – negativities, if you will, from which surely we would have to learn if we want to maintain a concept of sovereignty for the future. If Butler develops their analysis of the camp initially in *Precarious Life* in a discussion of the Guantánamo Bay detention centre, they recently return to it (and in particular to the notion of "indefinite detention") to discuss the refugee crisis in the Mediterranean, and it seems that the consideration of the law's role in such sovereign situations remains of the utmost importance today, more than a decade after 9/11. In view of ongoing discussions about, for example, the US/Mexico wall today, I also consider the wall (and, more broadly, fortification) as a key technology of sovereignty and analyze both its building and destruction – both the striation and smoothening of space, in the terms proposed by Gilles Deleuze and Félix Guattari – as part of how sovereign power is wielded. I tie Wendy Brown's critical analysis of the sovereign politics of the wall to Eyal Weizman's work on walls in forensic architecture and suggest, following recent scholarship by Guillaume Sibertin-Blanc, that Schmitt is a major interlocutor in Deleuze and Guattari's thinking about striated space and smooth space. This enables me to reassess the sovereign politics of the wall – both the building of walls and their destruction – today.

Part 2 also analyzes the situation of black life in the US through the lens of contemporary theories of sovereignty developed in Black studies. Reading together works by Ta-Nehisi Coates, Achille Mbembe, and Frantz Fanon, I ask whether a future of sovereignty can still be possible for black life. This means, as I discuss in a chapter on the police, revisiting Fanon's project of national liberation, which still inspired the Black Panthers at the time of the Civil Rights movement, in a time when White Power appears to have made the "American Dream" its own (as Coates in his criticism of the so-called "Dreamers" lays out). Finally, I also turn to sovereignty's fully technicized realization in the drone to consider how it dismantles the critical potentiality that is rooted in our vulnerability. But is the rejection of sovereignty that Chamayou proposes in response to this really the solution? Doesn't such a rejection risk throwing out the baby with the bathwater, as the expression goes?

My discussions of drones, the police, walls, and the camp in part 2, as well as of left-liberal takes on popular sovereignty in part 3, are framed through a constellation of references that I engage with in detail in part 1. There, I start with the work of Carl Schmitt, which has been used by some on the left (e.g., Chantal Mouffe; but one also finds echoes of this – in some cases arriving via Mouffe – in general audience books such as Rachel Greenwald Smith's *On Compromise*,[28] which uses Schmitt as part of a questioning of liberal compromise) to embrace the shift from biopolitical liberalism to sovereignty today (Mouffe argues in this situation for a political liberalism, a liberalism that would be politicized through sovereignty). I explore Schmitt's work and some of the problems it raises in part through its connections to Walter Benjamin (in particular, Benjamin's difficult essay on violence) and Giorgio Agamben's rarely discussed work on stasis or civil war. More surprisingly, perhaps, I also uncover echoes of Schmitt in Foucault and ask how these are to be squared with recent charges

A Backward Foreword · xxiii

regarding Foucault's "neoliberalism." While other theories of sovereignty could of course be engaged here, I turn to what, for some readers perhaps, is the hackneyed Benjamin-Schmitt-Foucault-Agamben constellation because it perfectly sets up the analyses provided in part 2 and because these references are needed to appreciate the approaches in vulnerability studies discussed in part 3. In other words, if I narrate the book's trajectory in reverse, as a "Backward Foreword," this is also because the choices made about the materials it covers early on were largely determined by the place where I wanted the book to arrive: *a critique of sovereignty from the point of view of vulnerability*.

While *Being Vulnerable* can be characterized as a short work of political theory for our time, I would more specifically present it as an intervention in vulnerability studies that (following some other major approaches in the field) seeks to bring contemporary discussions of sovereignty and vulnerability together. In a time when "post-critique" is all the rage, *Being Vulnerable* explicitly presents itself as a critique, which is a methodological and political choice that is closely related to the materials I cover. I am thinking of Benjamin's "Critique of Violence" essay, for example, or of Mbembe's *Critique of Black Reason*, which is a key resource in part 2. As I explain in the book, a critique in the Kantian sense seeks to distinguish between legitimate and illegitimate uses of reason. If Benjamin calls his project a critique, it is because he covers in his essay (in Max Weber's tracks) the differences between legitimate and illegitimate uses of violence. But Benjamin also does more in the essay, which is why in the original German it is not called "Critique of Violence" but "*On* the Critique of Violence" ("Zur Kritik der Gewalt"): at the very end of the essay Benjamin proposes the notion of "divine violence," which turns what one might want to call the "negative" part of critique (the fact that it always takes place *within* limits) into a "positive" transgression (a going *beyond* limits).

As I show, "sovereignty" is haunted by such a beyond, particularly in the exceptionalist articulation it receives in Schmitt. But much of its trouble also comes from there. If my critique considers sovereignty's beyond, its transgressive dimension, it is ultimately more interested in staying within – partly because I think the left has been too quick to reject sovereignty and partly because, from a political point of view, it is my position that sovereignty needs immanent, popular, democratic critique if we do not want it to be fully appropriated by the right.

While *Being Vulnerable* thus seeks to be a scholarly intervention in debates about sovereignty and vulnerability, it also seeks to provide –

for a general audience – not just an analysis of the political present but a proposal on how to live one's life within it. This is the affirmative part of the book's project, which I sometimes think of in manifesto-like terms. Today, it seems particularly important for the theoretical political left to put forward proposals that would counter those proposals coming from the right. Along the way, I also consider the more radical approach of stopping to participate in such countering altogether – of "look[ing] for something else,"[29] to echo Frantz Fanon, whose work takes on an important role in part 2. The subjects of biopolitical liberalism are exhausted. Sovereignty is repoliticizing them. But what sovereignty? If the left no longer seeks to participate in that conversation – if it doesn't critically take hold of what one may call the *resurgent politics of sovereignty* today – it may be doomed.

PART ONE

A Critique of Sovereignty

I

Carl Schmitt Ups the Ante

Let me return to the seemingly backward historical and political claim with which I started – a claim that reconsiders, as I have discussed, the relation between sovereignty and biopolitics – namely, that we live in a time when the "society of sovereignty" (to critically borrow Byung-Chul Han's terminology) is back. In the aftermath of 9/11, the work of the German conservative legal and political scholar Carl Schmitt was frequently used to back up this claim. But I return to Schmitt two decades into the twenty-first century to consider his work in light of what one might refer to as the century's ongoing crisis of vulnerability. As was the case after 9/11, Schmitt's centrality to the analysis presented here is not without controversy given his affiliation with Nazism (Hannah Arendt called him a "convinced Nazi").[1] Nevertheless, some scholars on the left have reconsidered Schmitt's theory and the criticism of liberalism from which it stems to repoliticize, or some might say "redemocratize," liberalism in view of the consensus democracy and apolitical relativism (not to say neoliberal opportunism – and I get to neoliberalism in the next chapter) that is left of it. Schmitt has thus unexpectedly proven to be an interesting force for the rethinking of democratic power in our time.

In the first part of *Being Vulnerable* I want to try to understand this phenomenon. My goal is, on the one hand, to show how Schmitt's position can, without too much trouble, be found in the work of other contemporary theorists of the political where one might least expect it: I demonstrate in particular that Michel Foucault's theory of the political carries a largely unacknowledged debt to Schmitt that may ask us to reconsider the gist of Schmitt's work. I present this reading of Foucault partly in view of the by now established left-liberal take on Schmitt that political theorists like Chantal Mouffe have pushed in their democratic thought. However, by mapping the stark differences between Schmitt's thought and that of one of Foucault's students, Giorgio Agamben, I ultimately seek to draw out the conservatism of Schmitt's thought in comparison to the more radical politics that can be found in Agamben and, more pertinently, in the work of Walter Benjamin, who is the linchpin in the debate between Schmitt and Agamben. Whereas Schmitt's exception is always folded back *within* the normative order, Benjamin instead considers an anomic force *outside of it*. It is no surprise that Benjamin's radicalism has proved more popular with the anti-sovereign political left, and, as such, it has been very effective. I also suggest, however, that today, after the 9/11 window has closed but amidst a continued resurgence of sovereignty, it may actually be Schmitt who is in fact more useful to a left that wants to be politically effective than the more radical politics of Benjamin. In view of Schmitt's dubious politics, this requires a reconsideration of Schmitt and the concept of sovereignty (both within his work and outside of it), something I begin here but intend to accomplish in particular in parts 2 and 3 through a focus on the concept of vulnerability.

To appreciate the recuperation of Schmitt's *Concept of the Political* by the liberal left, one must appreciate how it operates within a distinction between politics and the political that to many of us is lost. If politics, or what the French call "la politique," refers to "the play of forces and interests engaged in a conflict over the representation and governance of social existence" (as Christopher Fynsk in his "Foreword" to Jean-Luc Nancy's *The Inoperative Community* defines it[2]), "the political" (or "le politique") refers to "the site where what it means to *be* in common is open to definition."[3]

How does Schmitt conceptualize this site? One can only do so, he proposes, "by discovering and defining specifically political categories."[4] In the case of the political, that category is the distinction "between friend and enemy."[5] Like a kind of land surveyor – let's remember that he is also the author of *The* Nomos *of the Earth*, which deals with the taking, distributing, and pasturing of land (and sea [he also considers air and even space!]) in international politics – Schmitt seeks to mark off the territory of the political from other territories such as the aesthetic (defined by the beautiful/ugly distinction), the moral (right/wrong or, in theological terms, good/evil), and the economic (profitable/unprofitable). While those other territories could become sites of tension – of aesthetic, moral, or economic conflict – they only become properly political in Schmitt's theory when they intensify into a friend/enemy conflict.

What is such a friend/enemy conflict? For this, Schmitt arguably connects to the text's beginning, where he dedicates his book to his friend who died on the battlefield – a dedication to which I return in part 3. The enemy, Schmitt explains, is not simply the other or the stranger; there is something "specially intense" about the enemy, in an "existential" way.[6] The enemy is a figure of "the most intense and extreme antagonism."[7] The figure "[receives its] real meaning precisely because [it refers] to the real possibility of physical killing" – "negation" in the "existential" sense.[8] Unsurprisingly, such a figure is most clearly revealed in a situation of war, which Schmitt defines as "the existential negation of the enemy" and "the most extreme consequence of enmity."[9] When conceptualizing the enemy, Schmitt thus has in mind not so much an individual as a group.[10] Importantly, he does not have in mind a private but, rather, a public enemy. This means that the biblical imperative to "love one's enemies" does not have sway in the political sphere: it refers, Schmitt takes care to explain, to the private enemy rather than the public one.[11] One can be a good Catholic and still go to war. He also mentions the possibility of the enemy being either an external or internal enemy; in the latter case, "war" becomes "civil."[12]

If the friend/enemy distinction, most explicit in war, is the distinguishing criterion for the political, then it is probably safe to say that many living in the West today have never been political subjects – not even in the potential sense in which Schmitt defines the enemy. Put differently, it is probably safe to say that many of us are subjects of what I have already called biopolitical liberalism rather than political subjects in Schmitt's sense. Politics, for us, is all about debate. We find dying for a political cause to be almost unthinkable. As I indicate, though, the state of biopolitical liberalism is on its way out in a sense that far exceeds the now closed conversation about 9/11: the politics of black lives in the United States, for example, is clearly not about liberalism, unless one accepts Domenico Losurdo's account of liberalism's "counter-history."[13] Black life's concept of the political is much closer to Schmitt's theory than to liberalism. Something similar may be true for the poor or the indebted, whose livelihoods are increasingly in danger because of their financial situation. They are slowly being killed by their poverty and debt. The question from a Schmittian point of view is when those tensions will intensify into a properly political conflict – that between friend and enemy, that of war. This will lead to a confrontation of one group with another: the 99 percent versus the 1 percent, for example, or the white supremacist and white separatist alt-right versus the BlackLivesMatter movement and its allies (which come, in part, from the class conflict in the US).

Schmitt's position is extreme but he sticks to it consistently throughout his book. It leads him to argue, for example, that "a world in which the possibility of war is utterly eliminated, a completely pacified globe, would be a world without the distinction of friend and enemy and hence a world without politics."[14] Pacificism only turns political, he suggests a little later on, when it goes to war. Only when Marxists are ready to go to war for the class struggle will Marxism turn political.

Another important argument is that it follows from Schmitt's position that "humanity as such cannot wage war."[15] Why not? Well, because it has no enemy – for everyone is human. A war for humanity is not possible – "at least not on this planet,"[16] Schmitt adds. Whoever evokes the concept of humanity to go to war "wants to cheat."[17] He warns that doing so can drive war "to the most extreme inhumanity."[18] In short, humanity is, for Schmitt, "not a political concept."[19]

When it comes to political institutions, however, such universalism – Schmitt's planetary universalism of the human – becomes a problem: he argues against an institution such as the United Nations (not Schmitt's term, of course – he speaks of the League of Nations) that would seek to bring all nation-states together in a single political unity. Such a unity, in Schmitt's view, cannot be political; such universality "would necessarily have to mean total depoliticalization."[20] The political universe, for Schmitt, is crucially a political "pluriverse,"[21] as he famously puts it, and he is careful to distinguish this "pluralism" from the easy "liberal" pluralism that he attacks earlier on in his book.[22]

Basically, Schmitt is construing here a concept of the political against the biopolitical liberalism of endless debate, which he despises. A good illustration of Schmitt's position, and of the battle of his concept of the political against liberalism, is a literary fable that Schmitt himself brings up – namely, Jean de la Fontaine's fable of "The Wolf and the Lamb." In this well-known fable, a lamb tries to dissuade a wolf from eating it as a midday snack. The lamb tries to do so through rational argument, by trying to counter the various reasons – none of which mentions the simple fact of hunger – that the wolf brings up to justify his taking of the lamb's life. Read as a political fable, as surely de la Fontaine's use of words like "majesty" and "sire" to refer to the wolf allow us to do,[23] one can suggest in the context of a reading of Schmitt that liberalism, in this fable, is the lamb. Schmitt, by contrast, lays out a concept of the political that can be identified more with the wolf. Read in this way, the fable would then tell us that, at the end of the day, liberalism will always lose out against wolf-like conceptualizations of the political. "So trial and judgment stood." One may think of this situation as deplorable – but that doesn't take away the fact that for many today, it quite simply *is* the political situation. They are being told to act as lambs (in other words, as subjects of biopolitical liberalism), but if, at the end of the day, the wolf is always victorious, why would they? Wouldn't they rather claim sovereignty instead?

To be clear, if de la Fontaine's fable perhaps evokes the state of nature more than the state of sovereignty, I do not mean to suggest by this that Schmitt's concept of the political is like the state of nature. I merely evoke the fable to evoke Schmitt's proximity to war (the wolf) rather than to reasoned debate (the lamb). However, if one reads Schmitt on war,[24] it is clear that "war" is *not* like the state of nature *at all* – that it is in fact very un-wolf-like, if the wolf is associated with the state of nature. Schmitt's interest in war is due precisely to the fact that it is carefully regulated, subject to all kinds of rules and determinations. When Schmitt brings up the fable, he in fact characterizes it as a fable of aggression, which presumably he condemns – even if we can also recognize a trace of his decisionist sovereignty in it. Sovereignty, certainly, is more aggressive than liberalism, even if it may not act exactly like de la Fontaine's wolf.

To some writing today, Schmitt's theorization of the political as structured by the friend/enemy distinction poses a welcome challenge to liberalism in the "'post-political' age."[25] Liberal-democratic consensus society erases "the antagonistic dimension" of politics,[26] which is Schmitt's focus. In the edited collection *The Challenge of Carl Schmitt*, for example, Chantal Mouffe takes on Schmitt, in spite of his dubious politics, for his concept of the political in order to elaborate "a truly 'political' liberalism" that would not strive for a rational, "final reconciliation."[27] Mouffe considers the latter to be impossible. "Democratic consensus can be envisaged only," she writes, "as a *conflictual consensus*."[28]

At the same time Mouffe adjusts Schmitt's thinking on important points, for instance, when it comes to his use of the term "enemy":

8   A Critique of Sovereignty

> Indeed, the category of the adversary is crucial to redefining
> liberal democracy in a way that does not negate the political in
> its antagonistic dimension. The adversary is in a certain sense an
> enemy, but a legitimate enemy with whom there exists a common
> ground. Adversaries fight against each other, but they do not put
> into question the legitimacy of their respective positions. They
> share a common allegiance to the ethico-political principles of
> liberal democracy. However, they disagree about their meanings
> and their forms of implementation, and such a disagreement
> is not one that could be resolved through rational argument.[29]

Schmitt's enemy, while still present, becomes an "adversary" in this passage, and clearly Schmitt's especially intense conceptualization of the enemy as the one whom one wants to existentially negate (the political is the sphere in which there always exists the real possibility of killing) has been rewritten here for the biopolitical liberal age. Schmitt's "antagonism" is even adjusted in Mouffe to "agonism," so that the pluralism of politics can be present among friends and does not need to be confined "outside democratic association," as Mouffe points out. In other words: Mouffe has plenty of issues with Schmitt, but she argues that liberal democrats nevertheless have much to learn from him if they do not want liberal democracy to disappear into post-politics.

While all of this is valuable within the limits of liberal democracy, it seems to me that Schmitt is also valuable beyond this, in the way I suggest in my foreword: *precisely as a theorist of the political as a sphere of war constituted by the possibility of real killing*. Mouffe wants to incorporate this into a repoliticized liberal democracy, but this move *does not recognize* the way in which Schmitt's focus on war – actual war – states something about our societies today, which are torn apart by terrorist attacks, police violence against black bodies, and the destruction of the climate (a point to which I return later). In other words, and contra Mouffe's softening of Schmitt: we *do* live in societies in which various enemies – including we ourselves in the Anthropocene – pose to us *the real possibility of killing*. This too needs to be acknowledged.[30] If we can perhaps still – though it takes more and more effort – forget about this in the West, such a forgetting is not possible outside of it, where sovereign violence is often the rule.

*

Concept of the Political is not the only text that scholars focus on when they try to demonstrate Schmitt's importance for the thinking of politics today. When it comes to deciding on whether the friend/enemy distinction is in play, Schmitt points out that no neutral third party can do this for you.[31] Only you can. Of course, Schmitt had already engaged this issue of the decision in his *Political Theology: Four Chapters on the Concept of Sovereignty*. In that book's first chapter, Schmitt declares in the stand-alone opening sentence that "sovereign is he who decides on the exception"[32] (in the German original, "Souverän ist, wer über den Ausnahmezustand entscheidet"[33]). The sentence reads like a sovereign decision itself. In it, Schmitt decides, as a sovereign author, who is sovereign. In English, the sentence is suspended between the words "sovereign" and "exception," which are the most relevant terms here. In German, the language is more precise (exception is "state of exception" in the original German) and the sentence is now suspended between "sovereign" and "decision," which foregrounds the decision rather than the state of exception. If we want to take from Schmitt's *Concept of the Political* a revitalization of politics in the era of biopolitical liberalism, we also have to confront the exceptionalist decisionism of his earlier work to see how we relate to it.

The project of Schmitt's chapter, of course, is to define sovereignty. Some would, no doubt, tend to look at the normal situation to do so: Who guarantees the rule of law? Surely, that is the sovereign. But Schmitt's answer is different. If one wants to find out in any given situation who is sovereign, one must find out who decides on the state of exception. This is why sovereignty is, in his view, a borderline concept: it can only be understood from the extreme limit (*"extremus necessitatis casus,"* an extreme case of necessity[34]). For Schmitt, the exception comes first ("the rule ... derives only from the exception"[35]); it "proves everything."[36] Understood in this way, the exception has something "vital" to it:[37] "In the exception," Schmitt writes with echoes of Nietzsche, "the power of real life breaks through the crust of a mechanism that has become torpid by repetition."[38] In order to understand what that mechanism is, one has to understand what happens in the state of exception.

The situation that the phrase "state of exception" refers to is very particular: it is a situation or state in which the law, through the figure of the sovereign, temporarily suspends itself in order to enable sovereign power to maintain order (and protect the law). This is not a situation of "anarchy and chaos,"[39] as Schmitt is careful to point out. It is not a situation in which the law is destroyed. Rather, we are talking about a constitutionally guaranteed temporary suspension of the Constitution ("according to article 48 of the German constitution of 1919"[40]), a situation in which the law recedes but order is maintained. One might want to call this "extraordinary order" in response to Schmitt's suggestion that it be distinguished from "ordinary order." The state of exception enables Schmitt to point to the phrase "legal order" to explain that, in a state of exception, the two terms that make up that phrase get forced apart, are "dissolved into independent notions," with the law receding to a minimum while order (absolute order, in this case) is maintained.[41] It is in such situations, Schmitt argues, that sovereign power is revealed. Schmitt does not tell us according to what criteria the sovereign decides on the state of exception. He does not have the audacity to lay this out – this can only be decided by the sovereign, based on the sovereign's "competency." What is certain, however, is that the state of exception is declared in the name of "public safety and order, *le salut public* [public well-being]."[42]

Schmitt argues that the decision on the state of exception has always been at the core of sovereignty. He finds it in Bodin, for example, in the sixteenth century, and while "the vivid awareness of the meaning of the exception" is maintained in the seventeenth century,[43] Schmitt notes that by the eighteenth it has gone missing: "the exception was something incommensurable to John Locke's doctrine of the constitutional state and the rationalist 18th century";[44] "emergency law was no law at all for Kant."[45] But, Schmitt argues, "it should be of interest to the rationalist that the legal system itself can anticipate the exception and can 'suspend itself'" – "from where does the law obtain this force, and how is it logically possible that a norm is valid except for one concrete case that it cannot factually determine in any definitive manner?"[46]

What Schmitt tells us, in 1922, is that the key activity of sovereign power is to decide on the temporary suspension of the law in the state of exception. To do so, sovereignty takes up a peculiar position inside/ outside of the law ("although [the sovereign] stands outside ... he nevertheless belongs"[47]). What makes sovereignty? The state of exception. What makes the state of exception? Sovereignty – or, more precisely, the sovereign possibility of the law's suspension – a kind of "violence"[48] – that becomes possible in highly specific cases that the law could not possibility anticipate (future situations, as Schmitt makes clear: "the precise details of an emergency cannot be anticipated"[49]). Thus, the exception makes the sovereign and the sovereign makes the exception.

Both *Concept of the Political* and the earlier *Political Theology* turned Schmitt into an important theorist for the post-9/11 era, which was characterized by various exceptional suspensions of the law in the name of a war on terror, in which the East was presented as the existential enemy of the West. Schmitt's work, and his association with Nazism, became identified here with the ways in which the US responded to the 9/11 attacks.

But *Concept of the Political* and *Political Theology* are hardly Schmitt's only books, and the post-9/11 take on Schmitt is hardly the only one that can be put forward. We need to continue rethinking Schmitt as the century moves forward. In his work, Andreas Kalyvas (to the dismay of some who would prefer Schmitt to be forgotten) draws attention to Schmitt as a democratic theorist and points out that the relation of Schmitt's work to democratic theory requires further investigation. Rather than seeing it as opposed to democratic theory, which many are inclined to do, Kalyvas, in an article titled "Carl Schmitt and the Three Moments of Democracy," proposes that Schmitt's work delivers "many interesting insights with important and pertinent implications for a democratic theory with a radical intent to come to the fore."[50] As Kalyvas sees it, one can distill from Schmitt's work "not only certain elements for the reconstruction of a substantive model of radical democracy, but also for a theory of democratic constitutionalism."[51]

Kalyvas's reading relies on chapter 18 of Schmitt's much less read *Constitutional Theory*, where Schmitt introduces "a penetrating description of the three different ways in which a people is related to its constitution: a people can be *prior to and above* the constitution, *within* the constitution, and, *next to* the constitution."[52] The first relation corresponds to democracy's "instituting moment"; the second to "the moment of normal, procedural, everyday institutionalized politics"; the third, finally, "denotes the intermediary moment of spontaneous forms of popular mobilization and informal direct participatory intervention that can exist side-by-side with the established democratic legal order."[53] By focusing on Schmitt's analysis of those three moments, Kalyvas aims to "challenge dominant interpretations of Schmitt's political theory" that have associated him with abusive sovereignty. His second aim is to productively expand democratic theory, specifically the thinking about a *radical, participatory version of democracy.*"[54]

Going against established interpretations of Schmitt, Kalyvas's article foregrounds, for example, Schmitt's insistence on sovereignty's unique capacity "to create new constitutions and new forms of political institutions."[55] The sovereignty that decides on the state of exception, in which one or more constitutional laws are suspended – for example, the sovereignty of a president, who might hold this power – is distinguished in Schmitt's work from the sovereignty of the people, which is foundational and related to the Constitution (rather than to constitutional law, which can be suspended; the Constitution can't, although the people have the power to create a new constitution). Thus, for Schmitt, in a democracy it is the people who are "the true, uncontestable sovereign,"[56] as Kalyvas points out, and are a democracy's "sole legitimate sovereign authority,"[57] and this is the typical situation in modern times. One should note the difference between such a reading of Schmitt as a democratic theorist and the reading of Schmitt as the theorist of a sovereignty that decides on the law's suspension in the state of exception.

Another interest of Schmitt's that Kalyvas foregrounds is "the institutionalization of the sovereign will": How, once order has been constituted, does a people "subject itself to laws and authorities that it has created?"[58] Kalyvas takes his cue here from David Dyzenhaus's reading of Schmitt, which notes that, "while the vitality of the exception looms large as the theme of *Political Theology*, it is important to keep in mind that Schmitt was not arguing for the total negation of normality."[59] Kalyvas notes Dyzenhaus's insight that "one of Schmitt's main concerns was how to contain and curb the creative, form-giving, constituent power of the sovereign will."[60] If this will wasn't contained, if the first moment of democratic power wasn't followed by a second, then constituted order risked being perpetually interrupted, rendering it unstable and ineffective. It would lead, Schmitt thought, to that order's "eventual abolition."[61] Here, too, the reading of Schmitt as a theorist of the sovereign suspension of the law certainly doesn't seem to cover the full picture – specifically, it doesn't cover the normative dimension of Schmitt's thought. Both Schmitt's interest in the sovereign will and in sovereignty's constitution-making capacity can help to explain how Schmitt's work can be recuperated today as part of democratic theory.

The potentially radical dimension of this recuperation becomes clear in the third and fourth sections of Kalyvas's article, where he considers the place of extraparliamentary sovereignty in Schmitt and draws out Schmitt's insistence that no constituted order can exhaust the sovereignty of the people, as marked by the sovereign decision on the Constitution. Instead, the constituted order is always subject to the agitations of popular sovereignty.[62] Schmitt's problem with liberalism is, precisely, that it has alienated us from this. In this context, Schmitt acknowledges spheres in society where the people can voice its sovereign will next to the Constitution – a para-constitutional, extraparliamentary, and crucially democratic politics of sovereignty. Kalyvas notes, on this count, that "the similarities between this argument and the tradition of the extraparliamentary left, for example, are striking and intriguing."[63]

In the fourth and final section of his article, Kalyvas develops this into a theory of "The Three Bodies of the Democratic Leviathan": constituent, constituted, and para-constitutional, with the latter marking Schmitt's surprising proximity to the radical left. One may of course add that there are similarities here between Schmitt's argument and the tradition of the extraparliamentary right as well – Anthony McCann's *Shadowlands*, which studies the 2016 occupation of the Malheur National Wildlife Refuge in Oregon by a group of armed right-wing protesters led by Ammon Bundy, shows us as much.[64] But that is the *obvious* point about Schmitt. What makes Kalyvas's article interesting is his insistence (beyond right and left, if you will) on the importance of this for a truly political democracy – and this is the more interesting something one gets from McCann's book, even if it is focused on the right.

While the originality, not to say idiosyncrasy, of Kalyvas's reading should be recognized, a reading of *Constitutional Theory* among other texts also indicates that it is valid. Schmitt's complicated relation to democratic theory can further help nuance why so-called left liberals have turned to Schmitt to revitalize and redemocratize liberalism today: Schmitt does not have to be forced into this position. He was arguably always already there.

2

Foucault with Schmitt

Government is their war against us; rebellion is our war against them.
Michel Foucault, *"Society Must Be Defended"*[1]

For now, I take my cue from Kalyvas and his provocative reading of Schmitt, to begin to explore the analytical promise as well as the democratic possibilities of Schmitt's work without, of course, leaving its associations with fascism and Nazism behind. As a second step in such a counter-intuitive process, I turn to the work of Michel Foucault, which is arguably much closer to Schmitt's thought than Foucault's readers have been willing to acknowledge. Following up on Kalyvas's use of the image of the Leviathan to discuss various kinds of *democratic* power in Schmitt, I would like to consider what Jacques Bidet, in *Foucault with Marx*, characterizes as Foucault's "wink to Carl Schmitt"[2] in his reading of Thomas Hobbes's classic theory of sovereignty, *Leviathan*. It is important that Bidet writes of a "wink," for Foucault hardly follows Schmitt's theory of the political, or his blatantly anti-Semitic reading of Hobbes's *Leviathan*. Instead, I would argue that Foucault's wink repurposes Schmitt for democratic theory, and it is for this reason that I consider it here.

Building on work by Peter Gratton and Mika Ojakangas, who have more explicitly considered the "intellectual kinship" of Foucault and Schmitt,[3] I also want to approach that kinship – if it is one – in view of recent debates about Foucault and neoliberalism, a political-economic-philosophical formation that Schmitt did not consider but that is an important part of our overall "sovereign" situation today. On the one hand, one could argue that it is precisely because Foucault was not Schmittian enough, because he was ultimately interested in biopolitical governmentality rather than sovereignty, that his late thought became open to neoliberalism (as scholars like Daniel Zamora have demonstrated).[4] On the other, it is unclear whether a stronger attachment to

Schmitt would have prevented such a neoliberal opening (if, indeed, it was one): while Schmitt may not have considered neoliberalism, I discuss how multiple scholars have drawn out the importance of Schmitt's thought for neoliberal thinkers and neoliberal policy at large. Especially in the era of "Trumpism," which continues to reign even after Trump's electoral defeat, it seems what is needed is not so much a sovereign decision for or against Schmitt or neoliberalism as a consideration of how (on the one hand) Schmitt's exceptionalist sovereignty and (on the other) neoliberal policy operate *together* to shape today's political moment. For this, it is useful to read Foucault with Schmitt, Schmitt with Foucault – no matter how odd such a pairing may seem at first sight.

By aligning, to the extent that it is possible, Schmitt with Foucault, I am hardly trying to uncritically recuperate Schmitt; rather, my goal is to explore Foucault's link to Schmitt to expand on the complexities of the contemporary turn to Schmitt.

✳

To begin, consider for a moment one of the most famous images of sovereignty, the frontispiece of Thomas Hobbes's *Leviathan*. Intended to capture Hobbes's social contract theory in a single image, the figure of the Leviathan that is shown here finds its raison d'être in Hobbes's theory of the state of nature. Roughly, and speaking in a way that I nuance later, state of nature theory posits that, in the beginning, people were living together in a state of nature. Pessimistic theorists of the political – like Hobbes – envision this as an undesirable state in which people are like wolves to each other.[5] Optimistic theorists of the political think otherwise. In both cases, people eventually come together to draw up a contract (hence, Hobbes's renown as a contract theorist) to determine how they want to live together. This contract is a set of laws or a constitution by which a group chooses to live. The group thus institutes what Hobbes calls a Leviathan, Commonwealth, or State, an artificial man who represents them. Such a Leviathan is designed, in Hobbes, against the possibility of civil war, but the fear that the state of nature might again erupt is always there in the Hobbesian model. We therefore live in fear – of both the civil war and of the sovereign who is meant to hold it at bay.

The frontispiece of Hobbes shows all of this. It shows a figure of sovereignty – I hesitate to call it an actual human being – spectrally hovering over a landscape. It is unclear where this figure is standing, whether it is part of the landscape or not. Certainly, it resides outside of the walls that mark the town over which it looms. In its right hand, the figure holds a sword, symbol of earthly power (sovereignty's right to take life or let live, as Foucault puts it). In its left, it holds a religious staff, symbol of spiritual power – and note that the staff appears to reach into the landscape over which the sovereign rises. With the exception of the head and the hands, the body of this sovereign is made up of the bodies of its subjects – those who instituted the sovereign and find themselves represented in the body of the king.[6] They all look up towards the sovereign, who gazes outside of the image, at the reader. This image needs to be read vertically: starting with the Latin quote from the book of Job at the top ("there is no power on earth that compares to him"), one lowers one's gaze towards the bottom half of the image, which is split between images of earthly power on the left and images of spiritual power on the right. In the middle hangs a curtain, perhaps hiding where the sovereign is standing (its feet, as has been shown,[7] would likely rest precisely where Hobbes's name is written on the curtain).

Now consider Michel Foucault's reading of Hobbes in *"Society Must Be Defended,"* a lecture course that is focused on sovereignty. Foucault forces one to adjust the state of nature narrative. The state of nature is not one of perpetual, actual war in the way we have imagined it. The problem in the state of nature, Hobbes suggests (according to Foucault), is "equality."[8] People are too equal in strength; there isn't enough difference. And this leads to a "primitive war" as "the immediate effect of nondifferences, or at least insufficient differences."[9] "If there were great differences, if there really were obvious disparities between men, it is quite obvious that war would immediately come to an end."[10] Why? Because it would be obvious who the strong are, and who the weak are, and either there would be a clash and the strong would win or there would be no clash because the weak would be smart enough to refrain from engaging in one.[11] To live peacefully, people need to institute inequality or difference. This is how the sovereign comes about – a radically unequal power, marking absolute difference. "Differences lead to peace."[12] This gets people out of the state of nature and its petty war of representations, its "anarchy"[13] and "theatre"[14] of minor differences.

Hobbes has three models of sovereignty: the first is sovereignty by institution (people come together and close a contract, institute a sovereign).[15] The second is sovereignty by acquisition (one country violently conquers another, which is defeated).[16] Interestingly, Foucault points out that, while we would call the latter conquest ("domination"),[17] for Hobbes it is ultimately not because the defeated will institute the new sovereign, will accept the conqueror as their sovereign. Why? Because they want to live. But this is not a bio-political will to live: it is institution bound up in fear (of death – we are firmly within the realm of sovereignty).[18] Hobbes compares the latter form of sovereignty to (and this is the third model of sovereignty in Hobbes that Foucault distinguishes) children's dependency on their mothers: they depend on their mothers to live or, rather, to avoid death.[19] On this basis, Foucault presents Hobbes as a theorist *against* war, as a theorist of peace who took war as the fundamental adversary in his work.[20] Hobbes sought to "eliminate" war from politics.[21]

Foucault then mobilizes English political history to drive a rift into Hobbes's work.[22] He refuses to allow the violence of conquest to be swept under the carpet. He practises a political historicism against Hobbes's state of peace. He follows the Levellers and the Diggers et cetera in their attempt to keep revolution and rebellion – "war *against* the state,"[23] as Melinda Cooper specifies in her reading of the lecture – alive. There is always an alternative; the norm was violently put into place. In sum: Foucault takes it up for war against Hobbes as a theorist of peace.

At the very end of his lecture, Foucault attacks "dialectical material-ism," evidence that he is also working through his relation to Marx in his Collège de France lectures (as Stuart Elden, for example, has shown[24]). Jacques Bidet, author of *Foucault with Marx*, explains that what Foucault is likely attacking here is a "'Hegelian' Marx, thinker of the totality and its historical unfolding to the point where social contradictions are overcome."[25] Foucault's attack, at the end of the lecture on Hobbes as a theorist who seeks to eliminate war, may be against Marx as a "Hegelian" thinker who ultimately sweeps the negative under the carpet.

There are plenty of other reasons, Bidet goes on, Foucault may have taken up Marx in this context: Marx's account of politics, which focuses on class struggle and the economic determinism that triggered it, is simply not nuanced enough for Foucault to paint an adequate political picture. Bidet notes, much later in his book, Foucault's criticism of Marx's use of the word "struggle," which "passes over in silence precisely what is meant by struggle."[26] This in particular resonates with Foucault's criticism of Hobbes as a theorist against war. Bidet writes that, in Foucault's view, "Marxism ultimately neutralizes [the politics is war] paradigm by performing a dialectical operation on it: at the end of the revolutionary process, after the final reversal of economic domination, antagonism comes to be re-absorbed within a new contractual order of joint concertation among all. But Foucault refuses this final utopia."[27] "Under the new form of state domination, he discerns the war that is begun ever anew."[28] "The Marxists' dialectic," in Foucault's view, "occults the fact of war."[29]

All of this makes Foucault appear as somewhat of a Schmittian – and Bidet indeed writes of "Foucault's wink to Carl Schmitt, for whom the fundamental [political] category is also that of war"[30] – who seeks to keep alive a political pluriverse – against Hobbes,[31] who defends a political universe. When it comes to a concept of the political, Foucault's reading of Hobbes shows that he is more with Schmitt than with Hobbes.

In order to accept such a wink, however, one has to overlook at least one important difference between Foucault and Schmitt. When it comes to Foucault's advocacy of politics as war, Foucault is recuperating from Hobbes a war *against the state*; but that is crucially *not* what Schmitt advocates. (As Mouffe has already pointed out, Schmitt locates the enemy *outside* of democratic association. He doesn't think a democratic pluralism *within*.) The source of Foucault's concept of the political may not have been Schmitt so much as the Black Panther Party, as Brady Thomas Heiner argues.[32] Melinda Cooper remarks on this difference to reveal, as she puts it, "some provocative points of intersection and discord" between Foucault and Schmitt, leading to the conclusion that, in fact, Foucault and Schmitt "were engaged in a violent argument with each other."[33] There is no doubt, I think, that she is right.

Yet scholars have nevertheless insisted on the Foucault/Schmitt connection. In a chapter of his book *State of Sovereignty* titled "Torturing Sovereignty," Peter Gratton points out that "the powers described by Foucault can all be recognized in Schmitt's analyses,"[34] and he concludes that sovereignty, according to Foucault, "would be an exceptional power."[35] Mika Ojakangas argues that "Foucault's analysis of power ... in some respects resembles that of Carl Schmitt" and writes of the "intellectual kinship of these two thinkers":

Despite the differences between their perspectives and between the form of their question ("how" [Foucault] and "who"

[Schmitt]), Foucault and Schmitt share the same structure of thought ... In this epoch of immanence, every order which is to be something other than mechanical and lifeless abstraction has to search for an irregular basis: the exception. For Schmitt, this exception is the sovereign decision, for Foucault, it is the resistance of the plebs. In the final analysis, however, the question is about the same thing, the same principle, the same borderline concept between form and formlessness, which constitutes form by escaping from it.[36]

Indeed, there is further evidence that could be brought in for this surprising alliance between Foucault and Schmitt. When Foucault's doctoral thesis supervisor, Georges Canguilhem, theorizes "the normal and the pathological," he writes that "the abnormal, [while] logically second, is existentially first."[37] While the actual source for this language may come from elsewhere (Bergson?), this reads very much like Schmitt arguing for the priority of the exception over the norm: the exception "confirms not only the rule but also its existence, which derives only from the exception."[38] It is Stuart Elden who, in *Foucault's Last Decade*, explicitly casts the problematic of the normal and the pathological as a "constitutional" one in the "legal, political, medical and biological" senses of the word.[39] Schmitt was of course a constitutional scholar, and while Canguilhem's focus may not have been legal or political, there appears to be an obvious resonance between the two, between Canguilhem (writing in 1943) and Schmitt – and between Schmitt and Foucault.

When Kirk Wetters considers this pairing – Canguilhem and Schmitt – in "The Rule of the Norm and the Political Theology of 'Real Life' in Carl Schmitt and Giorgio Agamben" – he notes the resonance but underlines the differences: Canguilhem would have had no patience, Wetters argues, for the "organicist metaphors"[40] that characterize Schmitt's theorization of the norm and the exception and, in particular, "the *decisively* political."[41] For Canguilhem the law and sovereignty are contained within the temporal sphere of language rather than in the realm of the absolute (as they are for Schmitt). This leads Wetters to characterize Canguilhem as "reformist," while it is Schmitt who, "in contradiction to his apparent and avowed conservatism," becomes "an inheritor of revolutionary political thought."[42] The association of Schmitt to revolutionary thought needs to be read through the lens of Kalyvas's work on Schmitt to be given any nuance (on this, see my chapter 1; I return to it in the next two chapters). As for Wetters's characterization of Canguilhem as the one who does not use organicist metaphors, it's worth noting Canguilhem has been criticized precisely for his organicism.

∗

But let me focus on the key question: Where does Foucault stand in all of this? To answer it, one must consider both Foucault's and Schmitt's relation to liberalism and neoliberalism. Needless to say, not all political struggle is "war," and perhaps Foucault was going too far in his affiliation with Schmitt by proposing "war" as a lens through which to analyze all social relations. On the other hand, perhaps "struggle" does not go far enough in capturing the particular intensity of the political? Schmitt, in his insistence on the exception, was raging against liberalism. He sought to recuperate a political pluralism that was different from the liberal one. Foucault, on the other hand, seems to praise liberalism in his lectures on it (as Bidet and others point out), even if he has also often been presented as a critic of liberalism (consider, for example, his criticism of the liberal, autonomous individual as an idea that presents not so much the absence of power but one of its products; it's what informs Foucault's project of a critical ontology of the self). The recent conversation has in fact been about Foucault's "neoliberalism" – his apparent enthusiasm for neoliberalism as a mode of government (within such a framework, Foucault's late work on the "care of the self" can seem complicit with the entrepreneurial subjectivity that is central to neoliberalism). Perhaps Foucault's stance on liberalism in his lectures is in part a consequence of his rejection of Marx – to be against the latter may have pushed him in the direction of the former. Few have noted, however, that it may also be a consequence of the fact that Foucault was *not* a Schmittian: for while he insists, with a "wink" to Schmitt (as Bidet suggests), on war as an analyzer of social relations and attacks Hobbes for sweeping war under the carpet, he crucially does *not* adopt such a politics of war as part of an analysis of sovereignty *but* within a theory of biopolitical governmentality. This is, one could argue, what opened him up to neoliberalism. How so?

In the fifth and final section of *The History of Sexuality*, Foucault suggests that there has been a transition in the mode of Western power from a model based on sovereignty, defined by the ancient right to take life or let live, to a model of biopolitical government, which seeks to make live or keep alive until the point of death, if needs be. The latter is a kind of power that seeks to "[exert] a positive influence on life, that endeavors to administer, optimize, and multiply it, subjecting it to precise controls and comprehensive regulations."[43] On the path from sovereignty to biopolitical governmentality one comes across disciplinary power, which he associates with an "anatomopolitics of the human body";[44] biopolitics, by contrast, operates on the people as population. The biopolitical model may be associated with capitalism, but no Marxist analysis is going to be of much help to sketch it out. For what a biopolitical analysis focuses on is sex or race, and the Marxist analysis ultimately always boils down to class. So if Foucault is interested in war, he is interested in a war that is waged in society on sex and on race – in sex and race wars. These are not actual wars, but in order to foreground war as an analyzer of sexual and racial relations, Foucault is able to foreground the domination that is operative in intimate domains of existence that, for example, in the case of sex, one may think are outside of power. It is not because we are able to talk about sex that we have become free in our relations to sex. Psychoanalysis or *Cosmopolitan*, for that matter, are no better than confession, and it is through our talk about sex that we are governed. Importantly, Foucault is focused here on sexuality rather than sex and argues that sex is a mere effect produced through the discourse of sexuality. It comes after the fact, is generated through the talk.

Now, while Foucault may be a Schmittian due to his attachment to war, his focus on biopolitics rather than on sovereignty also propels him in a very different direction – in fact, in the direction of the liberalism and, in particular, the neoliberalism that Schmitt likely would have hated. This is clear in the lecture courses that follow *"Society Must Be Defended,"* in which Foucault shifts from discussing sovereignty to analyzing the pastorate (*Security, Territory, Population,* in 1977–78) and liberalism (*The Birth of Biopolitics,* 1978–79) – they step in, even, for the notion of biopolitics, which he had promised to analyze. In a way, Foucault is *not Schmittian enough*; or, rather, it is where he is not a Schmittian that he becomes open to the neoliberal attraction. For it is arguably Foucault's focus on sex and race, his interest in minorities, his pluralization of the Marxist perspective, that risks putting him in alliance with so-called "progressive neoliberals" or also a "neoliberal Left" as, for example, Daniel Zamora and the contributors to *Foucault and Neoliberalism* have shown.

In his contribution to this collection, Michael Behrent points out that Foucault considered neoliberalism to be very "far from inaugurating a new form of fascism"; instead, he suggests "it should be seen as a distinctly nondisciplinary form of power" (and Foucault was attracted by this, given his criticism of disciplinary forms of power).[45] In neoliberalism, Foucault found himself "intrigued with the ways in which a particular discursive framework – one that at the time was aspiring to hegemony – might accommodate difference and minority practices."[46] Foucault, as Mitchell Dean in his contribution points out, is not a thinker who "seeks freedom from *all* sorts of power but rather an alternative to *particular kinds* of power and regulation."[47] In this sense, neoliberalism works where sovereignty and disciplinary power fail. It is Nancy Fraser (referenced in Jean-Loup Amselle's contribution to the volume) who reminds us of this kind of "progressive neoliberalism" in the aftermath of Trump's election and suggests that there is a way in which diversity discourse and identity politics in the US have gone hand in hand with the neoliberal takeover – Fraser provocatively reads Clinton's election and rule as the culmination of this.[48]

Dean in fact clarifies that, on this count, neoliberalism differs not only from "sovereign power exercised through law, or ... disciplinary society with its norms, or even of the general normalization of a biopolitics of the population."[49] Here is Dean again: "Thus, Foucault here distinguishes the neoliberal program from those forms of regulation and power such as discipline, that subjugate individuals through the production of subjectivity – that is, through tying individuals to the truth of their identity, e.g. the occasional criminal, the recidivist, the dangerous individual, the invert, etc. For Foucault ... neoliberalism does not subjectify in this sense. By not doing so, it opens up the space for tolerating minority individuals and practices and optimizing systems of differences."[50] In other words, if biopolitics enters into Foucault's thought to name a problem – the shift in the history of Western power from the sovereign right to take life and let live (with the law as central to such a right) to the biopolitical project of making live and letting die (operative not so much in laws as in norms targeting sex and race) – neoliberalism (a form of power that accommodated sexual and racial differences and, *pace* Fraser, works through them) may have started to operate in his thought as that problem's solution. This does require one to understand that, in Foucault's thought, control does not amount to oppression, a reading that is unfortunately not as widely accepted as it should be.[51]

The question then becomes whether a continued attachment to sovereignty (a more Schmittian point of view) would have prevented this turn to neoliberalism from coming about. How does Schmitt's theory of the state of exception relate to today's neoliberal environments (this question seems particularly important in order to understand "Trumpism")? Might a Schmittian concept of the political, and the focus on exceptionalist decisionism (rather than on the norm) that it brings, *also* have connected to a neoliberalism that does not operate within "anarchy and chaos" but within a suspension of the law that is enabled by the law, giving absolute power to those sovereigns acting in a present future that the law was unable to anticipate?

In their illuminating book on neoliberalism, Christian Dardot and Pierre Laval seem conclusive on this when they quote Karl Polanyi's *The Great Transformation* and note, after teasing out the various state interventionist-strands in liberalism, what they call "intervention for *market operation*": "The economic liberal can, therefore," Polanyi writes, "without any inconsistency call upon the state to use the force of law; he can even appeal to the violent forces of civil war to set up the preconditions of a self-regulating market."[52]

It should probably be underlined here that Philip Mirowski, one of the foremost authorities on neoliberalism, has a section early on in his book *Never Let a Serious Crisis Go to Waste* titled "Learning from Carl Schmitt," in which he discusses Friedrich Hayek's – and, more generally, what he calls "the Neoliberal Thought Collective's" – reliance on Schmitt and, in particular, their "claiming the power to exercise the Schmittian 'exception.'"[53] "In too many ways to enumerate here," Mirowski writes, "the reaction of both economists and the NTC [Neoliberal Thought Collective] to the global economic crisis is a case study in the applications of Schmitt's doctrine of the exception."[54] Quoting Renato Christi's book on Schmitt, he agrees that, "in truth, Hayek owed much to Schmitt, more than he cared to recognize": "For Hayek and the neoliberals, the Führer was replaced by the figure of the entrepreneur, the embodiment of the will-to-power for the community, who must be permitted to act without being brought to rational account. While he probably believed he was personally defending liberalism from Schmitt's withering critique, his own political 'solution' ended up resembling Schmitt's 'total state' more than he could bring himself to admit."[55] William Scheuerman had already discussed this "unholy alliance" between Hayek and Schmitt in an article from 1997.[56] Around the same time that Mirowski's book came out, Thomas Biebricher analyzed Schmitt's exceptionalism as a key feature of neoliberalism.[57]

Grégoire Chamayou's more recent study of "authoritarian liberalism" marks a major contribution to such thought. In the chapter titled "The Sources of Authoritarian Liberalism" in *The Ungovernable Society*, Chamayou writes: "Foucault's celebrated course on *The Birth of Biopolitics* has mainly given us a vision of neoliberalism as a governmentalization of the state, as the dissolution of the old frameworks of sovereignty into market forms. This is true, but only in part. To better understand the ambiguity of neoliberal politics in its relations to state power, we need to study the other side too."[58] And he goes on to mention the centrality of Schmitt to such a project. Finally, Dario Gentili's *The Age of Precarity* also participates in such an investigation of the connections between neoliberalism and sovereign exceptionalism.[59]

It is a sign of the importance of Schmitt in Mirowski's study that, late in the book, he associates his book's title with Schmitt's exceptionalist theory of sovereignty: "It is here," he writes, "that it is most obvious that they [the neoliberals] take their Schmittian heritage to heart. They know what it means to never let a serious crisis go to waste."[60] Finally, note that one of Mirowski's references to Schmitt comes in a section of his book dedicated to Foucault, where he blames Foucault, in part, for not taking seriously enough how neoliberals "reserve to themselves the right of deployment of the Schmittian exception."[61]

Here we can finally also return to Melinda Cooper, who notes, on the one hand, that "the neoliberal politics pursued under the rubric of the 'Washington consensus' can be understood as an extreme extension of the classical liberal critique of sovereignty"[62] – in other words, it can be understood as a politics *against Schmitt*. On the other, however, "neoliberal economic imperialism could be described as the art of profiting from crisis in the deregulated space of global financial flows,"[63] and, on that count, it comes *closer to Schmitt* and his theory of the state of exception. Indeed, when Cooper concludes that "neoliberalism has invented another instrument of violence, over and above the territorial state-of-exception [*familiar to us from Schmitt*]: an ever-present state-of-emergency threatening to actualize in any region of the globe that falls short of the rigors of international competition,"[64] she is trying to underline the usefulness of *an updated Schmitt* for thinking about neoliberal politics. It is precisely in "insecure times," as the title of her article puts it, that "tough decisions" are presented as necessary. Schmitt is central, in other words, to the neoliberal moment. None of this makes the recuperation of Schmitt as an important thinker today any easier. Most importantly for my argument, it shows that to turn to Schmitt hardly means to turn away from neoliberalism – for Schmitt's approach to sovereignty remains at the heart of that form of power, even if it has sometimes been presented in tension with, or even in opposition to, it.

*

In a different mode, Naomi Klein's *The Shock Doctrine: The Rise of Disaster Capitalism* provides plenty of further evidence for this link between Schmitt and neoliberalism.[65] Klein shows how neoliberalism has used the state of exception to further its cause – how neoliberalism has implemented itself and maintains itself through states of exception or what she calls states of shock. Shock can happen to us, as when natural disaster strikes. Such shock is, partly, beyond our control (though this should never be assumed very easily – we know, for example, that more could have been done in New Orleans to keep the Lower Ninth Ward safe from the breaking of the levees during Hurricane Katrina). One thing Klein shows is that neoliberalism knows how to turn such unexpected, uncontrollable shock into profit. But there is more: she also shows how neoliberalism has forcefully implemented states of exception or states of shock in order to realize itself as a global economic regime. This is not about a natural disaster striking beyond our control: this is about a willed disaster that is brought about in order to put certain economic policies into place. After all, and going back to Schmitt, the key thing about the state of exception as he theorizes it is that someone – the sovereign – brings it about.

This goes back to the origin of the state of exception in theology, as the miracle. It is God, in the Hebrew bible, and Jesus, in the New Testament, who bring about miracles. The miracle, therefore, always remains within the scope of a theological agent, the father or the son. To draw this out means to draw out the agency within the miracle and the state of exception: they are something that is done, that is made, that is brought about. Schmitt, of course, places such agency in the hands of the sovereign, a figure who can be traced back to the Messiah and to God before him. But today, after the death of God and the waning of sovereignty post-Second World War, such a transcendental (and in the case of Jesus immanent-transcendental) place has become empty and this "vacation" (from the Latin *vacare*, "emptying out") has created room for other kinds of sovereigns or messianic figures to step in.

Claude Lefort of course already knew that, with the decapitation of the sovereign in the French Revolution, sovereignty became an empty place – a site, to speak in Nietzschean terms, where the will to power is played out.[66] But Schmitt makes us see the exceptionalist dimension of this, that it is the site to decide on the state of exception/ the miracle that is up for grabs. Today's neoliberals are "petty sovereigns"[67] who have stepped into this place in order to enforce states of exception/miracles to realize their policies. This is what Klein's book shows us.

Neoliberalism might, in its general perception, appear to largely operate outside of the state, through a shrinking of the state, deregulation, et cetera. The fact of the matter is different: neoliberalism is not outside of sovereignty –it works hand in hand with a sovereignty that is exceptionalist, that defines itself through the power to suspend the normal rule of law. This is, as Schmitt writes, the political "life" that breaks through the boring crust of the law.

It is here, to return now to Foucault, that we begin to understand the biopolitical dimension of the state of exception, which, in its association with the miracle, marks a way of bringing life within the law – but as the law's outside. Articulated biopolitically, Schmitt's theory – designed against liberalism – arguably gives us a theory of neoliberalism, something that the development of Foucault's Schmittianism in the late 1970s also puts us on the tracks of – even if Foucault himself appears to have been blind to it. We are arriving here, in other words, at a mediation of sovereignty and biopolitics that enables us to see the biopolitical element in Schmitt's concept of sovereignty, and the sovereign element in biopolitical neoliberalism. It's a mediation, or even a deconstruction, that resonates with Chamayou's notion of "authoritarian liberalism" and other approaches that have attempted to think together Schmitt and neoliberalism, and – though this pairing is obviously not equivalent – Schmitt and Foucault.

The pairing of Schmitt with Foucault enables one to see two things. On the one hand, it helps along our understanding of Schmitt as a radical democratic theorist who highlighted the continued political activity of the people within the constituted order, something that Foucault in his reading of Hobbes was also interested in. To arrive at this, however, one must transpose Schmitt's theory of politics as war *within* the state, not as civil war but as para-constitutional politics. One should acknowledge that this is already a creative rewriting of Schmitt.

On the other hand, the more problematic dimension of Schmitt's theory – his theory of sovereignty as the power to decide on the state of exception – persists in the pairing of Schmitt with Foucault as well and leads, in fact, to a consideration of what David Harvey calls "the neoliberal state" and, specifically, the combination of neoliberalism with authoritarianism (as, for example, in Harvey's account of Deng Xiaoping's neoliberalism).[68] If Foucault enables us to see that Schmitt can be an ally in thinking radical democratic politics, he also reminds us of the dark side of Schmitt's work and how it is operative in the contemporary neoliberal moment that Schmitt, in his time, did not consider.

3

Giorgio Agamben's Civil War

To speak of Carl Schmitt as a radical democratic theorist no doubt strikes many as preposterous. Schmitt was a conservative, they counter; there wasn't an ounce of radicality to him. If Andreas Kalyvas can recuperate Schmitt as a democratic theorist, it is precisely because Schmitt *wasn't* radical. Kalyvas does this by highlighting how Schmitt was interested in the sovereign normative power to form new constitutions (democracy's first phase) and how the normative order is able to limit the sovereign will to constitute – that is, how the sovereign is able to self-limit (democracy's second phase). Both of these are conservative aspects of his thought, drawn out by Kalyvas to attenuate for the exceptionalist, law-suspending emphasis in *Political Theology*. If the para-constitutional power that Schmitt, in his *Constitutional Theory*, acknowledges as part and parcel of constitutional democracies seems to come close to a more radical politics, it should be noted that, within Schmitt's system, it is tolerated only as a continued expression of constituent power – in other words, within the dynamic of constituent and constituted power. As such, though it may be democratic, it can only with difficulty qualify as truly radical.

In the terms developed by Dimitris Vardoulakis, one could say that, in Schmitt, "sovereignty" ultimately always settles whatever trouble "democracy" brings – constituted power ultimately always settles constituent power, the revolutionary potential or (also) the potential for civil war (in Greek, *stasis*) that it holds.[1] For Vardoulakis, sovereignty thus presupposes democracy in the dynamic relation between sovereignty and democracy – and he is emphatic that it is a relation. If it is not, in other words, if one is forced to choose either/or, sovereignty wins – democracy comes first ("stasis before the state," as the title of his book has it). From such a point of view, it may also be clear why Joan Cocks, in her far-reaching criticism of sovereignty, proposes we think of any kind of sovereignty as a "settler" sovereignty (even if it risks diluting the notion and its application in historically specific colonial contexts): because its key function is to "settle" a democratic trouble that can never be settled.[2] I for my part find it interesting that, in Schmitt, democracy takes place within the limits of sovereignty. What might we take from that insight today, within the contemporary resurgence of sovereignty? This is not so much a question of ceding to sovereignty at the expense of democracy; it's more about thinking sovereignty's democratic potential in response to its anti-democratic tendencies.

Even in Schmitt's immediate context, more radical theorizations of power were of course available. One need only consider, for example, the extraparliamentary theory of power that Judith Butler associates with the work of Walter Benjamin. As I discuss in the next chapter, in his essay "Critique of Violence" Benjamin insists on the anomic outside of what he calls "divine violence," whereas Schmitt – in his conservative response to Benjamin in *Political Theology* – uses the concept of sovereignty (defined as the power to decide on the state of exception) to fold such an outside back within the law. In this chapter, and continuing the discussion of Hobbes's *Leviathan* that I offer earlier, I want to show specifically how one of Michel Foucault's students, the Italian philosopher Giorgio Agamben, plays out Thomas Hobbes against Carl Schmitt to lay out a more radical political theory. As such, Agamben comes close to the position of one of his main influences, Walter Benjamin. It is ultimately through a detailed consideration of the tension between Benjamin and Schmitt (which I provide in the next chapter) that Schmitt's particular position can be understood and that what I consider to be his appeal for the political left today can be explained.

Agamben develops his analysis of Hobbes in a lecture he gave at Princeton University in October 2001, shortly after the 9/11 terror attacks. The lecture begins with a description of the frontispiece of Hobbes's book and lays out some aspects of the image that I discuss in the previous chapter. The lecture also includes a media-historical section about an optical device of which Hobbes was aware and to which he may have been alluding in the frontispiece to his book – namely, a scopic apparatus unifying in a single optical illusion multiple other images and thus projecting a unity from difference.[3]

30   A Critique of Sovereignty

Agamben suggests that Hobbes's own Leviathan may be such a device, in other words, an artifice that makes the projection of unity possible.

But the consequences of such a reading are huge: to accept it would mean to accept that Hobbes is aware of the fact that the body politic whose unity he defends is really an optical illusion. However, wouldn't this go against *Leviathan*'s central project: to write against the division of the religious civil war that was supposedly the book's foundational trauma? Wasn't this division the historical event against which all of the Leviathan was designed?

As he himself acknowledges, Agamben provocatively wants to reconstrue Hobbes "from scratch" as a thinker of the multitude, as a thinker within a political theoretical tradition to which he is usually opposed (Hobbes is usually associated with thinking "the people" rather than "the multitude").[4] If Hobbes thinks the people, Agamben argues, he does so only as an instant when it appoints a representative body: a sovereign. Hobbes thinks the people only as the constituted instant of constituent power. In that same instance, at that very point, however, the people also immediately disappears into the people-king, the *populus-rex*, which is its representative body or constituted power, and the people/body politic dissolves into what Hobbes calls the dissolved multitude, the *dissoluta multitudo*. This dissolved multitude comes about within the moment of political institution and continues to exist after it. The gap between this multitude and the *populus-rex* can intensify into a civil war situation (the Leviathan versus the Behemoth that is evoked in Agamben's lecture title: "Leviathan and Behemoth"). If the multitude wins this war, it becomes what Hobbes calls a *disunited multitude*. And from that state, a new people/body politic can be instituted – though again, only for a moment. In that moment, the people vanishes once more, the dissolved multitude comes about once more, and so on. Far from disappearing in Hobbes's book, the historically specific Civil War is permanently present as a more general civil war, and Hobbes (Agamben argues) is not at all reluctant to admit this.

The circular model that is described here, and that is diagrammed in Agamben's lecture,[5] is the model of earthly power. It explains why the people in the frontispiece of Hobbes's text are situated outside of the city, because "the people" names the multitude constituting itself as a people outside the city for a moment. (In this sense, the frontispiece really needs to be read in photographic terms, as a snapshot. The people-king is, to use Benjaminian language, what flashes up at a moment of danger – the danger *not* of the dissolution that immediately follows it *but* of the people-king itself.) After that moment, the people dissolves into a multitude that resides in the city, but as what Agamben calls an "unpolitical" element,[6] an element with no political significance. Contrary to the optical illusion or failure of the body politic, however, the multitude is real. What is real, in Agamben (and, Agamben argues, in Hobbes), is the unpolitical, internally excluded life of the multitude: politics' internal outside, its exception.

Agamben's lecture ends with some difficult pages on the eschatological, or what he also calls the messianic, dimension of Hobbes's project. This is where an explicit contrast with Schmitt opens up. In his book on Hobbes, Schmitt critically reads this dimension of Hobbes's project as metaphorical, as Agamben points out; but Hobbes insists that when he speaks about the Kingdom of God, he speaks about a real – not a metaphorical – kingdom. What to make of this? Agamben suggests (contra Schmitt) that it must be taken literally: for Hobbes, "true" political representation will only come about in the kingdom of god – in other words, as part of an eschatological, salvational history in which the successful body politic appears at the end of time. For the non-believer, this of course means that effective political representation will never be possible. Hobbes is both a thinker of the multitude as unpolitical element and of this salvational history. For Agamben, Hobbes's point that true political representation will only come about at the end of time is a marker of the fact that life is, ultimately, unpolitical.

Agamben develops his thinking about Hobbes several years after his key work *Homo Sacer* has already come out. Reading *Homo Sacer*'s pages on the paradox of sovereignty enable us to understand that he considers the multitude – which is inside the city only by virtue of being outside of it – to be in a position of exception. Agamben lays out his thinking about the exception through a reading of Schmitt, whose work he follows but also disagrees with to a certain extent. He challenges, for example, the way in which the exception in Schmitt is presented as a kind of life breaking through the crust of the law as if from the outside. For Agamben, a more correct reading would be that this outside is actually folded within the law and marks the law's core operation – it would be a more conservative understanding of Schmitt's outside. Moreover, Agamben argues that the law *operates by* producing the excepted element that Schmitt also calls "life." If in Schmitt one can perhaps still find a clear distinction between outside and inside (after all, Schmitt does define sovereignty as the power to decide, for example, on the friend/enemy distinction, and the enemy is clearly outside of democratic association, as I discuss in chapter 1), in Agamben's reading of Schmitt those spatial markers become part of a Moebius strip, get folded into each other in such a way that such a distinction is no longer possible.[7] It is clear that Schmitt doesn't think the outside as *truly outside*.

This also becomes very clear in Agamben's critical reading of set theory in the work of Alain Badiou. Agamben notes that there are two categories that Badiou takes from set theory, membership (being present) and inclusion (being represented). A combination of these different categories can lead one to think various situations: the norm (present and represented), excrescence (not present but represented), and singularity (present but not represented).[8] One can think, for example, of a US citizen present in the US, a US citizen living outside of the US, or someone living in the US who does not have political representation. In Badiou's thought, the exception gets defined with the third situation, that of singularity, and Agamben in fact associates Badiou's thought (he mentions specifically Badiou's thought of the event[9]) with Schmitt on this count. But Agamben argues this is a mistake: instead, the exception should enable us to think a fourth situation where someone is represented *as unrepresentable*, is included *as excluded*, produced *as such* even – is folded within something *only by virtue of being outside of it*.[10] Who is this particular subject?

In his book, he proposes a concrete figure for it, a figure he takes from Roman law: *homo sacer*, or the sacred person. The sacred person could not be sacrificed; if such a person were killed, they were killed with impunity – no punishment was meted out for the murder. A sacred person was outside of both religious law and human law.[11] But the status of that outside deserves to be assessed: after all, Agamben finds this figure *within* human law. In other words, human law includes law about a figure that is outside of such law. *Homo sacer* is included within law only by virtue of being excluded from it. Who is this figure? The sovereign, Agamben argues, takes up such a position. But the sovereign forms a couple with *homo sacer*, who takes up a similar position on the other side of the law (from below, versus the sovereign's from above). Obviously, *homo sacer* is a very specific figure. Again, who, concretely, might take up such a role in our societies today?

One might suggest – and I return to this at length in part 2 – that young African American men are one example of the sacred beings of US politics today. Present and represented, members and included (the

Giorgio Agamben's Civil War

latter at least in theory – many issues make this difficult or are even deliberately designed to prevent this), they are nevertheless killed with impunity. There is no punishment meted out for their killing. In this sense, they are like *homo sacer*: present within human law but not represented by it; represented as unrepresentable. Young African American men mark a specific bearer of this sacred life that Agamben calls "bare." And one must note that the designation "bare" can hardly do to capture the specificity of such sacred life since a key element of its being "sacred" is the fact that it is "raced," in other words, hardly "bare" (as Alexander Weheliye points out[12]). But Agamben would want to make another, more general point: the situation of young African American men in the US today marks the situation that virtually *all of us* are in in our relation to the law. No one's life coincides with their political life. No one coincides with their citizenship. Citizenship was something that was granted to us. As a result, it can be taken away. Some may resist this: clearly, *not all of us* are in the position of young African American men in the US. *Virtually*, Agamben says, we all are. This is another way of saying that the position of black life in the US *is* the universal position. The unfortunate tension that has been created between "Black Lives Matter" and "All Lives Matter" is, from an Agambenian point of view, fallacious.

Agamben's argument goes back to the root of his political philosophy, which is the fact that the Greeks used two words for life: *zoe* and *bios*. Whereas the former marks the simple fact of living common to all humans, animals, and gods (the Greek gods had very human traits – they were jealous, adulterous, murderous), the latter refers to ethical and political life – the form or way of living common to an individual or group. If *zoe* is the fact that I have to eat to survive, *bios* may refer to my preference for pasta over potatoes; biological life versus the good life. *Zoe* is state of nature; *bios* is life after the contract. However, when *bios* is stripped away, one does not just go back to *zoe*. One is produced, rather, as what Agamben (after Benjamin) calls "bare life" or "naked life" – politicized *zoe*.[13] Life in the state of exception is bare life.

While such life is generally produced by stripping *bios* away, in some cases it can also be produced by forcing *bios* onto *zoe*. This is the case, as Eric Santner points out, with Terri Schiavo, the Italian American woman who went into an overcomatose state and had a legalo-political battle be played out around her persistent vegetative life – a battle to keep her alive.[14] This is the contemporary, biopolitical version of another state of exception politics that is an older form of sovereignty and that wields death (Agamben, by the way, mentions Karen Quinlan, another overcomatose woman, as a case of *homo sacer* at the very end of his book). There are forms of biopolitical sovereignty that also operate by stripping life away: this is, for example, what happens in Guantanamo Bay – life is not killed there but kept alive to the point of death. This, too, is biopolitics, enforced by stripping *bios* away. All of this is still very different from the camps, which are a site of old, thanatopolitical sovereignty in addition to being a biopolitical site for the optimization of Aryan life. I turn to the camp as one of four paradigms of sovereignty in part 2.

Now, Agamben's point is not just that this kind of life at times breaks through the crust of the law. He argues, rather, that this is the rotten core of the law. No one is born a citizen, so as a result one is always internally excluded within such a political category. This is how sovereignty works, its core operation is to generate this kind of life. The model for understanding the law, Agamben provocatively argues, is thus Auschwitz, where such internal exclusion was brutally on display. Far from being an anomaly, Auschwitz made explicit the logic of ban or abandonment that is at the heart of how law/rights/the state/sovereignty operates.

Who are the subjects in the state of exception? All of us. Who is the multitude? All of us. This is the difficult but potentially emancipatory lesson of Agamben's work. Why difficult? Because it reveals the vulnerability of our position as subjects and citizens. Why emancipatory, from a certain point of view? Because it puts us in touch with the civil war situation that, in Hobbes, leads to a new body politic.

∗

It is unclear, however, how Agamben expects us to respond to this radical criticism of law – and this is in fact where the issue lies. Should it lead to a rejection of the law? Should it lead to a new engagement with it that may lead to better representative structures? Even if such structures are always a failure?

Consider here, in the context of the example of black life in the US today, Brady Thomas Heiner's article "Foucault and the Black Panthers."[15] What do the Black Panthers do in response to the racism they find in the law? They rewrite the law – the Declaration of Independence, the US Bill of Rights. One can ask, today, what good this has brought, given the continued vulnerability of black lives in

US politics. But what is the other option? Complete rejection of the law? Wouldn't this lead to the anarchy and chaos that Schmitt was keen on keeping outside of his concept of sovereignty?

Agamben's notion of destituent power was meant to create a way out of this impasse. It breaks, if you will, the tunnel vision created by the diagrammatic circle represented in Agamben's lecture, which goes from civil war to disunited multitude and then back to people-king. But why would the negative of a civil war necessarily be dialectically resolved into a new constitutive moment? Does one have to submit to this cunning of sovereignty? It is to escape this sovereign lure (to recall the work of Dimitris Vardoulakis) that Agamben proposes the notion of destituent power.

According to Agamben, destituent power is "completely set free from the sovereign relation of the ban that links it to constituted power."[16] As the anonymous collective the Invisible Committee explains: "The notion of destitution is necessary in order to free the revolutionary imaginary of all the old constituent fantasies that weigh it down, of the whole deceptive legacy of the French Revolution. It is necessary to intervene in revolutionary logic, in order to establish a division within the idea of insurrection."[17] "For there are constituent insurrections," it continues – recalling, perhaps, Schmitt's theory of an insurrectionary constituent power next to the Constitution – "and there are destituent insurrections."[18] It gives May '68 as an example and contrasts it with *Nuit debout*, which "was troubled by the old constituent itch."[19] (The French assembly movement *Nuit debout* and its lead philosopher, Frédéric Lordon, are frequent targets in this treatise of the radical left.)

But what does it mean to destitute? "Its characteristic gesture," the Invisible Committee writes, "is *exiting*."[20] It is "to *disengage from*" the struggle; this doesn't mean abandoning it, it clarifies, but "[fastening] *on to the struggle's positivity*."[21] "Escape, but while escaping look for a weapon," as Deleuze already put it. The whole project lies "*in the fight itself*."[22] The university must be destituted by "[establishing], at a distance, the places of research, of education and thought, that are more vibrant and more demanding than it is"; the judicial system must be destituted, and we should "learn to settle our disputes ourselves, applying some method to this, paralyzing its faculty of judgment and driving its henchmen from our lives"; medicine must be destituted so "we know what is good for us" and don't leave that judgment to a surgeon; finally, the government must be destituted "to make ourselves ungovernable."[23]

Apart from the fact that it is not quite clear how "ungovernable," in the final example, can be written back into the previous examples (which hardly seem to indicate "ungovernability" to me), one might also have a hard time seeing how what is presented here as destituent power is not, in fact, constituent power, setting up new places of teaching and learning, new ways of settling disputes, knowing about our health and sickness. One understands that they don't seek to set up institutions but what the Invisible Committee calls "forms."[24] Yet something about the first three examples does not sit well with the notion of the ungovernable that appears in the last – they appear to have more government in them than the Invisible Committee might want. To me, it doesn't seem so much that constituent and constituted power are left behind here as that a destituent relationship is being proposed between the two.

Read in this way, Agamben's theory of civil war or stasis would appear to be close to a sharp criticism that Vardoulakis has developed of it, in which he notes that Agamben in fact neglects to discuss "democracy" in his theory of civil war.[25] For Vardoulakis, stasis underlies all political praxis, and it is identified in his work specifically with what he calls the democratic "dejustification" of sovereign violence.[26] Rather than succumb to the sovereign lure, then, Vardoulakis envisions a dynamic, critical, and political relationship between "democracy" and "sovereignty" that takes the name of civil war or stasis – but not the unpolitical kind that Agamben proposes. In Agamben, Vardoulakis argues, "sovereignty" – the old sovereignty – eventually wins since Agamben's desire is to break the relationship with sovereignty, an exclusionary gesture that is characteristic of sovereignty itself. Vardoulakis, by contrast, insists on the democratic unsettling of sovereignty and faults Agamben for ignoring it. In *Being Vulnerable*, I am recuperating sovereignty from the rubble as well, considering how it may be democratically reclaimed under the current conditions of its troubling resurgence.

Although my position is thus ultimately different from Agamben's, I nevertheless want to continue tracing his more radical contemporary articulation of power, specifically in its association with anarchism – an association that Agamben has hinted at but has not developed in his work so far. In part 3 of this book, anarchism reappears in the form of a theory of democracy that posits a lack of exceptions in view of democratic equality. It posits an "unexceptional politics," to recall Emily Apter's work.[27] Unexceptional politics, as Stathis Gourgouris

Giorgio Agamben's Civil War

explains, imagines a democracy without *archè*, without foundation or (pre-established) rule. This means that no one is by nature more qualified to found a rule, or more qualified to rule, than anyone else.

To now return to the central term of my analysis: sovereign is not so much who declares a state of exception as who is without exception – unexceptional. *If a people founds and rules without exception, it is sovereign.* To be sovereign is to be unexceptional. This is Schmitt, in the sense that it maintains the concept of sovereignty – but Schmitt turned inside-out.[28] A democratic Schmitt.

For now, one can clearly see how Agamben is a Foucauldian. Following Foucault's insistence that politics is war, and following Foucault's "political historicism," Agamben continues in the tracks of statements like "all law is written in blood" (Foucault) et cetera. Agamben thus continues what I have presented to be a Schmittianism that can be found in Foucault. But Agamben and Foucault also strongly differ in their reading of Hobbes. Foucault presents Hobbes as a theorist against war, who seeks to eliminate war; Agamben says that Hobbes, without much reluctance, keeps civil war alive as a key component of this political theory – as a theory of generalized civil war, even. He does this because he is making a plea for the real kingdom of god to come about at the end of time – any earthly kingdom that we produce in the meantime is no more than an optical illusion. In other words, Hobbes for Agamben becomes a thinker not so much of the people as of the multitude that never coincides with the people, is only included in the people as its internal outside, its exception.

Apart from the fact that Schmitt is a thinker of the people and not of the multitude, and leaving aside for the moment Agamben's notion of destituent power, this reads like Schmitt's theory of a constituent power that is never exhausted by a constituted power – it reads like a radicalized version of what Kalyvas understands to be the third moment of democracy in Schmitt. Schmitt, however, would not say that, as such, constituent power and constituted power are at war; it's rather that Agamben seeks to expose the realm of democratic association to be rooted in the war against an enemy that Schmitt situates outside of such an association. With the notion of destituent power, however, Agamben seeks to go further than this and break the diagrammatic circle of constituent/constituted power, leaving both democracy and sovereignty behind. For Schmitt, and many others, this would go too far. In Agamben, it is of course that radicalization that leads to his eventual rejection of sovereignty – a rejection that had been slumbering in his work but played itself out in devastating ways during the pandemic.

Although Schmitt situates the enemy outside of democratic association, his theory of the exception is anything but a thinking of the outside. In fact, it proposes a constitutional understanding of the exception: the Constitution includes the possibility of its own suspension. This is why the state of exception proves so useful for Agamben, as a mechanism of internal exclusion, even if Schmitt may want to make it appear as if the outside of the exception truly comes from the outside. All of this reveals that Schmitt is in no way a radical but, rather, a conservative. Agamben develops his own radicalism in opposition to Schmitt. Its true influence, as I now go on to show, is not Schmitt but Walter Benjamin. The thorny question of which influence is more relevant today remains.

4

Radical Benjamin

An important text has been missing in this conversation so far, and one that can help us determine Carl Schmitt's exact position, is Walter Benjamin's "Critique of Violence" or, as it is titled in the German, "Zur Kritik der Gewalt," "On the Critique of Violence."[1] Benjamin writes this text in 1921, and Agamben argues (in *State of Exception*) that Schmitt was responding to this text when he wrote *Political Theology*. Benjamin responds to Schmitt, in turn, with his book on the origin of the German "Trauerspiel," which includes footnotes to Schmitt's *Political Theology*. The rest is history: Schmitt becomes a "convinced Nazi" (Arendt); Benjamin commits suicide on the run from fascism.

Most of Benjamin's important text covers what he calls "legal violence." What is a critique of violence? Benjamin does not just mean a criticism of violence here. He is not taking a position against violence in this text, or criticizing violence in this or that way. He is practising, rather, a critique in Immanuel Kant's sense of the word. He is trying to distinguish between legitimate and illegitimate forms of violence, in the same way that Kant is trying to distinguish between legitimate and illegitimate forms of reason. How to determine whether violence is legitimate or illegitimate, legally founded or not? To engage in a critique of violence, which Benjamin presents as a moral assessment of violence, a couple of problems have to be dodged. First of all, such a project needs to be pursued outside of the means/ends distinction. Usually the ends are used to justify the means: violent means are legitimate, for example, if the ends are just. Both natural law and positive law, Benjamin points out, are caught up in this means/ends distinction. He states several times that he wants to take violence outside of the means/ends sphere.[2] He wants to focus on the means alone, cut off from the ends. This leads him to reconsider the difference between sanctioned and unsanctioned force,[3] between legitimate and illegitimate violence. His position is that violence is deemed unsanctioned or illegitimate when it is in the hands of the individual. This is because law must be preserved against such individuals. This explains, Benjamin argues, the public admiration for "the great criminal,"[4] who is an individual who practises violence. He also mentions the example of the great strike and comes back to strikes later in his text. Strikes that seek to overthrow the law will be confronted with military violence. The latter is sanctioned, the former unsanctioned violence. Military force needs to preserve the law, it is a law-preserving force, to be distinguished from a law-making force. Against the great criminal, the law has capital punishment, a sanctioned violence that is legitimately used as a deterrent, to keep violence out of the hands of the individual. Capital punishment, in Benjamin's view, reveals that "there is something rotten in the law" because it practices a violence *in the name of the collective* that it seeks to deny *to the individual.*[5] One could call this the paradox of legal violence, after Giorgio Agamben's "paradox of sovereignty" ("I, the sovereign, who am outside of the law, declare that there is nothing outside the law"[6]). Benjamin also discusses the police in this context noting that it is in democracies, where the police are not invested with "the power of the ruler in which legislative and executive supremacy are united," that the existence of the police "bears witness to the greatest conceivable degeneration of violence."[7]

The origin of every contract, Benjamin writes, "points toward violence."[8] Still, non-violent conflict-resolution is possible in both the private and the public sphere. In the public sphere, it comes from conferences, understanding, the realm of language, even if Benjamin also shows through a short commentary on fraud that even the realm of language has become infected by violence. The text then shifts to discuss two forms of strike: political strike and proletarian general strike (a distinction Benjamin takes from Georges Sorel). The former is violent and law-making because it merely brings a change of masters; the second, even though it destroys state power (he writes, "vernichten," "ausschalten," and "aufheben" – the difference between all three is worth considering), is non-violent because it leads to a "wholly transformed work" ("eine gänzlich veränderte Arbeit"[9]). He calls the second "anarchistic."

It is only after this that Benjamin appears to come to his key question, and not even quite yet. What kinds of violence, he asks, exist outside of those envisioned by legal theory? This is where we arrive at the "On" or "Zur" moment in his title. He has done the critique. This is where he seeks to leap beyond mere critique, where the critique begins to turn into a transgression. At first, he suggests that mythical violence will bring such a beyond. But it turns out that all mythical violence is ultimately "identical with all legal violence."[10] A true beyond is only found in what Benjamin calls "divine violence," which he considers to be opposed to myth (as the Gods, he writes, always are). Divine violence is law-destroying, it destroys boundaries, it expiates, it strikes. Mythical violence, on the other hand, makes law, sets boundaries, works through guilt and retribution, and threatens. "Educative violence," "erzieherische Gewalt,"[11] is mentioned as an example of such a violence outside of legal violence – but it is not quite clear what it is, exactly, or how it is outside of the law. His final paragraph characterizes such violence as "waltend,"[12] translated as "sovereign."[13]

I want to elaborate for a moment on the difference between the German and English titles of Benjamin's essay, between "Critique of Violence" and "On the Critique of Violence," since it is crucial to the political project of this book. As we saw just now, Benjamin is hardly only doing "critique" in his essay. After spending quite a bit of time discussing how the distinction between legitimate and illegitimate violence might be made, he seeks, in the final part of the essay, to outline a realm that would lie beyond such critique. This is why his text is ultimately an essay that is not limited to the critique of violence but speaks about the critique of violence in order to ultimately accomplish something else. Mythical violence is brought in to do this, but cannot. It gets subsumed under legal violence. Divine violence – characterized as "sovereign," in the English translation – is what pulls off the transgressive leap beyond.

The reference when it comes to the term "Kritik" would likely be to Kant and his attempt to distinguish between legitimate and illegitimate uses of reason in *Critique of Pure Reason.* As we know, "critique" in Kant, while it lays out such a distinction, ultimately always stays "within" what is legitimate. It does not take the leap beyond. It is precisely on this count that Foucault, in his essay "What Is Enlightenment?," disagrees with Kant. Enlightenment, for Kant, famously refers to "man's release from his self-incurred tutelage," with tutelage being "man's inability to make use of his understanding without direction from another."[14] "Dare to think!" or "Sapere aude" ("To think, dare!" – the Latin has the word order in reverse and foregrounds the thinking rather than the daring) is therefore the motto of Kant's Enlightenment.[15] However, Kant also proposes another motto in the text: "Argue all you please, but obey!"[16] At the end of the day, for Kant, you have to pay your taxes, even if he encourages argument about taxation. Kant is able to propose both those mottoes due to the fact that he makes a counter-intuitive distinction between what he calls the private and the public uses of reason. By the private use of reason, he refers to, for example, a priest who speaks from the pulpit, and who in that public function must stick to what the Holy Book and the Church tell him. That is his private use of reason. But as a scholar, Kant writes, that same priest may go home and write a treatise that argues with the Church or he may debate publicly with other "citizens of the world" and challenge aspects of the holy doctrine. It is not just that he *may* do this. For Kant, it is an *essential* aspect of humanity that one does this. Those who do not do it are, in Kant's view, barely human.

There is, in other words, a way in which in Kant the opening that the Enlightenment presents – dare to think! – immediately gets folded back into a structure of obedience – but obey![17] This is odd because as the opening line of Kant's essay states, Kant was interested first and foremost in a way out, an exit. But as soon as he points to the exit sign, he also closes the door. It was Foucault who, in his response to Kant – he engaged Kant's essay again and again in the final decade of his life – turned out to be very frustrated with this. Foucault recognized the value of Kant's text but challenged its conservatism. The question for Foucault was: How can the project of critique be turned into a positive transgression? How can we use critique to become something other than what we already are? This he calls "the undefined work of freedom."[18] This is where Foucault – contrary to Kant – finds the core of the Enlightenment. He articulates this not only in the Enlightenment essay but in his late work on the "care of self."[19]

What kind of "sovereign" violence does Benjamin have in mind at the end of "Critique of Violence"? It is hard to tell. What can be said is that the realm of legal/mythical violence, the realm of critique, is interrupted by, or perhaps is not so much interrupted by as begins to border here upon, something else – a realm of violence outside of law and myth. Benjamin calls it "waltend" or "sovereign." The translation is worth noting. It is supposedly when Schmitt comes across this text, and its theory of a sovereign violence that transgresses legal/mythical violence, that he writes *Political Theology* as an attempt to rein such violence back in. Indeed, Schmitt folds it back within the law through the theory of the state of exception. This is a conservative move in response to Benjamin's radicalism.

How does Agamben relate to this? Recall that he thinks (mistakenly, in my view) that Schmitt is still too attached to an outside with his theory of the state of exception, which he presents as "life" breaking through the crust of boring law. Instead, Agamben argues, such "life" is at the core of the law's operation – that is how the law works. There is nothing "outside" about it. It makes Schmitt sound more radical than he actually is. It makes it possible to discern in Schmitt a trace, still, of the "divine violence" that in Benjamin transgresses the sphere of the legal/mythical. Agamben in a sense completes Schmitt's "taming" move by revealing how the production of internal exclusions is the key operation of the law. But that does not mean that he lets Benjamin go: au contraire. He in fact eventually returns to Benjamin's notion of divine violence as a criticism of Schmitt and his theory of the state of exception. Agamben embraces the outside of divine violence against the more normative aspects of Schmitt's thought.

This is where another text of Benjamin's becomes useful, his "Theses on the Philosophy of History," in which he distinguishes between the state of exception of fascism and what he calls "the real state of exception" ("wirklicher Ausnahmezustand"[20]).[21] Much of Benjamin's text concerns "history" and can thus be considered within a continuation of our engagement with Foucault's discussion of history in his lecture on Hobbes. Note Benjamin's particular conceptualization of history: as something that "flits by," "flashes up," et cetera.[22] It has been noted that here history is conceptualized in the language of photography.[23] But one should probably *also* note that this is the language of the exception: history is exceptional because it flashes up instantaneously – it is the historians' responsibility to attend to it, to care for it. It is in its exceptionality that history risks becoming "a tool of the ruling classes."[24] It is in its exceptionality that it risks being written by the victors. The scope of this process is disconcerting: not even the dead will be safe from it, as Benjamin writes. There is war that underlies history.

But Benjamin also sees something else in exceptionality: "it is our task [Aufgabe]," he writes, "to bring about a real state of emergency, and this will improve our struggle against Fascism" – with the latter being associated with "the oppressed" and "the [fake?] state of exception."[25] In other words, exceptionality seems to go two ways here: both in the direction of Fascism and then in the direction of something else that might defeat fascism. What this something else is, we do not know. The theses make clear that it has something to do with writing history otherwise: bringing theology into historical materialism (as he proposes in Thesis I), rethinking the idea of "progress" (which he captures, negatively, by the image of the Angel of History being pulled into the future, with its back towards the future, beholding a single catastrophe, its wings caught in a storm blowing from "Paradise" – "this storm we call progress," the last word dripping with irony).[26] And it has something to do with rethinking messianism, which Benjamin reconceives from a traditional messianism that's focused on the end of time into an alternative, *weak* messianism (Thesis II) that would contract the future into the now (as in the famous statement that "everything will be as it is now, just a little different"[27]). In historical terms, this means crystallizing a certain configuration of thoughts into "a monad,"[28] into "now-time."[29] This is a slowing down or arrest, a "stop," that – against the accelerationism of "progress" – presents "a revolutionary change in the fight for the oppressed past."[30] The "continuum of history" – one single catastrophe – is thus "blasted open" and a new sense of history, a new calendar, is established. This process is captured, in Thesis XVII, as an "Aufhebung" – a cancellation or destruction that also preserves.[31]

Going back to "Critique of Violence," one might also surmise that Benjamin had already theorized this "real state of exception" in 1921 as "divine violence" – the "sovereign" violence beyond the sphere of legal/mythical violence that writes contracts in blood. In other words, Benjamin may be theorizing a greater state of exception against Schmitt's state of exception that would be able to end the fascist state of exception with which Schmitt had become associated.

Agamben appears to be attracted by such a "real state of exception" as the solution to the problems with the "normal" state of exception that he criticizes. As he suggests in his reading of Hobbes, "all of us" are in the state of exception in relation to the flashing instant of the people-king, which as soon as it has come about dissolves into what Hobbes calls the dissolved multitude, an unpolitical element. The general situation that is described here is one of precarity and vulnerability. But it also introduces the possibility of the civil war that, in the Hobbesian circle of constituted power, lies at the origin of any new institution of a people-king. As such, it is the revolutionary, rebellious reality of any established power that dissolves as soon as it is instituted (as Agamben in his reading of Hobbes insists). In other words, the "real" state of exception, which sounds theological and perhaps messianic in Benjamin, has nothing of the theological to it: it is quite literally what Benjamin calls "real," the reality of our unpolitical existence (in contrast with the optical illusion of our body politic). Theology is "the real kingdom of god" that, in Hobbes's theory, will come about at the end of time. But Agamben is not doing theology: by uncovering the real state of exception in Hobbes, he points out that the dissolved multitude marks the real antidote to the fascistic illusions of *all* government. Benjamin, I would argue, is his ally in this, even if in Benjamin this antidote is still called "waltend" – sovereign – a term that Agamben rejects. What in Benjamin still appears as a sovereignty against sovereignty becomes in Agamben an unpolitical reality *outside* of sovereignty. This is the reality of Agamben's generalized civil war, realized by the power he calls destituent.

To sum up, we find the following *escalation of thought*: in "Critique of Violence," Benjamin proposes a divine violence that would exceed the mythical violence of the law. In response, the conservative Schmitt proposes a concept of sovereignty that is, ultimately, folded within the law – as an outside. Agamben in his criticism of Schmitt not only sides with Benjamin, whose "Theses on the Philosophy of History" can be said to offer a greater sovereignty against Schmitt's sovereignty; he also takes Benjamin even further in his assertion of a generalized civil war and rejection of democracy and sovereignty in favour of destituent power. Due to his attention to Schmitt, Agamben preserves the descriptive usefulness of Schmitt when considering our contemporary situation. But by radicalizing Benjamin and rejecting sovereignty he also removes us from the possibility *of critically taking on today's sovereign resurgence* – of operating within it rather than without it. My argument is that this has become an untenable position. Rather than taking inspiration from Agamben's civil war and destituent power, or even from Benjamin's divine violence, today's left needs to critically intervene within the resurgence of sovereign power. For that, and in spite of all of his problems, it may be useful to return – once more – to Schmitt. In the next part of this book, I work through four "Paradigms of Sovereignty" to see where such a project might lead.

PART TWO

Four Paradigms of Sovereignty

5

The Camp

If Giorgio Agamben emerges in part 1 of this book as a radical critic of sovereignty – even with Walter Benjamin, as I show, the case is not as clear – this radicalism is perhaps due to the paradigm that Agamben himself offers for sovereignty:[1] the concentration camp.[2] Acknowledging that his is a philosophical rather than a historical position, Agamben insists that something of the logic of the camp is paradigmatic of Western modernity, a paradigm whose operations he also traces back to classical times (Roman law). But how can one equate one of the key accomplishments of modern political thought, "sovereignty," with Auschwitz?

Many would point out the outrageousness of basing a study of sovereignty on such an aberrant example. Those are likely the theorists of sovereignty who are focused on the norm, on sovereign power as the guarantor and protector of the norm.[3] But Agamben is a (critical) Schmittian and, following Schmitt, starts from the statement that in order to understand sovereign power one must look at the exception rather than the norm. This explains his focus on Auschwitz, on the exception, to understand sovereign power. Ultimately, these two different positions are part of a shared perspective, namely, a transcendental perspective on sovereignty as the power that guarantees *and* suspends the law. Agamben captures this with the "paradox of sovereignty": "I, the sovereign, who am outside of the law, declare that there is nothing outside the law."[4] This formula takes recourse to the law's suspension in order to guarantee its universal application within a territory.

It is worth noting that, by focusing on the exception, Agamben does seem to get something right, namely, that a legal "within" is always declared from an "outside," from a position that is not quite yet included in the "within," even if the "within's" retroactive scope applies to it (as in the paradox of sovereignty). Of course, that outside will, according to many, not be called a state of exception: it will be referred to as a state of nature, the pre-political situation from where a contract is closed. But we can probably agree that when it comes to those "states of nature," they are phantasy-like projections back into political history, constructions of pre-political states that never really existed as such. Nor did the "savages" that are said to have populated them. In this sense the state of exception, as the real dissolution of any established political order (dissolution that, as Agamben has taught us, becomes explicit in, for example, a civil war situation), is the real trace of this phantasy state in the political body – the violent, foundational trauma that power's illusion seeks to occlude. In this sense, while logically second, existentially the exception *does* come first – and Agamben is right in foregrounding it, even if limiting it to Auschwitz drastically narrows down the range of possible examples. ("We, the people" could also have done as such an example). Agamben, however, seems to want to judge everything by the negative. His work produces, one is tempted to say, an inflation of the negative.

This was illustrated by the philosopher's response to the Covid-19 crisis,[5] which sharply criticized the exceptional measures implemented as part of what he considers a civil war in order to flatten the virus's curve; again and again, Agamben doubled down on a theoretical argument without acknowledging the need to prevent the virus from spreading in order to save lives. While Agamben's responses caused much controversy, including a full-page opinion piece titled "The Coronavirus Philosopher" in the *New York Times*,[6] they should not have come entirely as a surprise given that he has mostly taken a hard-liner's position on sovereignty as a power whose essential activity he considers to be the biopolitical production of bare life. In this, sovereignty reveals its structural affinity with the concentration camps, which in their biopolitical production of bare life in turn express what Agamben considers to be the "paradigm of the modern."[7] The modern's law or *nomos* (as he also refers to it, with echoes of Carl Schmitt) adds up to what many consider to be one of modernity's most horrific aberrations: Auschwitz.

It's a position that, since the late 1990s when Agamben's work started to receive a wide English-language readership thanks to Daniel Heller-Roazen's translations, has caught a lot of flak: defenders of

The Camp

modernity, sovereignty, and even biopolitics alike have held Agamben accountable for his flattening claim. If the camp expresses the logic of modernity specifically, then why tie that to sovereignty, a power that, while it arguably finds its first sustained articulation in thinkers like Jean Bodin and Thomas Hobbes, obviously has a longer history than that? Doesn't Agamben's own focus on Roman law in his study of sovereignty acknowledge as much? But can one really talk about sovereignty with respect to Roman law? Didn't the modern articulation of the concept bring a difference with respect to that law? Is there really a kinship or continuity here? Surely all of modernity doesn't add up to the camp? To talk about the camps as biopolitical doesn't seem to make a whole lot of sense either when one thinks of them as death-camps specifically (from that point of view, they strike one rather as examples of a *thanato*-politics, a death-politics rather than a politics of life); instead, one would have to consider the camps as sites where a kind of life is optimized – Aryan life. On all three counts – biopolitics, sovereignty, modernity – one can apply pressure to draw Agamben's provocative position on sovereignty into question.

Agamben's association of sovereignty with fascism during the pandemic recalls Michel Foucault's discussion of "the state" (together with "the people" a typical repository of sovereign power) in *The Birth of Biopolitics*, where Foucault criticizes what he characterizes as a diluted analysis that "allows one to practice what could be called a general disqualification by the worst."[8] Criticizing those who suffer from "state phobia" and in their affliction conflate fascism with the welfare state,[9] Foucault delivers a stinging critique that, one could argue, applies to Agamben:

> As soon as we accept the existence of this continuity or genetic kinship between different forms [*formes*] of the state, and as soon as we attribute a constant evolutionary dynamism to the state, it then becomes possible not only to use different analyses to support each other, but also to refer them back to each other and so deprive them of their specificity. For example, an analysis of social security and the administrative apparatus on which it rests ends up, via some slippages and thanks to some plays on words, referring us to the analysis of concentration camps. And, in the move from social security to concentration camps the requisite specificity of analysis is diluted.[10]

In other words: the state *cannot* be limited to the concentration camp. To claim a continuity between the latter and (in Foucault's example) the welfare state is merely a pathology of the state phobia that Foucault calls out. To consider the pandemic, then, and to call the state's response to the pandemic "fascism" – which is exactly what Agamben, a dedicated reader of Foucault, did – would be "to practice ... a general disqualification by the worst." It means to put into circulation an "inflationary critical value."[11] Specifically, Foucault suggests that it does not distinguish carefully enough between "different *forms* of the state" (emphasis added). One perhaps unexpected consequence of such a lack of careful distinction is that Italian newspapers "often sympathetic to [the anti-immigrant League party of Matteo Salvini" (as Christopher Caldwell puts it in the *New York Times*) turned out to be receptive to Agamben's resistance to the pandemic.[12] The philosopher calling the state's response to the pandemic fascist, then, was embraced by the fascists. (Agamben's answer to this was that it is not because a fascist says that 2 + 2 = 4 that mathematics are proven wrong: "A truth remains such, whether it is expressed by the Left or enunciated by the Right."[13])

I would like to seize on Foucault's use of the word "form" to consider more closely how it operates in Agamben's thought. This might seem like a counter-intuitive move: Agamben has in some recent debates about form been cast as an anti-formalist – as one of those vitalists, quite common in the recent history of continental philosophy, who have taken it up for life against form and have thus lost track (as those scholars would argue) of the political benefits of form.[14] But this overlooks the important, and multiple, roles that form plays in Agamben's work. Strange as it may sound, Agamben is somewhat of a political formalist – but not a very good one. *And it is this failure of political formalism in his work that risks preventing the development of the affirmative politics of sovereignty that I am pursuing in this book.*

I would argue that Agamben's political formalism fails for at least two reasons: first, the positive articulation that the notion of form receives in his work, in the term "form-of-life" that his work affirms, has never been fully developed and has thus remained something of an enigma to Agamben's readers (there are good reasons to think that Agamben might embrace this, as I will explain, but it has added to the confusion around the role of form in his work); the second reason, which I develop at length in my book on the plasticity of sovereignty,

The Camp   53

is that Agamben, possibly as a consequence of his rejection of aesthetics early on in his work, does not think political form plastically
enough. The political form of "sovereignty" appears to be caught in a
straightjacket in Agamben's work that prevents it from being thought
in its various articulations, some negative to be sure (as, for example, in
the abusive form of sovereignty called tyranny), but some also positive
(it would be difficult to argue that the entire history of sovereignty as
a political concept has amounted to nothing more than a series of
"camps," with Agamben looking on as some kind of Benjaminian
"Angel of History" moving backwards into the future, his wings
caught up in the storm of what is called progress ...; some of it *was*
actually progress, one would have to acknowledge – but without the
irony that Benjamin attributes to this term).

Against the inflationary critical value of "the camp" as a paradigm
to judge all political forms, I thus propose – and it feels somewhat
absurd that I need to formulate this as a proposition – to distinguish
between the state's response to the pandemic and fascism. I will push
this even further and think the state's response to the pandemic as *a
sovereign practice of care*. I don't dispute that, on the surface, some
of the techniques and technologies of such a practice may resemble
those of a sovereign practice of control that might, in another historical context, be the techniques and technologies of fascism. As such,
these techniques and technologies are worth analyzing in their specific
contexts and with their specific purposes. But "resemblance" is not a
strong critical relation (if all you have is a hammer, everything looks
like a nail), and surface reading is not strong critical reading.
Aestheticizing sovereignty means recognizing the plurality of its political forms and being able to critically distinguish between those that
are for the better and those that are for the worse. If such a distinction
is no longer possible – an "if" that seems to have become the mark of
our time – we will truly have become post-critical.

DO WE REALLY ALL LIVE IN A CAMP?

If Auschwitz marks the exception for Agamben, his analysis of the
camp does not end with the state of exception. In *Means without
End* – a title that echoes Benjamin's "Critique of Violence" and its
triple rejection of "ends" for the project of a critique – Agamben
defines the camp as a state of exception *that has become the rule*.[15]
The latter is an important addition. A camp is *not just* a state of

exception *but* a state of exception that has become the normal way of doing things. Normally, this should not happen with the state of exception: it should be declared temporarily, and then be undone. But Agamben argues that, more and more, power has operated through states of exception in such a way that the exception that lies at the heart of power's operation has by now effectively become the rule. It is this particular situation that he names "camp." We have moved, in the history of Western democracies, from the city-state of Athens to the city-as-camp – to Auschwitz. Again, this is a philosophical and not a historical argument: Agamben would be the first to recognize that most of our lives are not comparable, historically, to the "lives" (if they can still be called that) of those in Auschwitz. But virtually, we are all in their position, he argues. As the internally excluded of the body politic, we all live in a camp.

This becomes easier to understand if we recall once more a short section early on in *Homo Sacer* where Agamben discusses the work of Alain Badiou.[16] As I discuss in chapter 3, Agamben lays out some terms that can usefully be mobilized to summarize his own theory of sovereignty. Following Badiou, Agamben crosses the terms "membership" and "inclusion," and "presentation" and "representation." A member may be present in a society, but they are included only if they are represented in that society politically. Agamben notes that Badiou defines as "normal" a situation in which there is both presentation and representation, membership and inclusion. "Excrescent" is a situation in which there is representation but not presentation: you may be politically represented in a state, for example, even if you are not present there. Badiou calls singular a situation of presentation without representation: the state of being a member/present without being included.

If Agamben spends a paragraph summarizing Badiou, however, he does so because he wants to go further. "What becomes," he asks, "of the exception in this scheme?"[17] In *Homo Sacer*, Agamben theorizes the exception as a situation of inclusive exclusion: of being excluded within. (The example, as he points out, is the exception's inverse: it names a situation of exclusive inclusion.) In Badiou, the exception would fall in the situation of the singular (present without representation), but for Agamben this is not so. The exception, he writes, is "the figure in which singularity is represented as such, which is to say, insofar as it is unrepresentable."[18] This does indeed go further than Badiou. If singularity can be turned into normality simply by

The Camp

providing representation/inclusion, with exception Agamben is interested in a figure who is included in a situation *as* unrepresentable.

Most of you reading this book are likely in a normal situation: present and represented (e.g., you are present in the US and a citizen of the US). Several may be excrescent: represented but not present (e.g., I am a citizen of Belgium, but I am not present there). Some may also be singular: present but not represented (you may be present in the US but not politically included in it – for example, if you are in the US without papers). These examples give rise to the question: Who is in the situation that Agamben calls exception?

Agamben's answer might surprise you, even if it also kicks in an open door: under the conditions of sovereignty, it is all of us. When he asks, "What is the figure of bare life as it has been integrated into the management of the pandemic?," his response is: "All men are, in this sense, potentially asymptomatic cases," and in this sense we all are bare life in relation to pandemic government.[19] Speaking more broadly, one might say that all of us as are politically included, only – he provocatively argues – by virtue of being excluded from the forms representing us. None of us coincides with the political representations that are supposed to protect us. The tie between nativity and nationality, between birth and political representation, is a retroactive projection that does not correspond to how things are. All of us are born without papers. Political representation is a symbolic identity that is added to our biological life afterwards. The fact that it was added means, more disturbingly, that it can be taken away. It's in this split between biological life and symbolic life, the simple fact of living and the political forms of life, between *zoe* and *bios* (as Agamben, following the Greeks, puts it), that our lives are produced as bare lives by the sovereign powers that govern it.

The goal of Agamben's project is to block this political machine, which – as his discussion of the split between *zoe* and *bios* shows – is also an anthropological machine, by thinking what Agamben calls a "form-of-life" in which the simple fact of living would coincide with the political form of life, and the sovereign split between biological and symbolic life, *zoe* and *bios*, would be overcome. This would render the phenomenon of the camp inoperative. Agamben has come closest to realizing this project in *The Use of Bodies*,[20] the last book of his *Homo Sacer* project, and various shorter essays that he has published since then. There is a utopian dimension to this project, in the sense that it imagines a place, or perhaps even just a space, where life would be able to be differently – protected but not through symbolic identities that were added to it and that, as a consequence, could be taken away. Protected as such. A life, as he would put it, that is its own form – that does not lack for a form that needs to be added to it. A good life.

If this sounds a little enigmatic or even mystical to you, that's because it is. And that may be part of the point: the enigma plays an important role in Agamben's early work, for example, his criticism in *Stanzas* of Western culture's celebration of Oedipus as the one who solves the riddle (why can we not let the riddle be?);[21] or in the section titled "The Idea of Peace" from his *The Idea of Prose*: "Not the appeal to guaranteed signs, or images, but the fact that we cannot recognize ourselves in any sign or image: that is peace – or, if you like, that is bliss more ancient than peace which a marvelous parable of St. Francis's defines as sojourn: nocturnal, patient, homeless – in non-recognition. Peace is the perfectly empty sky of humanity; it is the display of non-appearance as the only homeland of man."[22] It does not seem to me that such a homeland, such a space or place, generally exists (though you may have experienced pockets of it). Over and over again, Agamben suggests that poetry and art hold the key to it. To those who are studying poetry and art, this may seem like an all too easy solution: How many times haven't we seen poetry and art brought in to save us from bad politics? We know very well, however, that there's no guarantee that poetry and art would be beyond the problems that plague politics. Still, there is something provocative about the hackneyed suggestion, which taps into poetry and art's speculative core, the fact that one of their essential abilities is that they are able to imagine things as otherwise than they are – in philosophical terms, that they are able to tap into the contingency of things. (This is, in my view, one of poetry and art's strongest connections to philosophy.) And so in this sense, poetry and art would have the capacity to put us in touch with a speculative reality that is not governed by the logic of sovereignty, a logic that – as per Agamben – cannot but produce bare life.

What to call such a reality, beyond its association with poetry and art? What to call life in such a reality? Agamben's work provides an answer to that last question: it's "whatever being,"[23] a term that circulates in his work as an equivalent to "form-of-life," and the positive counterpart to the negatively valued bare life. His answer to the former question is more complicated. I have suggested,[24] and others have also made this claim, that if Agamben's name for the inclusive

The Camp

exclusions of sovereignty is "exception," the term "state of exception" actually carries a double valence in his work, one negative, the other positive. The negative one names the sovereign state of inclusive exclusion, one that Agamben historically marks (via Schmitt) as theologico-political. Schmitt, indeed, turns the decision on the state of exception into the key characteristic of sovereignty. The positive state of exception is marked by Agamben, this time after Walter Benjamin, as "messianic": it is the collectivization of whatever being's form-of-life, most likely as some form of anarchism (as the closing sections of *Use of Bodies* allow one to conclude[25]). In his late work, Agamben ties anarchism to the notion of destituent power, a power or, perhaps better, a capacity that would dismantle the Western political logic of constituent and constituted power that echoes the hylemorphic logic of *zoe* and *bios* that he considers to be the core of sovereignty.

Apart from the double – or even triple, if we acknowledge bare life in its difference from *zoe* – role of life in the above summary of Agamben's thought, the double role of form is also worth noting. It appears both in the explanation of *bios*, which Agamben translates as the form of life (as opposed to the simple fact of living), and in the notion of form-of-life, which is supposed to overcome the nefarious distinction between *zoe* and *bios* that, as Agamben sees it, lies at the root of all of sovereignty's trouble. Both those notions of form have a very different relationship with life. The first, *bios* as form of life, is marked in Agamben's work as the sovereign internal exclusion of life (*zoe*) from ethical and political form, thus rendering it into bare life. The second, form-of-life, establishes that contraction of life and form otherwise, realizing life itself as a form. What exactly is meant by this in Agamben's work is difficult to figure out, as I have already indicated. But we do sense in this a tension between life and form that is arguably a key feature of much recent thought. While in the eyes of some, this may add up to a defence of life against form, a pushing of form towards life – a reading that's certainly understand-able given Agamben's criticism of the split between *zoe* and *bios*, the simple fact of living and the political form of life – one may also want to pursue (as I intend to do here) the hyphenation in the other direction and consider life's pushing towards form to see what understanding of form this might yield. Agamben is typically considered a vitalist; but this has prevented a reading of him as a formalist, someone who may also invite us to rethink the notion of form through its hyphen-ation with life.

TOWARDS AN AFFIRMATIVE (AND NON-FASCIST) SOVEREIGNTY OF CARE

Philosopher Judith Butler recalls this argument – "Agamben writes, 'We are all potentially exposed to this condition' [i.e., the condition of bare life in the state of exception]"[26] – in their text "Indefinite Detention" about the contemporary camp in Guantánamo Bay, Cuba. "Camp" is the name used for the facilities there: they are not prisons, the people who are kept there are not called prisoners (they are detainees).[27] By that nomenclature, power is trying to prevent "normal" law from applying to its subjects – it is trying to prevent their rights from being effective. In other words, the normal rule of law is suspended in the Guantánamo Bay camp, and this is how the capture of human bodies is accomplished there. The exception has become "Standard Operating Procedure," to recall Erroll Morris's documentary about the Abu Ghraib prison photographs that Butler also discusses.[28]

Horrible as they may be, Guantánamo Bay and Abu Ghraib are obviously not Auschwitz. This should be a point we can all agree on. Nevertheless, in spite of the historical difference, one can make a structural argument that the legal paradox that enables Guantánamo was also operative in Auschwitz.

Butler is ultimately interested in that legal "end of the business" – a position that they pointedly oppose (but also complicate at the end of their text) to that of Donald Rumsfeld who insists: "I'm not a lawyer. I'm not into that end of the business."[29] Butler's position in "Indefinite Detention" is worth tracking. They start with Foucault's notion of governmentality/government, the late modern form of power that becomes dominant over sovereignty: this is the biopolitical power that operates on populations, through statistics, norms rather than laws, that is invested in sex and race, has no clearly assigned source of power, governs through allowing people to live their lives "freely," et cetera. Today, according to Foucault, sovereignty has waned; biopolitical governmentality has taken over. Butler begins by saying that Foucault may have been too quick to insist on sovereignty's "devitalization" in this context. The rise of governmentality does not necessarily mean the devitalization of sovereignty.[30] Instead, it may be that it is only sovereignty in its traditional sense, as the guarantor of law, that has waned. Exceptionalist sovereignty as Schmitt theorizes it may thrive in the governmental (and, one should add, neoliberal) environment.

The Camp   59

I have already shown that it is partly *this* that opened up Foucault to neoliberalism. It is also what prevents a narrowly Foucauldian perspective from explaining Guantánamo. Butler seeks to right this situation: sovereignty has "[emerged] as a reanimated anachronism within the political field unmoored from its traditional anchors … with the vengeance of an anachronism that refuses to die."[31] In our day and age, "prerogative" power is not solely reserved for those holding the executive seat. In a time of governmentality, where power has become much more diffuse, there are plenty of "managerial officials with no clear claim to legitimacy" who are exercising it.[32] "Petty sovereigns abound," they write, "reigning in the midst of bureaucratic army institutions mobilized by aims and tactics of power they do not inaugurate or fully control."[33] They refer to this as a "resurrected sovereignty," "a lawless and prerogatory power, a 'rogue' power *par excellence.*"[34] One imagines that Schmitt would have been horrified by this; it is not his vision of sovereignty at all. At the same time, such a perspective is not covered by Foucault's theory, which leaves sovereignty aside. It is no wonder, then, that Butler ultimately turns to Agamben as a philosopher who has thought through the results of this, which is the creation of "a paralegal universe that goes by the name of law."[35]

What is going on here? In Butler's terms, we find a "spectral sovereignty" that is "reanimate[d] … within the field of governmentality" – a Schmitt who has to be thought with Foucault, or a Foucault who has to be thought with Schmitt. "The state produces, through the act of withdrawal, a law that is no law, a court that is no court, a process that is no process."[36] This is precisely what they find in Guantánamo, where, as they write at the beginning of their text, detainees are not granted "the right to legal counsel" or "the right to trial";[37] "the rights to counsel, means of appeal, and repatriation stipulated by the Geneva Convention have not been granted to any of the detainees in Guantánamo."[38] Instead, subjects are caught within a state of indefinite detention; in some cases they are held without having done anything wrong (in a kind of "Minority Report" situation – arrested before having committed a crime – to recall Philip K. Dick's science-fiction story). Importantly, this is not an "anarchical" situation.[39] It is clearly still *conditioned*, somehow – but in an *unconditional* way. It is probably Agamben, again, who has most clearly laid out this paradox.

"Indefinite detention" for Butler ultimately does not name an exceptional circumstance "but rather the means by which the exceptional circumstance becomes established as the naturalized norm," "part of a broader tactic to neutralize the rule of law in the name of security."[40] This is how they arrive at Agamben's statement that potentially, we are "all ... exposed to this condition."[41] All of us are potentially bare life.

Further on in Butler's text, this leads to a reflection on the notion of "the human,"[42] which echoes Agamben's point that bare life is neither human nor animal life but a kind of third. Butler notes that bare life risks being associated with animal life. But it is important to see that it is different from it. Animal life hardly fits the description given of bare life, as, for example, in the case of the extreme concentration camp prisoner, the "Muselmann." Bare life is, rather, a figure against which both human and animal life can be defined.

For the purposes of this book, however, I want to jump to the closing pages of the text, where Butler considers what argument should be construed against the problematic situation they describe. "One might conclude," they write, "with a strong argument that government policy ought to follow established law"; "And in a way," they continue, "that is part of what I am calling for." "But," they are quick to note, "there is also a problem with the law since it leaves open the possibility of its own retraction."[43] In addition, in some cases it only extends the rights it guarantees to those who are members of recognized nation-states. What about the Palestinians, for example, whom they bring up shortly afterwards? How are their rights guaranteed? It seems impossible to simply respond to the problem of the state of exception with a call for the (same old) law, in the same way that it seems impossible to respond to the problem of the dehumanization of bare life with a simple insistence on the human.

In the same way that the law should be recognized as a tool that includes the provision of its own suspension, leading to the state of exception and thus casting all of us as potential bare life, the human is a category that internally excludes all of us – a category with which none of us fully coincides (there are aspects to our lives – our aggressions, for example; our sexuality; faith; et cetera – that seem to situate us at the limit of what is generally thought of as "human"). It would be more effective to rethink the category of the human from below – "*I* may not be human, but neither are *you*" – rather than to reinforce it from above.

What would be the analogous move with the law? We can see what it would *not* be: reinforcing the law from above, at the risk of continuing or creating ever more exceptions. But what would it mean to rethink the law from below, precisely from the position of those who

The Camp 61

are internally excluded from it? This might mean to start with what Agamben calls the "unpolitical" element of the multitude – its destituent force. But in order to do what? It may be here, precisely, that the "good" state of exception opens up, in the messianic time when, according to Benjamin, "everything will be as it is now, just a little different"; where the strike does not destroy work but enables the workers to take up a "wholly transformed work."[44] As I argue elsewhere, there are elements in Agamben's work that point in this direction, even if his choice of the camp as the paradigm of sovereignty generally forces him to be more radical.

After all, when the focus is on "work," such a "good" state of exception is probably easier to imagine – even for those who are no fans of work – than when the focus is on the extreme example of the camp. While Agamben with the paradigm of the camp may have captured something about the logic of sovereignty, it would be difficult to argue that sovereignty can be reduced to that. Instead, the concept demands a much more nuanced negotiation that is able to recognize different aspects of its power and how sovereignty has operated in different situations. With the camp, which presents absolute negativity, this is not possible. For such a properly critical project, less extreme paradigms of sovereignty can be helpful. In the next chapter, I focus on "The Wall" as one such example.

As I indicate in *Plastic Sovereignties*, Catherine Malabou has done very important work in the discussion about form. In "Grammatology and Plasticity," for example, Malabou labours hard to distinguish her theory of plasticity, and the formation of form that it seeks, from Derridean deconstruction, pointing out that the formation of form entails "a power to shape meaning that exceeds [the] graphic displacement" that is central to deconstruction and that is perhaps most memorably captured by Derrida's notion of "différance,"[45] a neologism that marks through a difference that is visible/written yet not audible/spoken (the famous "a" instead of the "e" of "difference") a displacement or deferral of meaning. Even though Malabou obviously does not deny such graphic displacement, she evidently also wants more – and thus she arrives, I argue, from Derrida's deconstruction (marked by his theory of graphic displacement) at a formalism that (as I show in *Plastic Sovereignties*) has great political potential. It's important to note that, as such, a formalism like the one I find in Malabou does not leave Derrida behind – it places a different emphasis, rather, foregrounding construction after several decades of critical praises of formlessness.

In *Unexceptional Politics*, Emily Apter describes and analyzes such a project in a discussion of Bruno Latour's criticism of Schmitt in his *An Inquiry into Modes of Existence*. There, Apter perceptively writes about how Latour "unexceptionalizes transcendent modes of the Political," advocating what Apter calls a "'small p' politics that speaks its own language, that defines distinct modes of acting or articulating politically that evolve and mutate."[46] It's at this point that a reference to my *Plastic Sovereignties* appears, a book that's brought up here as part of an approach that, in Apter's closing words in the chapter from which I have been quoting, "promotes thinking pragmatically and philosophically."[47] This works well to describe, I think, the political formalism of what (after Apter) one might call unexceptionalism, the way it can overcome the age-old distinction between form and the formless that has hindered not just thought but also politics.

Following such a thought, one thus ends up with what can be characterized as a living notion of form – a mindset in which life and form are no longer opposed but in which life already provides form and form enables life. This is not so much Agamben's form-of-life but what one might call a *life-of-form* – a different way of looking at form. Considered within such a framework, sovereignty is not so much a power that formally constrains life or biopolitically produces it as something less than life (bare life, naked life, life in its privative mode). Unexceptionalism seeks to tap into sovereignty's plastic possibilities as a political form by unworking its biopolitical production of a life that is less than life. Sovereignty is thus pushed towards its plural formations, which in turn open up the critical task of their assessment – of the critical assessment of sovereignty's multiple forms, to hearken back to the term used by Foucault in the passage I quote at the beginning of this chapter.

There, Foucault indicates that it would be a post-critical mistake to consider the politics of all of those forms to be the same. While fascism and the welfare state may both be forms of the state (and here already there is much to discuss – fascism is often considered to be an excess of the state, for example, but Foucault is actually going to draw that into question in his lecture), Foucault argues that it would be a mistake to consider them to be the same, to suggest that there is a kinship or continuity between them just because they are both forms of the state. To consider a political formalism of sovereignty means to acknowledge those differences and take them as a challenge for thought.

The Camp   63

I return, then, to Agamben's remarks about the coronavirus pandemic with which I started: Is the sovereign power that is obviously active in that situation as part of an attempt to prevent the virus from spreading, and thus to prevent suffering and save lives, fascistic?

On the one hand, we find many of the ingredients here of Agamben's theory of sovereign power. The pandemic has clearly shown us the workings of a state that, in order to optimize and even save the lives of some, lessens the lives of others, and some might even argue renders them "bare" (a life lived outside of social proximity can hardly qualify as a "good life" in the classical sense of the term; it is a life that has had its form of life forcibly removed, something that, understandably, we have all found extremely difficult to accept – because we are social beings). One complication, of course, is that in the case of the pandemic, we are *all* at risk of suffering and death; in other words, it is a situation in which we are all rendered as bare life in order to, paradoxically, optimize our own lives. This is supposed to be a temporary, exceptional measurement – but Agamben fears (and is right to fear, I think) that its traces will last long after the pandemic has ended. In other words, we may be living through a time that will have long-lasting effects on our social lives, which is (by extension) on our being-human.

But does this situation qualify as a camp?

Part of the problem is that, if the only concept you have is the camp, everything will look like fascism to you. It seems impossible within the framework of Agamben's thought to read the above ingredients as part of a sovereign practice of care, a situation in which disciplinary power would not so much be the mark of a camp as of a city that, as a city-state but also at the level of the people, is pursuing the care of everyone. When "care" is evoked in Agamben's reflections on the pandemic, it is only with reference to Nazi eugenics;[48] the pandemic can only be seen as a collapse of all ethical and political values.[49] Dear reader, did it feel like that to you when you were home-schooling your children, seeing your elders on zoom, taking care of those close to you who got sick, quarantined when you yourself got sick, and got to know better those few of your friends with whom you continued to socialize because it was worth the risk?

Let us grant that it is not always easy to mark the difference between care and control. But in situations like the pandemic, it does seem that the difference needs to be charted not only in recognition of the gravity of the situation but also – and precisely – to better understand the practices of control operative in this situation (practices that, in many cases, were already felt before the pandemic arrived) and that might become further embedded in our lives once the immediate need for care has passed.

The reductive approach to political form that Agamben's remarks about the pandemic express reveals an unwillingness to do so. Paradoxically, this means that Agamben is no longer able to distinguish true emergency situations. In a thought in which the exception has become the norm, there are no longer any exceptions. This means, effectively, that a situation like the pandemic can no longer be thought. This is not only a loss under pandemic conditions: it will actively hamper our understanding of new forms of control once things go back to "normal" again.

6

The Wall

Never believe that a smooth space will suffice to save us.
> Gilles Deleuze and Felix Guattari, *A Thousand Plateaus*[1]

If the camp is arguably extreme as a paradigm for sovereign power – as the architecture that would capture the core of sovereign power – one may object less to "the wall" as such a visible, spatial marker of sovereignty. Political theorist Wendy Brown thinks about the wall in this way in *Walled States, Waning Sovereignty*. After pointing out that sovereign walls are a global phenomenon, one that can be found both at the limit of sovereign nation-states and within them (as in the case of gated communities, for example), Brown distinguishes between three paradoxical dimensions of walls. First, she notes that, while agents "across a wide political spectrum – neoliberals, cosmopolitans, humanitarians, and left activists – fantasize a world without borders … nation-states, rich and poor, exhibit a passion for wall-building." "Second, within the ostensibly triumphant political form, democracy … we confront not only barricades, but passageways through them segregating high-end business traffic, ordinary travelers, and aspiring entrants deemed suspect by virtue of their origin or appearance." Finally, in a time of what Brown characterizes as "incorporeal power," she highlights the "stark physicalism of walls." In short: walls open and block; combine "universalization" (democracy) with "exclusion and stratification"; and combine "networked and virtual power" with "physical barricades."[2]

Indeed, Brown focuses on the wall as a paradoxical architecture for a time in which the nation-state is no longer "the dominant political actor."[3] She labels this a "post-Westphalian world," that is, a world after the 1648 Westphalia peace treaty that ended the Thirty Years' War and established a balance of power between sovereign nation-states. This does not mean, as Brown is careful to point out, that sovereignty has become "finished or irrelevant": "'Post' indicates a very particular condition of afterness in which what is past is not left behind, but, on the contrary relentlessly conditions, even dominates a present that nevertheless also breaks in some way with this past. In other words, we use the term 'post' only for a present whose past continues to capture and structure it."[4] So what does sovereignty look like today, and how does the sovereign architecture of the wall help us to understand it?

Brown notes, first of all, that sovereignty "has always been something of a fiction in its aspiration and claim to" a number of qualities (Lauren Berlant, too, has pointed this out). She lists: supremacy, perpetuity, absoluteness and completeness, non-transferability, and specified jurisdiction (she later adds decisionism, with reference to Carl Schmitt[5]). Those attributes, however, "have been severely compromised" in recent times by: "growing transnational flows of capital, people, ideas, goods, violence, and political and religious fealty"; "by neoliberal rationality"; "by the steady growth and importance of international economic and governance institutions"; "by a quarter century of postnational and international assertions of laws, rights, and authority."[6] Sovereignty has not been eliminated by those, but Brown argues it has migrated into the realms of "capital and God-sanctioned political violence."[7] The result of this is that "sovereign nation-states no longer exclusively define the field of global political relations or monopolize many of the powers organizing that field, yet states remain significant actors in that field, as well as symbols of national identification."[8] Walls, Brown argues, "are iconographic of this predicament of state power."[9]

What lies behind their construction? "Counterintuitively," Brown suggests, "it is the weakening of state sovereignty ... the detachment of sovereignty from the nation-state." "The new walls," then, "are icons of [nation-state sovereignty's] erosion."[10] They may appear as intense markers of sovereignty, but actually "they reveal a tremulousness, vulnerability, dubiousness, or instability at the core of what they aim to express." Brown notes that those qualities are actually considered to be "antithetical to sovereignty." The walls thus present us with what Brown calls a "visual paradox": "What appears at first blush as the articulation of the state sovereignty actually expresses its diminution relative to other kinds of global forces – the waning relevance and cohesiveness of the form."[11] As such, those paradoxical walls blur "the distinction between the inside and outside of the nation itself";[12]

The Wall 67

they "do not and cannot actually exercise [the power] that they also performatively contradict";[13] there is something "theatricalized and spectacularized" to them that "brings into relief nation-state sovereignty's theological remainder"[14] – the awe it is supposed to evoke. If those protective aspects of sovereignty are waning, this understandably comes with some nervousness on the side of the subjects that sovereignty is supposed to protect, and the wall is also a marker of that.

In the rest of her chapter, Brown engages in a comparative discussion of two cases: the Israel Security Fence and the US/Mexico Border Barrier. Regarding the former, she notes that the fence has a number of features that enable us to think of it not so much as a wall as "a technology of separation and domination in a complex context of settler colonialism and occupation." She notes, with reference to Eyal Weizman's work, how the wall is actually "discontinuous and fragmented."[15] After pointing out its "temporally and spatially ad hoc and provisional qualities," she suggests the wall is actually *more of a barrier than a border*: removable and reroutable, this fluidity is an essential part of its operation, which Brown characterizes after Azoulay and Ophir as a "suspended political solution."[16] Brown notes, without mentioning Carl Schmitt by name, that "the notion of 'suspended political solutions' underscores the literal suspending of law, accountability, and legitimacy and the introduction of arbitrary and extralegal state prerogative that occurs on states of emergency" – in other words, it underscores the Schmittianism of the peculiar sovereign politics of the wall. To speak of a wall as a kind of "suspense" is, of course, a contradiction in terms: the very point of a wall, as architect Daniel Libeskind already evoked in 1986 with his *City Edge* project in Berlin – a suspended wall – is that it is not suspended, not internally in deconstruction, et cetera. But one sees here how precisely the wall's suspendedness and "inward dehiscence" (to quote Mark Taylor writing about Libeskind) becomes part of its operation today, in the "post-Westphalian world."[17] Thus, Brown concludes that the Israeli wall "like the others, both performs and undoes a sovereign boundary function, just as it performs and undoes" other aspects of phantasmatic sovereignty. "If the Wall is a bid for sovereignty, it is also a monstrous tribute," she writes, "to the waning viability of sovereign nation-states."[18]

She notes the same is true for the US/Mexico Border Barrier – "it stages a sovereign power it does not exercise"[19] – but her comparative analysis also draws out important differences. For one, "while the Israeli wall issues from and deepens contradictions generated for

68   Four Paradigms of Sovereignty

sovereignty by expansionist colonial occupation, the US barrier issues from and deepens the contradictions generated for First World sovereign integrity and capacity by neoliberal globalization."[20] The wall is an "ineffective bulwark" against this.[21] It's a wall meant to block "flows of people, contraband, and violence," which are the hallmarks of an era after "state sovereignty, but before the articulation of instantiation of an alternate global order."[22]

In the closing pages of the chapter I'm discussing, Brown's argument takes a political anthropological turn when she considers Greg Eghigian's notion of *homo munitus* – the fortified person – as the walled subject of the walled nation-state-in-decline. The chapter ends, interestingly, not with the reinforcement of the argument that walls confine but evokes, quite puzzlingly given what has preceded, "the comforting walls of a house."[23] While the wall confines, then, and confines today in the peculiar ways that she has laid out, Brown also evokes here that the wall can comfort – that, in some cases, one might *desire* a wall. But not the wall that confines and imprisons. Her chapter thus becomes *a negotiation of walls*, a consideration of how walls can also provide comfort *rather than* confinement, if such a thing is possible.[24]

✻

This suggestion of another kind of wall is interesting to consider, especially in view of how the destruction of walls has played out in post-1968 theory and, today, in politics – and I am thinking specifically about the Israel/Palestine conflict, which is central to Brown's chapter. Eyal Weizman, the architect and theorist whom Brown quotes at one point in her chapter, describes in his work the kind of "walking through walls" that the Israeli Defense Forces (IDF) practice in their urban warfare against the Palestinian guerrilla. Brigadier General Aviv Kochavi calls this kind of warfare "inverse geometry" because it reorganizes "the urban syntax by means of a series of micro-tactical actions" that turn the private into the public.[25] Basically, "soldiers [avoid] using the streets, roads, alleys and courtyards that define the logic of movement through the city, as well as the external doors, internal stairwells, and windows that constitute the order of buildings; rather, they were punching holes through party walls, ceilings and floors, and moving across them through 100 metre-long pathways of domestic interior hollowed out of the dense and contiguous city fabric."[26] The military refers to this tactic as "swarming" or

The Wall 69

"infestation," a metaphor it borrows from "aggregate animal forma-tion"[27] but that also has a tie to Artificial Intelligence.[28] Swarming resonates with Azoulay and Ophir's theory of the barrier as a "suspended political solution" as it "turned inside to outside and private domains to thoroughfares." Again, one hears echoes here from Schmitt, and perhaps in particular Agamben and his discussion of sovereignty's paradoxical "threshold" position inside/outside. But as the private/public inversion also indicates (Schmitt *insists* on the distinction, as one should recall), this is obviously no traditional exercise of sovereign power: "Fighting took place within half-demolished living rooms, bedrooms, and corridors. It was not the given order of space that governed the patterns of movement, but movement itself that produced the space around it."[29] The city in flux.

The fact that Kochavi defines this as a reorganization of urban "syn-tax" reveals to what extent he considers this to be a kind of linguistic model of warfare that "interprets" space, "and even [re-interprets] it, as the condition of success in urban war."[30] According to Weizman, this "makes apparent the influence of post-modern, post-structuralist theoretical language" in the IDF's way of waging war. Weizman men-tions Deleuze and Guattari as well as Debord as specific influences. He also mentions Derrida and the work of the deconstructive architect Bernard Tschumi, who would be considered part of the same school as the already mentioned Daniel Libeskind. Post-1968 French theory turns out to be critical to the development of the contemporary Israeli military apparatus and its practice of breaking through walls when it wages urban war. This kind of urban war is, Weizman writes, "the ultimate post-modern form of warfare."[31] Sovereignty is clearly still exercised here, but it is exercised after its postmodern deconstruction, in what one might want to call its "liquid" form.

For those of us who love post-1968 French theory but are critical of the Israeli military and other militaries who have learned from it (including the US military), the revelation that some of the IDF's lead-ers are actually students of theory may be disturbing. And yet, it was of course Derrida who already taught us that one can never guarantee a text's reception – a letter may be sent with a particular receiver in mind, and even with a particular message in mind, but there is no guarantee that it will ever arrive with that receiver and communicate its intended meaning. Weizman's point about the "military use of theory for ends other than those it was meant to fulfill" confirms one of the key premises, I would say, of Derridean deconstruction. If anything, it might make us look differently, perhaps, at the kind of stuff that postmodernism and deconstruction brought down. Of course, this is not a nostalgic project that would seek to bring those things back exactly as they existed in the past, and with the same problems that 1968 targeted. The project would be, rather, to bring about some kind of transformed wall that would both avoid the problems of the phantasmatic sovereign wall that Brown describes and the destruction of walls that postmodernism and deconstruction (at least in Weizman's reading) seem to advocate and that has become – like the wall – a powerful tool of the military. Post-1968 theorists are not likely to take it up for domesticity, what Brown calls "the comforting walls of the home," but surely even the highest of high theorists must cringe at the description by Aisha, a Palestinian woman, of the wall of a family living room being blasted to pieces only to have the IDF storm in, with the children screaming and panicking et cetera: "It is impossible to imagine the horror experienced by a five-year-old child as four, six, eight, twelve soldiers, their faces painted black, submachine guns pointed everywhere, antennas protruding from their backpacks, making them look like giant alien bugs, blast their way through that wall."[32]

The problem is not theory's alone. Weizman discusses art in the 1960s and 1970s being complicit with these developments. Specifically, he mentions Gordon Matta-Clark's "unwalling of the wall," a project that developed between 1971 and 1978, during which "Matta-Clark was involved in the transformation and virtual dismantling of abandoned buildings."[33] This project was labelled "anarchitecture," presumably to draw out its anarchic roots – its affinity with the rule of no rule, the rule without rule of "anarchy" (but I have to revisit this rather naive notion of anarchy in part 3). Buildings were sliced, as Weizman writes; holes were opened up "through domestic and industrial interiors."[34] In the meantime, neoliberalism was on the rise as an anarchitectural force, at least when it came to state architecture. Today, with the middle class on its way out, in the aftermath of the 2008 securitized mortgage market crisis (the *housing* market crisis, it should be noted), can it really still make sense to aspire to the slicing of buildings and the breaking through walls? Rather than destroying homes, shouldn't one find ways for people to be able to hold on to them?[35] At the end of his chapter "Evacuations: De-colonizing Architecture," Weizman evokes land art (earthwork) as a kind of art that mobilized, in the 1960s and 1970s, various of the issues that

The Wall 71

Weizman's discussion of inverse geometry warfare brings to the fore – such as the inversion of inside and outside, for example.

In the face of the kind of warfare Weizman describes, then, which relies on inverse geometry in its reorganization of urban architecture, a kind of warfare that practices "walking through walls," might one not reaffirm the value of the wall as a creator of a potentially comforting domesticity (as evoked by Brown), a potentially protective space where the subject can be "at home," "chez soi" (as they say in France – it is a phrase that Derridean deconstruction has targeted for the sovereign phantasm that it projects), and protected (but not in the sense of "munitus," "fortified") from precisely the violence that the IDF wages on the private? Might there not be an affirmative politics of the wall – and not the sovereign phantasm of the wall as Brown lays it out – that can be waged *against* the IDF's urban warfare? Might not such a politics have us re-evaluate the post-1968 theory moment and draw out some of its limitations when it comes to postmodernism, deconstruction, and various other destabilizing movements? While those have accomplished important work, is destabilization really what is needed today? Might not the time have come to invest theoretically in form, stability, frame, structure, architecture, and – why not – the wall as something that is potentially good and that might even be connected to the politics of art, which has all too often been associated with the wall's destruction? *Don't we all need at least a little bit of confinement to be able to live?*

*

In *State and Politics: Deleuze and Guattari on Marx*, Guillaume Sibertin-Blanc explicitly presents D + G's thinking about the state and sovereignty, and, in particular, striated space versus smooth space, as opposed to Carl Schmitt's thinking about sovereignty in *The* Nomos *of the Earth*. As Sibertin-Blanc points out, when D + G attempt to think the smooth space of a nomadology of the earth, they can be understood to do so in opposition to Schmitt, who proposes the earth or specifically the taking of land as the origin of state and sovereign power. "Nomos" only derives its meaning, he argues, from a "spatialization," a "localized" and "localizing" "territorial act" of land-taking through which state and sovereign power is established.[36] State and sovereign power thereby take on an earthly foundation – the distribution of the land justifies, so to speak, their power. For D + G, by contrast, "the nomos is a process that undoes the divisions and distributions of the existing spatial order and which, so to speak, *defounds* them. It does not counter them with a new order of territorial takings or captures and a new system of delimitation, it produces and inverts a type of space that makes it unlimited, and makes its capture impossible."[37] Nomads, he points out, "hold" a space rather than "taking it," and it is because of this that they need to be opposed to sovereignty and state power: "One can only hold a space that cannot be taken, or that resists being taken (partisan war), precisely by becoming unlimited, in other words impossible to circumscribe in fixed limits, delimitations of contour and interior sharing, dimensions, and unvarying directions."[38] Such a nomadic, "unlimited space" is called "smooth."[39]

Sibertin-Blanc notes the peculiar understanding of "smooth" that we confront here: "We would then say," he continues, "that a space is 'smoothed' by what happens in it ... not when it is homogenized but on the contrary when the constant markers that allow modes of occupation of space to be related to constants of objectivation are placed in variation."[40] "Space is striated," on the other hand, "by walls, enclosures, and roads between enclosures"; "nomad space is smooth, marked only by 'traits' that are effaced and displaced with the trajectory."[41] While D+G continue a thinking of state and sovereignty, then, it is a thinking that can be opposed to Schmitt's notion of sovereignty as based in a nomos of the earth. Taking the land, Sibertin-Blanc correctly notes, restates "the decision of the situation of the exception" that Schmitt had already theorized in 1922 as well as "the constitutive act that reestablishes the normative orders constituted."[42] "Nomos in the Deleuzian, and therefore nomadic sense," then, "works on the contrary like an instance of illimitation. It makes the earth the great Deterritorialized but also the highest deterritorializing power: not the foundation of divided, jurisdictioned, economically invested territories, but on the contrary that which opens territories onto their outside, their disinvestment, or their transformation."[43]

Now, interestingly, such a space is "not unknown to Schmitt. The paradigmatic figure of it in *The* Nomos *of the Earth* is maritime space; another is the tactical space of the partisan, given the importance Schmitt gives partisans in decolonialization struges and revolutionary wars."[44] "Significantly," Sibertin-Blanc adds, "Deleuze and Guattari see maritime space as a typically nomadic smooth space"; in this, it is similar to "the desert."[45] In conclusion, smooth space therefore "contains a subversion of the very Stateness of politics"; turning space

The Wall

73

into smooth space is a "political act that aims to neutralize another politics implied by this type of space." With a footnote to Eyal Weizman's "Walking through Walls," Sibertin-Blanc adds that this is why it is very important to take note of "State armies appropriating some guerilla tactics, which transfers techniques and knowledge of asymmetrical war or war by the minority to the repressive apparatus."[46] It is worth noting, of course, that D + G associate nomadology with what earlier in their book they call the "war machine," which exists between what they describe as the two heads of sovereignty – its fear-inspiring, binding head, and its contractual, juristic head.[47] The war machine and nomadology exist in excess of those, between those, beyond them – as their outside.[48] In this sense, the "nomos" that D + G theorize comes close to Benjamin's divine violence, which troubled Schmitt so. Schmitt is all about organization, although his work has the crisis of organization built in; D + G propose "the body without organs," even though that body and the smooth space it presents is not so much contrary to striation but striation intensified (fractally, as they explain).[49] It is from this perspective that they also criticize Kant, whose notion of critique I, too, criticize (from a transgressive point of view) at the end of part 1: "Kant was constantly criticizing bad usages," they write, "the better to consecrate the function."[50] Kant's critique of bad forms of reason was ultimately to reinforce good forms of reason. Schmitt's response to this makes total sense: he notes, dismissively, that "emergency law was no law at all for Kant." For Schmitt, however, *it is* – it is law, he folds the emergency within the law with his theory of sovereignty. Nomadology, D + G's nomos, aims for something else – just like Benjamin's notion of divine violence. One can only imagine Schmitt shuddering with horror when reading *A Thousand Plateaus*.

In both the case of walls and of breaking through walls, then, we are dealing with what one could call a *pharmakon* (and Brown suggests as much about walls when she adds a preface to her book's second edition): something that could either be a cure or a poison. Walls can be comforting, in which case breaking through walls is violent; but walls can also violently confine, in which case it is necessary to break through them. If this seems like a relativist conclusion, it hardly is: rather, it makes walls and the destruction of them appear as critical notions whose political effects need to be thought through in each situation. Sibertin-Blanc makes this very clear in the final section of his chapter on Schmitt. Nevertheless, and generally speaking, walls *can* be associated with a striated politics of sovereignty and the Schmittian nomos of the earth, whereas their destruction can be said to smooth space into nomadic (and Deleuzian) earth (sea, desert). The question would then become what politics is needed, for us, today, in response to the challenges that face us. If we are sceptical of the walling in and out that political phenomena like Brexit, Trump, or the rise of the right in Europe are doing, it seems impossible in view of Weizman's account to simply level the destruction of walls against this; indeed, *it may be because we have been too critical of walls that a certain nostalgia for the wall has taken over.* The problem with such a nostalgia is that it has not absorbed the lessons of the un-walling that, for example, critical theory has been doing for years.

At the same time, and again in view of Weizman's account, it may be that critical theory should learn a lesson or two from these vicious returns of the politics of the wall, realizing that perhaps human beings need a certain degree of walling to be comfortable. The latter is not an extremist political point that can be easily situated on the right. It seeks to cut across the political spectrum in the hope of bringing the demand for walls and the criticism of walls together into a different kind of wall. It is Sibertin-Blanc who points out that, as a theorist of the state, Schmitt thinks the state in crisis; D+G, on the other hand, maintain a degree of order in their theory of smoothening. And yet, these positions are all too easily presented as clear opposites, with Schmitt being for the wall and D+G against. In fact, and while their political positions are clearly different, both are more nuanced than such a clear opposition, and through that nuance they may reveal a hesitation within the human subject when it comes to its consideration of the walling and unwalling – towards unwalling in the case of those who love the wall, and towards walling in the case of those who want to break it down. It is, I think, in that hesitation that our political hopes lie: not only for a different kind of wall but also for a different kind of unwalling – which is, ultimately, also for a different kind of theory.

7

The Police

In *Between the World and Me*, Ta-Nehisi Coates shows, although he does not use these terms, that black life in the United States is caught up in a state of exception.[1] In his discussion of black life's exposure to sovereign power, he focuses on the pair black life/police in view of the ongoing police shootings of young black men – in some cases, children – in the US. As Coates notes, perhaps the most troubling element, apart from these people's deaths, is that they are killed with impunity: "These shooters were investigated, exonerated, and promptly returned to the streets, where, so emboldened, they shot again."[2] It is the element of impunity that clearly renders black life in this situation "sacred," in Giorgio Agamben's understanding of this term in the context of his work on sovereignty: outside of human law, exposed to be killed without legal consequence ("vogelfrei," as I argue elsewhere[3]). It is this element that turns black people's "fear to rage": the fact that the murderers "cannot be subpoenaed … will not bend under indictment."[4] In this chapter, I propose to turn to the police, then, and its related internally excluded/excepted/sacred figure of black life, as a paradigm of sovereignty.

That we are talking about a situation of sovereignty here is partly made clear in Coates's text through the specifics of the police killing upon which he focuses, which involves an officer from Prince George's County (in Baltimore state) and a young black man called Prince Carmen Jones. Prince Jones is shot one night, while going to visit his fiancée, by a cop who claims Jones was trying to run him over with his jeep. Jones had been approached by the cop, gun drawn; the cop had been undercover – in other words, was in plain clothes – and had shown no badge. He was, in other words, "a man in a criminal's costume" (as Coates points out),[5] and Coates confesses with horror: "I knew what I would have done with such a man confronting me, gun drawn, mere feet from my family's home."[6] The suggestion is, presumably, that he would have done the same: he, too, may have tried to run over the cop. The point about the "criminal's costume" is sharpened a few pages later, when we finally find out something that Coates obviously knew from the onset: "The officer who killed Prince Jones was black."[7]

It is hard to overlook the sovereign overtones of the confrontation (one prince versus another). To be clear: while Coates presents the lives of young black men to be caught up in a state of exception, he also insists that in the US this exception has become the rule. "In America," he writes later on, "it is traditional to destroy the black body – *it is heritage*."[8] In other words, America is another name for a place where the state of exception of black life has always been the rule. It is another name for what Agamben, working within a European frame of reference that ignores the situation of black lives in the US entirely, calls a camp: any situation in which the exception becomes the rule. The police, indeed, "reflect America in all of its will and fear," as he notes earlier on, "and whatever we might make of this country's criminal justice policy, it cannot be said that it was imposed by a repressive minority. The abuses that have followed from these policies – the sprawling carceral state, the random detection of black people, the torture of suspects – are the product of democratic will."[9] The charge, if we put Coates and Agamben together, is harsh: *democratic America equals black Auschwitz*. Or, without Agamben's frame of reference: slavery never ended.[10]

The latter phrasing of course more specifically evokes "the plantation" rather than "the camp" as a paradigm for analysis, and several of the authors whose work I engage in this chapter highlight the tension between those two paradigms, even if they also use them together (as in Achille Mbembe's theorization of necropolitics, for example, which I discuss below). By working between the two paradigms, I do not mean to suggest that the historical events they reference are "the same" or even that they are the same "as paradigms." As Adom Getachew and Chris Taylor remind us in a dialogue titled "The Global Plantation," scholars have insisted on their differences and on the limits of European theory that the focus on the camp (rather than the plantation) as a model of thought reveals (Taylor mentions specifically "the frequent Caribbeanist complaint that Agamben takes the camp, not

The Police 77

the plantation, as the paradigm of modernity"[11]). Due to my focus on "the police," however, I am inclined to work first and foremost within the paradigm of "sovereignty" (and its associated paradigm of "the camp"), a focus that is also borne out in the references that are mobilized in this chapter, even if "the plantation" also enters into tension with those paradigms and asserts itself as a perhaps more historically specific way of conceptualizing the situation of black lives in the US. In this sense, the theoretical point of view here can be said to be influenced by thinkers such as Taylor and Getachew, and, as such, it reflects the importance of work in Black studies for the reconceptualization of sovereignty that I envision in this book.[12]

In the Prince Jones killing, we confront a particular perversity of what I here call black Auschwitz, namely, black-on-black violence, which is fuelled, Coates suggests, by what he calls "the Dream." By this, he means white people's Dream, the Dream of a white America. He calls those who share such a Dream, "Dreamers." Black people in the US carry not only "the burden of living among Dreamers"; they also have the "extra burden of your country telling you the Dream is just, noble, and real, and you are crazy for seeing the corruption and smelling the sulfur."[13] Perversely, it is "the Dream" that may in part explain the instance of black-on-black violence that Coates is analyzing: it is "the Dream" that may explain the cop's reaction to Prince Jones, in the same way that it is "the Dream" that may explain Jones's reaction to the cop. Part of the "criminal's costume," in other words, and one can hardly call it a *costume*, is the *blackness* of both the victim and the murderer – a blackness that "the Dream" criminalizes and that makes black people kill each other due to white people's fear. When Coates shudders in horror at the realization of what he would have done – *the same* – he is also shuddering in horror at the extent to which "the Dream" has infected *him*, the extent to which it has turned *him* against his own people. *Between the World and Me* is an attempt to puncture this "Dream," to force something between the reality of Coates's life and the psychotic construction of "the Dream" in which it is caught up.[14] In *Between the World and Me*, Coates is attacking a white sovereignty not just in terms of the physical violence that it wields but in terms of the psychic phantasy that backs it up.

To be a black man in the US means that the police "had my body, could do with that body whatever they pleased."[15] Coates ties this situation to the history of slavery in the US and, thus, to the history of European colonialism and the relentless and ongoing "plunder of black life" that they present. Obsessed with the Civil War, in which 600,000 people died in a conflict over the practice of slavery, Coates notes: "it had been glossed over in my education, and in popular culture, representations of the war and its reasons seemed obscured ... as if ... someone was trying to hide the books."[16] There is a way in which it seems, therefore, as if the Civil War never happened – and certainly when considering the situation of black lives today, this appears to be what Coates is forced to conclude. The heritage of destroying the black body, far from having ended with the Civil War, continues.

In this chapter, I negotiate the continued relevance of sovereignty for the situation of black life in the US today. Following Achille Mbembe's theorization of necropolitics, I distinguish between two sovereign inscriptions of black life within sovereign power: one (conservative) associated with G.W.F. Hegel's dialectics, the other (radical) with George Bataille and the break with dialectics. I then turn to Frantz Fanon and Mbembe's reading of Fanon (in *Critique of Black Reason*) to show how this tension between Hegel and Bataille can already be found in Fanon's plea for absolute (radical rather than dialectical) violence, which is, however, formulated as part of a constructive (more conservative) call for national liberation that would rein this violence back in.

That said, the constructive element of Fanon's project was hardly conservative in any straightforward way: he had in mind a national liberation based on the creation of a new man, one that thus preserved traces of both the Bataillean and Hegelian inscriptions of black life in sovereign power that Mbembe distinguishes. "Sovereignty" in Fanon must be negotiated between those two traces.

It's worth adding, as I discuss below, that the relation between black life and sovereignty may in fact exceed both: neither Hegelian dialectics nor Bataillean transgression, perhaps the para-ontological understanding of blackness can find political meaning here as a continuous unsettling that's neither with Hegel nor with Bataille and that is, as such, precisely – as David Marriott argues – *non-sovereign*.[17] Such an unsettling would stand closer to Afropessimist criticisms of sovereignty.

One must also beware in this context of the standard narrative that "equate[s] decolonization with the transition from empire to nation-state"[18] – of the view of decolonization as "a moment of nation-building in which the anticolonial demand for self-determination culminated in the rejection of alien rule and the formation of nation-states."[19] Against such accounts, the already-mentioned Adom Getachew emphasizes "anticolonial nationalism as *worldmaking*" and as moving precisely beyond the limits of the nation-state as the Eurocentric paradigm of the political unit.[20] It's not so much that the importance of the nation-state is rejected in such an approach, as Getachew (in spite of some of the stronger formulations in her book) also makes clear; it's that anticolonial nationalists were not "solely nationbuilders" but also "worldmakers" in ways that went beyond the limits of the nation-state.[21] There is still sovereignty here, but one that has passed through critique and has been thought otherwise.

Mbembe's "critique" reveals such negotiations as well in that it appears to be torn between a more conservative articulation that would remain within critique's limits and a more radical one that would seek to transgress them. The risk of transgression, however, is great: indeed, in his most transgressive moments, Mbembe seems to promote the kind of exceptionalist sovereignty that Coates's work exposes.

More than fifty years after the founding of the Black Panther Party in 1966, and at a time when the "horizontalist" Black Lives Matter movement is violently clashing in the US with new "vertical" formations on the right, this chapter asks whether there can be a future for sovereignty when it comes to black life in the US. Can there be an Afro-Futurism of sovereignty? Can Fanon's call for national liberation and the articulation it was given in Black Panther politics still take on new meanings today? Can there be a dream of sovereignty – and it should probably be recognized that sovereignty, to a certain extent, is always a dream – that is not a white Dream? Who are its dreamers? What might they dream? Such questions seem particularly important today, when sovereignty has re-emerged on the right. Liberalism is exhausted. Sovereignty is making a come-back as part of a repoliticization against liberalism and neoliberalism (though this last point is contestable).[22] But where is this sovereignty going to go? Unless the left participates in this conversation and rethinks sovereignty from within, it may not stand a chance against the right's revitalization of sovereignty's old spectre.

*

Coates's references to the history of slavery and colonialism enable us to characterize the situation in the US that he analyzes not only as a state of exception and, more specifically, as a camp but also as a necropolitical situation, to use Achille Mbembe's productive notion.[23]

Indeed, Mbembe focuses on those histories to develop the notion of necropolitics, which he situates closely – perhaps too closely – to the work of both Agamben and Michel Foucault. I say "perhaps too closely" for while Foucault in his work on power distinguishes between sovereignty as the power to take life or let live (the power of death) and biopolitics as the power to make life (to foster, generate, optimize it), Mbembe's notion of necropolitics brings those two aspects of power together as one. Mbembe is compelled to make this deconstructive move due to the situations (and the particular histories) he is looking at, which include slavery and colonialism – both situations to which neither Foucault nor Agamben pay much attention. As scholars like Paul Gilroy or Alexander Weheliye point out,[24] Foucault uses the term "colonialism" largely metaphorically; by characterizing the object of sovereign power as "bare" life, Agamben is incapable of thinking the importance of race in biopolitics. Both of these notions are important in Mbembe's discourse, and this forces him to take up some distance from both Agamben and, in particular, Foucault, to whom he is nevertheless indebted. He does not share their Eurocentrism, and this produces a shift in the theory. One way to summarize this would be to say that Mbembe, for his investigation of biopolitics, is operating from the position of those who die. He is interested in the "wounded or slain body" and how it is "inscribed in the order of power."[25]

On this last count, Mbembe considers two different inscriptions: the Hegelian one and that of Bataille. In Hegel, whose dialectical model Mbembe focuses on, the human being confronts death in negating nature by creating a world. It is through this exposure that the human being "truly *becomes a subject*."[26] To become a subject, then, "supposes upholding the work of death," in the sense that life "assumes death and lives with it."[27] Death can thus become part of an "economy of absolute knowledge and meaning."[28] Negation drives the dialectic forward, but this forward movement is also the negation of the negation. There is death but it can productively become part of life.

Not so in Bataille, whose work Mbembe discusses in contrast: "Bataille firmly anchors death in the realm of absolute expenditure," an expenditure that he calls "sovereign."[29] For Bataille, sovereignty thus breaks with the Hegelian dialectic, a break that is marked through its relation to death: "it is the refusal to accept the limits that the fear of death would have the subject respect."[30] The sovereign world, for

Bataille, "is the world in which the limit of death is done away with,"[31] as Mbembe quotes. Sovereignty therefore becomes a name for "the violation of all prohibitions": "Politics, in this case, is not the forward dialectical movement of reason [as in Hegel]. Politics can only be traced as a spiral transgression, as that difference that disorients the very idea of the limit. More specifically, politics is the difference put into play by the violation of the taboo."[32] But how does Bataille's position relate to necropolitics?

In the opening paragraphs of his text, Mbembe distinguishes between what he appears to characterize as the violence of sovereignty and what he refers to as "the power of absolute negativity." The latter he glosses with Arendt and her claim that the concentration camps introduce us to a negativity of death that is outside of the life/death binary. Necropolitics, it seems, investigates such a negativity, the power of such absolute negativity, in the sense that it investigates the "camp" in which life – and in particular black life – is caught up. At the same time, however, necropolitics and the biopolitical sovereignty that it names are presented in Mbembe's text along Hegelian lines, as conservative in the sense that they refer to "*the generalized instrumentalization of human existence and the material destruction of human bodies and populations.*"[33] In other words, they refer to the way in which dead bodies *can* become part of an economy of knowledge and meaning.

I would characterize such an economy here based on the associations that Mbembe sets up as the economy of slavery and colonialism. But it is also the economy that Coates confronts in his close reading of the death of black lives in the US. It is Mbembe who, in combination with Coates, enables us to mark this contemporary American situation as the situation of slavery and colonialism continued. But Mbembe can arguably *also* show us, via Bataille, that such a Hegelian situation need not be the only one. There is also the absolute expenditure of death, which would *not* allow such instrumentalization of black death as part of the white people's Dream. In other words, while Bataille appears to be associated with the absolute power of negativity that is in turn associated with the state of exception of the camp, there is also a way in which Bataille can become associated with another state of exception that would break with all of this.

*

Mbembe's negotiation of Hegel and Bataille thus connects to Frantz Fanon and the peculiar role of dialectics in his work. With Fanon, of course, there is no doubt: we are in the colonial situation, it is the colonial situation – the French presence in Algeria – that he, as a Martiniquan/French citizen, confronts. I am thinking in particular of the chapter from *The Wretched of the Earth* titled "Concerning Violence" (in the Constance Farrington translation)/ "On Violence" (in the Richard Philcox translation).[34] Born in Martinique, Fanon had studied psychiatry in France and had been assigned to a hospital in Algeria. He quits his job there and joins the Front de Libération Nationale, the anti-colonial resistance fighters – as a Martiniquan/French citizen, not as an Algerian, not as Algeria's colonial subject (even if he identified with the latter and ultimately became Algerian).[35] There is dialectics in Fanon's text, but one feels that it is stuck in the basic opposition without synthesis: colonized confronts colonizer violently, but no progress, no compromise, no rational deliberation is possible ("Challenging the colonial world is not a rational confrontation of viewpoints," he writes).[36] Indeed, Fanon's text is an affront to liberalism (Fanon writes about "the liberal intentions of the colonial authorities,"[37] for example) – he rather snarkily attacks liberalism's "gentleman's agreement"[38] – and to the ways liberalism can be tied to colonialism to make history "move forward" (to evoke the Hegelian narrative).

Against this, Fanon asserts "absolute violence":[39] the need to kick the colonizer out and decolonize (which, as he notes, involves many levels of existence). It is a call "for total disorder,"[40] "tabula rasa."[41] "Every obstacle encountered" must be "smash[ed]."[42] "Any method which does not include violence" must be rejected.[43] There is only one way to affirm that decolonization has been successful: Do those who used to be the last now come first?[44] The point is to take the colonizer's place.[45] If this is not accomplished, nothing has been done.

It is true that there are moments in the text where the usefulness of violence also appears to be drawn into question, as when Fanon writes: "the question is not so much responding to violence with more violence but rather how to defuse the crisis."[46] Indeed, Mbembe notes in *Critique of Black Reason* that "Fanon was conscious of the fact that, by choosing 'counter-violence,' the colonized were opening the door to a disastrous reciprocity."[47] But the general orientation is unmistakable: violence is needed to end the madness. Absolute violence – non-dialectical violence. Tabula rasa. Absolute break. Cut.

The Police   83

Out *and* out, as Philcox renders "absolue" (the translation is flawed, but its repetition of the "out" is useful here – it does render the outside-ness of ab-solute). Looking forward to Mbembe, this reads like Bataille's absolute expenditure applied in the colonial context. In his reading of Fanon, Mbembe also recognizes that he proposes violence as the only way forward.

Nevertheless, it is not quite the *only* way. For it is crucial that the broader, *constructive* context in which, for Fanon, this destruction takes place is that of "national liberation, national reawakening, restoration of the nation to the people or Commonwealth."[48] In short, it is that of … sovereignty. This is in many ways a remarkable point, and one can understand it, of course, in view of the fact that the colonized are, precisely, without their own nation-state. And it is certainly not as if Fanon were not aware of the problems of nationalist politics, of what he calls "the pitfalls [mésaventures] of national consciousness." But in this chapter he consciously leaves the portrayal of "the rise of a new nation, the establishment of a new state, its diplomatic relations and its economic and political orientation"[49] aside to focus on the violent break.[50] What will happen, however, when the absolute violence, the out and out violence for which he calls, is reined back in, is folded back into the national liberation that he calls for at the beginning of his text? What will happen when it becomes sovereign *in that way* again?

Bataille of course calls his absolute expenditure "sovereign" in response to such a "conservative" folding within, precisely to attack the old sense of sovereignty. To an extent, these questions point to the problem of all revolutions, which ultimately fold their constituting power back into constituted power. How to run with constituting power appears to be the question. And more radically even: how to run with power, apart from the constitutional gesture?

"National liberation." Can we even think in those terms still today? Could we call for a project of national liberation in response to the colonialism that the US, today, continues to practise on the black lives that live within its borders? We can think of the project of the Black Panthers, which involved a close study of law and, in some cases, a rewriting of key documents of US political history (the Bill of Rights) as an attempt towards national liberation *from colonialism and slavery*. But *within the limits of* national sovereignty. (They were a political party, after all.) An attempt to cleanse sovereignty from colonialism and slavery, to claim a sovereignty *outside of the white people's*

84 Four Paradigms of Sovereignty

Dream.[51] Violence clearly has a role in this project. But what is its end? Is it an end? Is it pure means?

Consider in this context Kadir Nelson's *New Yorker* cover "After Dr. King," an alternative image of sovereignty: a black body of sovereign power – the body of Dr Martin Luther King Jr, seemingly seated in contemplation or prayer, hands folded and eyes fixed upon the future[52] – that gathers within it the unhappy subjects who question the established sovereignty's competency to protect them. While it gives us an image of black sovereignty, it is important to note that this figure is that of Martin Luther King. Can the *New Yorker* cover be imagined with Malcolm X on it?[53] (Ta-Nehisi Coates notes Malcolm's association with violence and his own dislike of it.) Or does the figure of King ultimately reconcile the violence of the subjects it carries within, and is Nelson's image the ultimate Hegelian reconciliation of political violence and the avoidance of civil war? Would the Malcolm X cover have offended the *New Yorker*'s liberal sensibilities too much (the force of Bataille is certainly stronger in Malcolm than it was in King)? Does the King image continue, in this sense, the old sovereignty – plenty of similarities, after all, between Nelson's image and the frontispiece of Thomas Hobbes's *Leviathan* – rather than bring the tabula rasa that Fanon calls for? And perhaps Fanon, too, when he folds violence back into "national" liberation, ultimately does not live up to the radicality of his own position: complete rejection of the nation-state.

Nelson's *New Yorker* cover "Say Their Names" can be seen as his most recent engagement with this problematic, this time in reference to George Floyd's murder, and with Floyd embodying what Coates calls the US "heritage" of violence against black bodies: Floyd's body becomes the sovereign body of a Leviathan that holds the bodies of those who died because of police violence or racial violence more broadly.[54] We see: Ahmaud Arbery, Tony McDade, Trayvon Martin, Laquan McDonald, Freddie Gray, Eric Garner, Aiyana Stanley-Jones, Botham Jean, Michael Brown, Sandra Bland, Yvette Smith, Alton Sterling, David McAtee, Walter Scott, Breonna Taylor, Tamir Rice, Philando Castile, Stephon Clark. But we also see: Martin Luther King Jr; Medgar Evers; Malcolm X; Emmett Till; Rosa Parks. The image includes depictions of the Rodney King beating, the March from Selma, the Tulsa Race Massacre. At the bottom of the image, perhaps suggesting that what we are still living through today has its roots there, are "the Unnamed" – the millions of black people who were

The Police 85

enslaved in the US – as well as Gordon, an escaped slave whose heavily whipped back was photographed, producing an image that contributed to the abolitionist movement.

Such visual renderings of the problematic of sovereignty can be found elsewhere as well. Consider, for example, Ryan Coogler's *Black Panther* (Disney, 2018), which problematically casts as its villain Killmonger, who wants to use the precious metal vibranium of King T'Challa's Wakanda to liberate oppressed black people worldwide. If I bring up the *Black Panther*, it is partly because Coates has been involved in the comic book's reimagining for the age of Black Lives Matter. The *Black Panther* poster, with the troubling tagline – "Long Live the King" – clearly inscribes the film's politics in the negotiations of sovereignty that I have opened up.[55] In this context, it is interesting to see that the only figure vying with King T'Challa's central position in the image as Wakanda's sovereign is Killmonger, who seems to almost outgrow Wakanda's Leviathan, split off from it towards the left, beginning to mark the fissure of a civil war, presenting the figure of a competing sovereign, sword in hand.

But Fanon, too, when he called for national liberation, likely did not want "that old sovereignty" again. That may be why, in his text, he also mentions "the creation of new men" as the result of the project of decolonization.[56] Everything must start, he seems to say, from the creation of a new people, a new human being. It is from there that a *new* sovereignty might come along. It is this point, specifically the notion of a new human being (rather than a new black man), that Mbembe focuses on in his *Critique of Black Reason*. It is Fanon who, in *Black Skin, White Masks*, says that "Black" is "only a fiction."[57] "For him," Mbembe notes, "the name referred not to a biological reality or skin color but to 'one of the historical forms of the condition imposed on humans.'"[58] Mbembe distinguishes Fanon's position on this count from that of his teacher, Césaire, one of the key thinkers of "Négritude." While Césaire as per Mbembe's account is obviously no Senghor (the other thinker of negritude), Mbembe still presents him as more essentialist than Fanon, in the sense that he affirmed a negritude that Fanon ultimately wanted to go beyond. Mbembe points out, however, that in Césaire's "Black" there was a universalism that was proposed, a universalism that could only emerge from "blackness" and the difference that it marks – a difference that reveals the world. For that revelation, blackness was essential. "But," Mbembe asks, "how can we reread Césaire without Fanon" (who wrote after him)?

86   Four Paradigms of Sovereignty

For him, it is difficult, if not impossible. And this has everything to do with the notion of "critique," which names Mbembe's project. As long as we are reading Césaire, we remain on the conservative side of critique, even if Césaire opens up the possibility of transgression. The transgression only arrives, however, with Fanon, who seeks to go beyond the notion of "Black" and imagines a world "freed from the burden of race" (a formula Mbembe repeats at least twice in his book – it closes the book as well).[59] "If there is one thing that will never die in Fanon," Mbembe writes, "it is the project of the collective rise of humanity ... Each human subject, each people, was to engage in a grand project of self-transformation, in a struggle to the death, without reserve. They had to take it on as their own. They could not delegate it to others."[60] The echoes here are multiple: *struggle to the death* – this is Hegel, of course, the master-slave dialectic. But struggle *without reserve*: this is Bataille's absolute expenditure, the break with economy. Finally, the project of *self-transformation*: here we get echoes of the Enlightenment project and the "care of the self" that Foucault was so interested in towards the end of his life (the stuff that, according to some critics, opened him up to neoliberalism[61]). It is no coincidence, I think, that the chapter I have been quoting from here is titled "The Clinic of the Subject," which, in addition to echoing Fanon's training as a psychiatrist, is a very Foucauldian title.

So a number of questions emerge: at the level of *subject formation*, Mbembe seeks to present Fanon as more Bataille than Hegel. But at the level of Fanon's *political project*, this distinction – Hegel or Bataille – is undecided; it seems that Fanon's call for national liberation is perhaps more Hegel than Bataille. To be sure, if a national liberation were to be built around Bataille's kind of subjectivity, then surely it would be very different from the old sovereignty and its dialectical transformation. We would get a break with dialectics here that would bring about a truly new sovereignty rather than its dialectically accomplished next step. If this comes with the project of total self-transformation, the question remains how this would relate to the neoliberal, entrepreneurial subject. While Fanon of course could not foresee this question, Mbembe does address it in his introduction, where he presents neoliberalism as one of "three critical moments in the biography of the vertiginous assemblage that is Blackness and race."[62] Neoliberalism, defined as "a phase in the history of humanity dominated by the industries of Silicon Valley and digital technology,"[63] has a "tendency to universalize the Black condition," by which he

The Police   87

means "practices [that] borrow as much from the slaving logic of capture and predation as from the colonial logic of occupation and extraction, as well as from the civil wars and raiding of earlier epochs."[64] It is a key component in what Mbembe calls "the *Becoming Black of the world*."[65] At no point does Mbembe discuss, however, how the language of self-transformation in Fanon could *also* become part of such a project.

There remains the third path that I allude to at the beginning of this chapter: the para-ontological understanding of blackness that would mark, next to both Hegel and Bataille, sovereignty's continuous unsettling – its *non-sovereignty*, as I suggest. Fred Moten develops the notion of the para-ontological (after Nahum Chandler and, by R.A. Judy's account, Oskar Becker[66]) in response to Western ontology, which is, he argues, a "white" ontology that under the guise of universality refuses to think blackness. As he puts it in a lengthy, beautifully lyrical and intensely political article titled "Blackness and Nothingness (Mysticism in the Flesh)": "Blackness is prior to ontology ... blackness is the anoriginal displacement of ontology ... ontology's anti- and ante-foundation, ontology's underground, the irreparable disturbance of ontology's time and space."[67] Blackness – not only in an identitarian way, as a condition that is particularly felt by black bodies, but also in a more general sense, as a structural condition that does not depend on one's skin colour (Moten distinguishes between "blackness and blacks"[68]) – is not covered by the ontological, and it is to move towards the philosophical thinking of blackness that Moten proposes his notion. The para-ontological, in such a project, captures what resides "next to" or "para" ontology. It captures the "nothingness" of blackness, the particular "nothingness" – which is evidently not nothing – that it marks. In my introduction, I suggest reading this position politically, as a para-sovereign position.

Moten turns in this context to Far Eastern thought and, specifically, to the notion of "wu" (無, "nothing"). Moten brings this daoist notion of an active emptiness together with a black para-ontology and politics of resistance that can – in his view – be associated with Fanon.[69] The thought of the dao, and specifically of "wu," is a thought that puts being on hold rather than "in the hold,"[70] as Moten's reference to the slave-ship has it. Yet it is also through its attention to "the hold" that Black studies (as Moten sees it) "disrupts"[71] the "nothingness" of Far Eastern thought, forcing "'the real presence' of blackness"[72] back into it and working both with and against the suspension that "wu" brings. There is, clearly, something to be learned from and resisted within the para-ontological. In the words of Abdelkebir Khatibi, another thinker of the dao, what's needed here is a "double critique,"[73] both of the para-ontological (as subject genitive: the para-ontological *suspends*, in the way that "wu" suspends) and of the para-ontological (as object genitive: the para-ontological *is suspended* by "'the real presence' of blackness").

Moten's choice (after Chandler) for an understanding of the preposition "para" or "next to" is worth pausing over in the context of my discussion of sovereignty because it marks a moving sideways rather than up or down or inside or outside. If up/down or inside/outside can easily be appropriated within the dialectical (Hegelian) and transgressive (Bataillean) models of sovereignty that I previously found in Mbembe, this is more difficult to do with the horizontal dynamic of the "next to," which posits itself on the same plane as whatever it preposes. But does this lateral unsettling take us out of sovereignty? It seems that even in the intervention of such a sideways move, the para maintains a hyphenation to the ontological, some kind of connection – that of a mere dash – to what it unsettles. Read politically, this would also apply, then, to the para-ontological approach to sovereignty, in which some connection to sovereignty would be maintained by the mere presence of a dash. There is always the temptation of overlooking this dash and rewriting this continuous unsettling as an outside – more radical than Bataille's, which still calls itself sovereign. Moten in fact flirts with such an outside. "On the one hand," he writes, "blackness and ontology are unavailable to each other"[74] – and the project of para-ontology seeks to remedy this situation. "On the other hand," he continues, "blackness must free itself from ontological expectation, must refuse subjection to ontology's sanction against the very idea of black subjectivity."[75] The more radical conclusion, then – following the invitation of this "other hand" – would simply be to reject ontology altogether, a rejection that would lead to non-sovereignty. But Moten might consider such a conclusion irresponsible from the point of view of a history in which whiteness and blackness have been co-constituted in ontology, through ontology, and in/through sovereignty. In other words: while blackness might desire the outside, it may not be afforded such luxury from the point of history. Indeed, none of us may.

*

"If we owe Fanon a debt," Mbembe writes, "it is for the idea that in every human subject there is something indomitable and fundamentally intangible that no domination – no matter what form it takes – can eliminate, contain, or suppress, at least not completely. Fanon tried to grasp how this could be reanimated and brought back to life in a colonial context that in truth is different from ours, even if its double – institutional racism – remains our own beast. For this reason, his work presents a kind of fibrous lignite, a weapon of steel, for the oppressed in the world today."[76] It is worth noting, in the context of a discussion of sovereignty, the potential complicity of such a discourse with exceptionalism and some of the problems this raises. This becomes clear in Mbembe's book. When, a few pages later, Mbembe turns to the politics of art in this context, he writes: "Here the primary function of the work of art has never been to represent, illustrate, or narrate reality. It has always been in its nature simultaneously to confuse and mimic original forms and appearances ... But at the same time it constantly redoubled the original object, deforming it, distancing itself from it, and most of all conjuring with it ... In this way the time of a work of art is the moment when daily life is liberated from the accepted rules and is devoid of both obstacles and guilt."[77] I can follow this final passage all the way up to its last sentence. But I do not think its grand, concluding statement – liberation from accepted rules, being devoid of obstacles and guilt – *follows logically*, or evokes *the same politics*, as the language of constantly redoubling, deforming, and distancing that Mbembe uses earlier on. I am concerned about how the final line promotes an exceptionalism – "liberation from the accepted rules," "devoid of both obstacles and guilt" – that the previous language actually dismantles. I like the dismantling better. It marks an *immanent criticism of sovereignty* that may be more efficient, politically, at dismantling sovereign exceptions than Mbembe's final sentence.

Given this conclusion, however, one should not be surprised by the final paragraph of the chapter: to be African, it proclaims, is to be "a man free from everything, and therefore able to invent himself. A true politics of identity consists in constantly nourishing, fulfilling, and refulfilling the capacity for self-invention. Afro-centrism is a hypostatic variant of the desire of those of African origin to need only to justify themselves to themselves."[78] Mbembe prefers here a world that is constituted by the relation to the Other – and it is the human that introduces that otherness into blackness, which he argues must be "clouded."[79] This will be the beginning – via Fanon – of the "post-Césairian era."[80] Again, one wonders whether "clouding" – a term he uses earlier in the chapter – can mean the same as "free from everything"; one wonders whether "post" can really refer to the radical break that seems to be alluded to here. Ultimately, *Mbembe's critique appears to be torn between a more conservative articulation that would remain within the critique's limits and a more radical one that would seek to transgress it.* Given that he relies for his critique largely on Fanon, this should come as no surprise, as I show that Fanon, too, is caught up within this tension of staying within (Hegel) and going beyond (Bataille). Everything in "On Violence" points to the beyond; and yet, the constructive part of its project – not addressed in the chapter – takes place "within" national liberation.

Ultimately, what haunts the difference between those two positions is the problematic of sovereignty itself: of its paradoxical association both with an outside and a within ("I who am outside of the law, declare that there is nothing outside of the law," as Agamben captures the paradox of sovereignty). And, of course, of an even greater sovereignty – absolute violence, absolute expenditure – that, as the sovereignty of sovereignties, may ultimately do no more than perpetuate sovereignty's exceptionalism.

Indeed, it may be that, for black life, the project of sovereignty is over, that Fanon's call for national liberation and the inspiration it provided for the Black Panther Party are a thing of the past, for good. Joan Cocks, focusing on the Israel/Palestine situation and Indigenous politics, lays out some very good reasons for this.[81] But if this is so – if sovereignty should indeed be seen as a thing of the past – it seems crucial at a time when sovereignty is going through a revival on the right, in open conflict with the "horizontalist" Black Lives Matter movement today, that new forms of collective organization be proposed *against* sovereignty. Are these non-sovereign forms of collective organization? Do they claim sovereignty *otherwise*? How do they effectuate their power?

8

The Drone

> The state and its laws do not operate by themselves, as if they are a self-moving machine (*to automaton*). They require the participation of the humans – they require the engagement of the citizens.
>
> Dimitris Vardoulakis, *Stasis before the State*[1]

And so we arrive, at the end of part 2 of this book, at the fourth paradigm of sovereignty that I propose to discuss: the drone. Associated with the Obama years of US global hegemony – a fact that continues to puzzle many, including Teju Cole who, in a short essay titled "A Reader's War," considers how Obama, the Nobel Peace Prize-winning president who reads literature and is thus presumably exposed to the ennobling effects of what is called "the humanities," could also be behind what Jeremy Scahill calls the "dirty" drone wars and their devastating consequences[2] – the drone combines in its paradigm aspects of the previous three: the camp-like exposure to killing with impunity that it marks; the uncertainty and even weakness of sovereignty that it reveals in spite of the phantasm of sovereign power it projects (in this sense, the drone is similar to the wall and a symptom of sovereignty's insecure power); and, finally, the ways in which the negative effects of drones are, outside of the post-traumatic stress disorder (PTSD) symptoms from which those controlling them suffer, disproportionately felt by certain parts of the global population whose lives are evidently considered to be worth less than the lives of others. In this sense, the drone also recalls my discussion of the police.

As a fully technicized realization of a sovereignty without a people, and a key instrument in a war that no longer needs soldiers and no longer makes victims on "our" side – let's exclude here those PTSD victims I have already mentioned – the drone presents us with a split between the people and the sovereign that allows the sovereign body to live on without a people animating it, as a machine without a ghost.

In this sense, it is the stark realization, neatly captured in an instrument of war, of Giorgio Agamben's civil war thesis, which (in a reading of Thomas Hobbes) understands the coincidence of people and king to exist for a mere moment only, as what, after Walter Benjamin, we may call a "flash," after which the normal state of affairs – the dissolved multitude, to recall the terms that Agamben borrows from Hobbes – returns. The difference is that here we encounter a situation in which that "flash" finds a way to keep going, far beyond its time, as a soulless, fully technicized war-instrument separated from a people. There is a disidentification that takes place in the drone that, while central to Agamben's discussion of the multitude, Agamben does not consider *from the side of sovereignty itself*: the drone is sovereignty disidentified from the people and somehow living on even if it is devoid of the life that is supposed to animate it. (Sovereignty without the people should, at least after the revolutionary shift to popular sovereignty, amount to nothing.) This is a hollow, sovereign shell that has lost its political meaning. And this situation has come about, most importantly for our purposes, by removing the vulnerability of the people from its make-up.

Perhaps the keenest analyst of this situation is Grégoire Chamayou, who, in the fifth and final part of *A Theory of the Drone*, titled "Political Bodies," points out that the drone (dialectically) solves a tension in sovereignty,[3] which has to do with "the state's relation to its subjects."[4] What is this tension? On the one hand, "according to social contract theories" (which find their source in the natural law tradition), people institute a sovereign to protect their lives. People obey the sovereign's commands because the sovereign protects their lives; their obedience is in exchange for protection. In war, however, this situation changes: it is the people who are called on to protect the sovereign, and this reversal also affects the relation of commandment and obedience, as we will see. In fact, the reversal of the maxim "Protego ergo obligo" ("I protect, so I am obliged") into "Obligo ergo protegor" ("I am obliged, so I am protected") reveals,[5] according to Chamayou, "the hidden principle of political domination," which is "You must obey me so that I am protected."[6] "And that is the case even if I don't protect you from anything anymore, above all not from myself."[7] "It is from that interpretative turnaround," as Chamayou points out, "that all the critical theories of protective powers take off" – and it is those critical theories that will be the focus of his further analysis and of the final part of this book.

The question that is raised here is basic: How can a state that claims to protect the lives of its citizens "without contradiction" call for "sacrifice in war"? According to Hegel, who inspires Chamayou in this chapter, "it cannot."[8] In other words, this is a tension that cannot be dialectically resolved. There may be multiple reasons for the contradiction. The contradiction may be there because the state "[attaches] too great a value to the life of [its] citizens"; or it may be, rather, that the state has become invested in a very "impoverished concept of what life is," placing the preservation of life at all costs above "the safeguarding of a far superior ethical and political life."[9] For both these biopolitical reasons, states will be averse to incurring losses in war and even to waging war. But it is not necessary for the contradiction that Chamayou diagnoses to lead to a biopolitical aversion to war: if only sacrifice *could* be avoided, in that case the thanatopolitics of war *could* be maintained – but *without sacrifices*. The drone presents us with this solution, which – again, Hegel would be horrified – *dialectically* solves the tension at the heart of sovereignty. Sovereignty's protectorate can be maintained because we are no longer required to die for it. The drone removes us, Chamayou argues, from our "ontological vulnerability"[10] – the founding presupposition of sovereignty: sovereignty presupposes a vulnerability that founds the protection it provides – that could have otherwise activated a critical attitude towards sovereignty. In Chamayou's view, it is "political vulnerabilization" (as distinguished from ontological vulnerability; our being-*made* vulnerable rather than our being vulnerable) that could become a "limitative principle" to sovereignty.[11] But, again, the drone "tends to somewhat deactivate that critical attitude."[12]

The drone removes us from the realization that sovereignty requires us to die for it, to sacrifice our lives in its wars. It is such a realization, Chamayou argues, that could become the source for a critical attitude towards sovereignty because such ontological and political vulnerability could make us question sovereignty's commandment. For if we normally, in peace, obey sovereignty because it protects us, this obedience is in question when, in war, we are called upon to expose our lives to death to protect sovereignty. Sovereignty's commandment, in such a situation, is put to the test. Its foundation – we obey because we are protected – becomes unstable. In such a situation, the people may very well conclude that "we won't do it, we don't want to die for that, not for this war, not in this fight, for it is not ours."[13] In this way, a split is introduced within the sovereign body, the people split off or

94 Four Paradigms of Sovereignty

disidentify from the sovereign, and we enter into the sphere of what, above, I call "civil war." However, the drone prevents that gap from coming about. It contributes to the unifying force of sovereignty.

But how does it do this? Interestingly, by removing people, the human being, from the technicized realization of sovereignty that it presents. Basically, sovereignty realizes itself today not through people fighting for it on the battlefield but through the inhuman apparatus of the drone. That is where sovereignty exists. The people have, quite literally, been withdrawn from it, even if that withdrawal has not yet quite articulated itself as a political force. And it is the drone itself that "tends to somewhat deactivate" that political withdrawal by removing us from our political vulnerabilization. It is in the final chapter of his book that Chamayou (in part through a reference to Hannah Arendt) begins to imagine the positive articulation of this situation – namely, the moment when the bodies that have been withdrawn from or actively withdraw from sovereignty would begin to act in concert to form a new political body. It is unclear, in Chamayou's book, what such a new body would be called.[14]

However, the fate of "sovereignty" as Chamayou criticizes it cannot be in doubt. Chamayou's final image for it is that of a "radio-commanded policing automaton" from 1924: "The robocop of the twenties was to be equipped with projective eyes, caterpillar tracks, and, to serve as fists, rotating blow-dealing truncheons by the weapons of the Middle Ages. On its lower belly, a small metal penis allowed it to spray tear gas at unruly parades of human protestors. It had an exhaust outlet for an anus. This ridiculous robot that pissed tear gas and farted black smoke provides a perfect illustration of an ideal of a drone state."[15] The description clearly ridicules "dronized" sovereignty. As Chamayou's evocation – and representation – of Hobbes's frontispiece in this context also shows (the image of Hobbes's artificial man is reproduced in Chamayou's book at this point), the drone thus marks a perversion of the unity between people and sovereign, for which Hobbes advocated, presenting us instead with a situation in which the sovereign has progressively become separated from the people and operates in our time as a "dronized" sovereign, an artificial man without people to support it. What to do with such a dronized sovereignty, with a state that in Emily Apter's reading of Chamayou "is invested in a cynegetic power, manifest ... in a cartography of manhunts, kill zones, and calculated halos of collateral damage?"[16] Chamayou concludes: "[Its] increasingly evident destiny would be to be dumped

The Drone 95

in a junkyard like any other piece of scrap metal."[17] He suggests, in other words, that we throw it out.

Again, the positive other side of this – what will the people do who have been withdrawn or have actively withdrawn from this dronized sovereignty? – remains unclear. However, the evocation of Arendt suggests that Chamayou envisions some kind of new formation of political collectivity, of what Arendt calls "action" or "acting in concert" after this. It is to these forms of new political collectivity, some of which may still be called sovereign, that I now turn.

Let me simply note, in closing, that, for Chamayou, such new political collectivity would emerge from the experience of political vulnerabilization. On this count – the focus on history rather than ontology – his work subtly differs from that of Judith Butler, who, in the preface to *Precarious Life* nevertheless suggests that, in response to the experience of "heightened vulnerability" that the US found itself in after the 9/11 terror attacks, the country could have found an opportunity to rethink its role "as part of the global community."[18] Unfortunately, the US did no such thing – it strengthened its "old" sovereignty instead. Moving forward, then, I intend to take the notion of a political collectivity that would be rooted in political vulnerabilization as a touchstone to think about new political formations and, specifically, formations of sovereignty today.

It is, indeed, such a turn towards vulnerability within sovereignty that another reading of Schmitt can enable us to achieve. For Schmitt's concept of the political, organized around the friend/enemy distinction, which is most explicit in war, opens with the memory of Schmitt's friend, who died on the battlefield. There is heroism in this, a recuperation of a political life against the endless debate of liberalism – masculinism versus liberalism's effeminate palaver. But the personal note, at the beginning of Schmitt's book, of the death of a friend is also a reminder of life's vulnerability, and Schmitt's rethinking of the concept of the political around the "real possibility of death" does more than just evoke the violent will to live, to avoid the existential negation that the enemy might bring: it also marks the possibility that one might die. As such, Schmitt's flexing of the sovereign muscle, like the walls that Brown discusses, becomes a marker of an anxiety that underlies it – of a vulnerability that haunts it, in the same way that civil war and the optical illusion of the *populus-rex* haunt Hobbes's theory of sovereignty. This is why Guillaume Sibertin-Blanc can present Schmitt as a thinker of the state (sovereignty) for whom the crisis of the state (democracy) is never far away. The Schmittian sovereign, then, while decisive on those states that pose an exceptional threat to our life, also brings us sovereignty at its most vulnerable – a vulnerability that we have forgotten in part due to the dronization of sovereignty that Chamayou lays bare. The challenge then would be, coming from Schmitt, to insist on this vulnerability studies perspective and to rethink the political from there – as a realm in which one does not always win but sometimes also dies, a death that may urge one to rethink sovereignty outside of the immortality phantasy, in which it is all too often caught up, as the collective power of and for the vulnerable.

PART THREE

Sovereignty and Vulnerability

9

Homo Vulnerabilis

The idea that he is likely to survive me I find almost painful
(Aber die Vorstellung, dass er mich auch noch ueberleben sollte, ist
mir eine fast schmerzliche).

> Franz Kafka, "The Cares of a Family Man"
> ("Die Sorgen eines Hausvaters")[1]

Given the discussion of sovereignty that I provide in part 2, it should come as no surprise that Chamayou's book on the drone can end by picturing sovereignty in the junk yard. The sovereignty that Chamayou thus discards is the fully technicized conclusion of a historical power that (as I show) has always been troubled and that, in the drone, finds some of that trouble laid bare. The focus of Chamayou's argument ultimately becomes the human being's "political vulnerabilization" – their being *made* vulnerable. It is from this vulnerabilization – rather than "ontological vulnerability," the founding presupposition of sovereignty – that human beings develop a critical, democratic relation towards sovereignty, a critical relation that the drone (because it enables us to forget about our vulnerability) risks deactivating. One important aspect of any attempt to rethink sovereignty today, then, would have to be vulnerability and, more precisely, vulnerabilization as a kind of starting point from where a critical sovereignty could become possible.

On this count, my use of Chamayou's work can connect to other recent efforts in the field of political thought: Judith Butler's already discussed work on "precarious life,"[2] for example, or Isabell Lorey's work – crucially not within the realm of sovereignty but part of a thinking of the multitude – on insecurity, precariousness/precarity, and vulnerability.[3] Where Lorey and Butler both differ from Chamayou, however, is that they seek to articulate, starting from the experience of ontological vulnerability, new forms of collective living. And in some cases – and here I think not only of Butler but also, in particular, of Wendy Brown and Bonnie Honig,[4] though not, importantly, of Lorey – they call such new collectivities "sovereign," as if to distinguish these sovereignties from the abusive sovereignties they criticize. In their attempt to think other sovereignties, these approaches take us back to the very origins of sovereignty in the realization of both the fact that human life is vulnerable (ontological vulnerability) and of contingent processes of political vulnerabilization. It seems to me that such an approach has some advantages: first, it can unwork those most obnoxious aspects of sovereignty that I have already laid bare here (its invulnerable/immortal, masculinist, and white core); second, however, it can enable one to hold on to those aspects of sovereignty that are arguably good – the powerful, politically effective collective organizing that it stands for; the institutions that it brings; the democratic impulse that animates it, especially in its popular (rather than monarchic) formation.

Before sovereignty is criticized into oblivion, we should probably also consider that one other force that has been very invested in the breaking down of sovereignty – or, more precisely, in sovereignty's transformation for this force's own benefit, its use and abuse – is neoliberalism. It's Wendy Brown who, in *Undoing the Demos*, criticizes neoliberalism's effect on sovereignty and begins to tentatively take on a defence of popular sovereignty in response.[5] As I indicate in part 1, sovereignty's relation to neoliberalism is complicated. While neoliberalism may be invested in the breaking down of popular sovereignty, scholars like Philip Mirowski show that it operates hand in hand with the exceptionalist sovereignty that is the focus of part 2. Brown is highlighting instead neoliberalism's relation to an alternative kind of sovereignty, one to be defended. Bonnie Honig is working in Brown's tracks when, in *Public Things*, she pursues this defence in a more pronounced way and faults Brown for not doing so.[6] Butler's *Notes Toward a Performative Theory of Assembly* can be read along similar lines:[7] we have here three contemporary thinkers who take it up for sovereignty in the face of its neoliberal destruction, but with an awareness of the criticisms from the left that old sovereign power has received.[8] The extent of this awareness may be up for discussion: Annie McClanahan and Sarah Brouillette resist, for example, the rather "pastoral" views of the post-Second World War moment that Brown, in her book on neoliberalism, projects.[9] Still, the political point is clear

Homo Vulnerabilis

and valuable, and can be summed up as a *critique*: Brown, Honig, and Butler are seeking to distinguish legitimate uses of sovereignty from illegitimate ones, and they perform this difficult but necessary work *within* the limits of the concept. If this appears to be a conservative move, one should note that it takes place in part to confront the (perhaps at first sight more progressive) project of neoliberalism to undo sovereignty. In addition, it should be underlined that at least in two of these cases – that of Honig and Butler – this project develops as an attempt to engage with contemporary protest movements and their desire to be politically effective. These critics wonder, more precisely, whether the horizontalism of such movements can be enough to accomplish the political task they have set for themselves.

On this count, the projects of the already mentioned critics can be said to line up with that of Naomi Klein, who, in *This Changes Everything: Capitalism vs. the Climate,* "confesses" that "the last five years in climate science has left me impatient."[10] She adds: "As many are coming to realize, the fetish for structurelessness, the rebellion against any kind of institutionalization, is not a luxury that today's transformative movements can afford."[11] "We collectively lack many of the tools that built and sustained the transformative movements of the past. Our public institutions are disintegrating, while the institutions of the traditional left – progressive political parties, strong unions, member-based community service organizations – are fighting for their lives."[12] While this is not an explicit plea for sovereignty, it does gesture in the direction of political verticality against which many contemporary protest movements appear to be (blindly) opposed.

Bruce Robbins traces the development of the role of the state in Klein's work, from her early work on sweatshops all the way to her recent book on the climate. He uncovers a turnaround in Klein's politics when it comes to the state and what one might want to call "sovereignty."[13] "Food sovereignty" explicitly comes up in Klein's book, and it is discussed in Honig's work as well. Honig also acknowledges – as I intend to do in the next chapters – native sovereignties as one site where the contemporary politics of sovereignty needs to be considered. While Brown mentions both, Honig charges that she does not seriously consider either.

But of course to reclaim sovereignty, to reclaim a power that has been burdened with so much abuse, one will have to rethink it. I have been suggesting that the point to which I want to go back is an anthropological one – a view of the human being as vulnerable;

specifically, and following Chamayou, I am interested in historical processes of political vulnerabilization that bring some important relief to a universalist philosophical notion like ontological vulnerability. (The importance of this difference was clearly exposed, for example, by the pandemic, in the sense that some lives were more vulnerable to the virus than others, and that increased vulnerability was in part the product of a history of political vulnerabilization that goes back for centuries. It was of course also the product of how bodies are politically vulnerabilized in the present, at the intersection of race and class.) I would like to rebuild sovereignty from there, using vulnerability as a guiding thread, as the element *with* which sovereignty is designed rather than the element *against* which it is designed. Traditionally, as we have seen, the sovereign protects us from our vulnerability (and therefore we obey the sovereign) or we protect the sovereign from its vulnerability (in times of war – but this puts the condition for our obedience into question, as Chamayou points out; this is the critical edge of our political vulnerabilization). In both cases, sovereignty operates in recognition of but also against vulnerability: our own, or its own. This is how ontological vulnerability is sovereignty's foundational presupposition. Chamayou suggests, however, that the critique of sovereignty opens up as soon as that "against" is disabled – in other words, as soon as the relation between sovereignty and vulnerability is reconceived, with vulnerability precisely *not* being something that sovereignty must, at all costs, keep at bay. Such a reconceived relation between sovereignty and vulnerability would change something at the level of the individual subject – of us, who expect the sovereign to protect us from our own vulnerability – and at the level of the sovereign, who seeks to remain invulnerable. Both the sovereign and the sovereignty-of-the-subject would, if the relation between sovereignty and vulnerability were reconceived, be drawn into question. With respect to political sovereignty, then, it may become the case that it requires not so much our defence *but our care*, as the kind of "public thing" that Honig talks about, or the infrastructures that Butler also singles out in their work about street protests. Those things are vulnerable, they address us and solicit our "care and concern" for their maintenance,[14] to use the terms Honig borrows from Hannah Arendt and Donald Winnicott. Such care and concern do not necessarily lead – and I would say in fact *should precisely not lead* – to invulnerable phantasms of sovereignty and the violence of such phantasms' defence.

Indeed, although vulnerability is arguably at the origin of the sovereign project as it can be found, for example, in Thomas Hobbes (and we have come across echoes of it in Schmitt, for example, through the memory of his friend who died on the battlefield), it is worth noting that it is *not* exactly vulnerability that Hobbes or Schmitt invite us to think about *but* the life/death-distinction (in other words, mortality/finitude rather than vulnerability). Sovereignty is defined, as Foucault summarizes it in the fifth section of volume 1 of *The History of Sexuality*, by the right to take life or let live. While such a formula evidently evokes death, a death that the sovereign wields through the sword that is prominently featured in the frontispiece of Hobbes's 1651 book, "death" is not exactly "vulnerability" since one's vulnerability does not refer to one's actual death but to the possibility of one's being wounded. As such, it falls more within the field of biopolitics, the politics of life – of making live and letting die. At the very least, it forces us to mediate between sovereignty and biopolitics, two forms of power that are often kept distinct.

Similar to one of those "-abilities" that Samuel Weber in his work on Walter Benjamin writes about,[15] vulnerability marks a possibility rather than an actuality, and, as such, there is something about it that escapes the decisiveness that Schmitt turns into the core of the concept of sovereignty. *There is something about vulnerability that is, precisely, non-sovereign.* To be vulnerable is to be alive with an awareness of the possibility that one might be wounded. To be wounded, as far as the actualization of that possibility goes, is still not to die – one can live with a wound, whether physical or psychological, without its being fatal. In that sense, the state of vulnerability and even the state of being wounded pose some challenges to the notion of sovereignty as well as that of biopolitics (the politics to foster, generate, optimize life) because it operates in part outside of the life/death binary that structures both those notions. Going back to Honig, and the psychoanalytic overtones of her work, I am thinking of a kind of care and concern here that takes place within the possibility of being wounded rather than a care or concern that nurses someone back to the illusion of perfect health: *interminable care.*

This has perhaps most efficiently been drawn out by Jasbir Puar in an article (which has since been developed into a book) titled "The 'Right' to Maim: Disablement and Inhumanist Biopolitics in Palestine," in which Puar launches with Frantz Fanon's notion of colonialism as "an incomplete death" in order to expose how the "deliberate maiming" practised by the Israeli Defense Forces troubles the Foucauldian notion of biopolitics (and, I would add, the traditional right of sovereignty as defined by Foucault).[16] After a discussion of Achille Mbembe's notion of "necropolitics," which as a politics that is focused on death does not cover the politics of maiming either, she eventually finds an ally in Lauren Berlant's notion of "slow death" to refer to the Palestinian situation of being "marked for wearing out, a gradual decay of bodies that are both overworked and under-resourced."[17]

Berlant is, indeed, one of the key thinkers of sovereignty's "phantasm," the fact that it has always been something that people have aspired to rather than an actually existing state ("we were never sovereign" operates like a silent refrain of Berlant's *Cruel Optimism* and one can see why as there is something cruelly optimistic about sovereignty's phantasy). In response to those, however, who still defend the notion of sovereignty, Berlant notes that she is "persuaded enough by these kinds of reservations not to push for a wholesale exorcism of sovereignty's spirit by a dramatic act of taxonomic substitution; legal and normative ghosts have precedential power, after all."[18] But she adds:

> even if we cede sovereignty to perpetuity as a fantasy that sustains liberty's normative political idiom, we need better ways to talk about a more capacious range of activity oriented towards the reproduction of ordinary life: from the burdens of contemporary compelled will that fuel everyday employment and household pressures, for example, to the pleasures of spreading-out activities like sex or eating, aleatory modes of self-abeyance that do not occupy time, decision, or consequentiality in anything like the sovereign registers of autonomous self-assertion.[19]

For this, she proposes what she calls "practical sovereignty," which "would be better understood not to take the mimetic or referred shape of state or individual sovereignty but a shape made by the mediating conditions of zoning, labor, consumption, and governmentality, as well as unconscious and explicit desires *not* to be an inflated ego deploying power and manifesting intention."[20] Puar does not take the "alternative sovereignty" route, but she lays out the notion of "maiming" as a kind of reversal of Berlant's slow death: "If slow death is conceptualized as primarily through the vector of 'let die' or 'make die,' maiming

Homo Vulnerabilis

functions as 'will not let die' and, its supposed humanitarian complement 'will not make die.'"[21] Another way of putting this is that maiming works through wounding, governs through the human being's ability to be wounded, its vulnerability, and that this kind of work, this kind of governance, is not covered by the focus on death. It is a question, rather, of projecting death into the life that biopolitics targets, of imagining precisely the "incomplete death" that Fanon draws our attention to, and rethinking the political situation from there.

Now, Puar makes this move in order to cast light on the Israel/Palestine conflict and the particular forms of sovereign governance she finds there. But with Berlant, who proposes a "practical sovereignty" in the same breath, developing on her comment that she is not pushing "for a wholesale exorcism of sovereignty's spirit," we are also invited to think alternative sovereignties starting from this position of vulnerability. In fact, this may be crucial precisely in a situation like the Israel/Palestine conflict, where the entire struggle according to many is about establishing a national sovereignty for Palestine while at the same time maintaining it for Israel (the so-called "two-state solution"). If we grant each party its wishes – a big IF, of course; how can it be done? – the question concerning what kind of sovereignty those parties will want still remains. At this point, before sovereignty has even been granted, it might seem premature to raise these questions; Edward Said, following Jean Genet, remarked that he would start criticizing Palestine (or, in Genet's words, "betraying Palestine") as soon as it became a state. It is Fanon who has brought us the project of thinking postcolonial liberation through the liberatory struggle of nationalism. But as the "On the Pittfalls of National Consciousness" chapter in *The Wretched of the Earth* also shows, Fanon was well aware of the potential problems nationalism might bring. Focusing on the "constructive" dimension of the project that Fanon in, for example, "On Violence" leaves aside, it would be important to emphasize that such a project could not simply be about the assertion of invulnerable/immortal, masculinist, and – in these senses – white life (it was Fanon, too, who alerted us to the "black skin, white masks" problematic); it could not be about flipping from colonialism and incomplete death into an unnuanced politics of postcolonial "life." Rather, there is a reverse side to colonialism's "incomplete death" that one could call this new politics' "incomplete life" – a life that is never thought as separate from its vulnerability, from its capacity to be wounded and to die. And it is from this reverse side of incomplete death – from this ontologically incomplete life – that the claim to an alternative, critical, democratic, and political sovereignty may become possible.

I am weary, in other words, of simply opposing to the politics of maiming, which is a politics that governs through rendering subjects disabled, an abl-ist politics that would mark the "normal" condition of life. The project would be to rethink sovereignty from what one could call *an ontological disablement* (a "being vulnerable," as my title has it), a fundamental non-ability or negative ability that would become the core of a revised concept of sovereignty. If there is something that sets vulnerability aside from the various abilities Samuel Weber discusses in his book, it seems to be precisely this negativity, the fact that the ability to be wounded does not name a philosophically positive "ability" as it seems all of the other abilities discussed in his book do. As an ability, vulnerability names the possibility of no longer being able, or no longer being able as one was before. It marks, then, precisely the possibility of our disablement, and, as such, it could also be a powerful position from which sovereignty could be rethought – as guided by this negative ability.

Isabell Lorey accomplishes something of the kind in *State of Insecurity: Government of the Precarious*. On the one hand, what Lorey lays bare is how today we are governed through vulnerability, through "precarization," in other words the production of "precarity." Precarity is thus "a category of order, which designates the effects of different political, social, and legal compensations of a general precariousness."[22] General precariousness refers to a "condition inherent to both human and non-human being"[23] – the ontological (though Lorey also partly calls it social, probably in view of the other categories) notion of vulnerability that I discuss earlier on. "Precarization" then "means more than insecure jobs, more than the lack of security given by waged employment. By way of insecurity and danger it embraces the whole of existence, the body, modes of subjectivation. It is threat and coercion, even while it opens up new possibilities of living and working. Precarization means living with the unforeseeable, with contingency."[24] Whereas Hobbes could still promise "protection and security," Lorey points out that this hasn't really been possible since Hobbes's time; in our neoliberal moment, she writes (jumping from 1651 to the 1970s and after), "neoliberal governing proceeds primarily through social insecurity, through regulating the minimum of assurance while simultaneously increasing instability."[25] It's a form of government that is "based on the greatest

Homo Vulnerabilis

possible insecurity" – "greatest possible" because it obviously can't "pass a certain threshold" without "endanger[ing] the existing order."[26] Following Foucault's analysis of neoliberalism, Lorey concludes that "managing this threshold is what makes up the art of governing today."[27]

In the face of this, however, Lorey asks an interesting question: "Where, within these governing mechanisms, [are] cracks and potentials for resistance to be found?"[28] It is obvious from Lorey's analysis that the "modern, male, bourgeois form of sovereignty,"[29] which was launched in the eighteenth century (and had its roots some century before then), is out – has been pushed out in part by neoliberal governance. But what has come in its place? Neoliberal governing *through* insecurity. Lorey opposes, in other words, Hobbes's sovereignty against insecurity and neoliberal insecurity. It's sovereignty versus neoliberalism (with liberalism as a kind of mediator along the path to neoliberalism). Again, she asks the question: "How can new practices of organizing that break through these forms of individualization be found today?"[30] "This is possible," she writes, "when precarization is not perceived and combated solely as a threat, but the entire ensemble of the precarious is taken into consideration and the current domination-securing functions and subjective experiences of precarization are taken as a starting point for political struggles."[31] She adds that doing so necessitates "reopening the field of concepts of the precarious."[32] The most revealing point is her conclusion that "the demand for a simple 'politics of de-precarization' no longer makes sense."[33] Indeed, such a politics would return us to what with Lauren Berlant we might want to call a phantasy of not being precarious, a phantasy of invulnerable/immortal sovereignty. It is, instead, from our vulnerabilization – and, more precisely, precarization – that Lorey wants to rethink politics:

> In a governmental perspective, precarization can be considered not only in its repressive, striating forms, but also in its ambivalently productive moments, as these emerge by way of techniques of self-government. In a historical era when contingency is not only subject in a new way to conditions of economic exploitation, the term governmental precarization can also cover a productive way of dealing with what is incalculable, with what cannot be measured or modularized, with what eludes government through insecurity.[34]

The attentive reader will have noted the D+G term "striation," which Lorey uses here to refer to "repressive" forms of precarization. Interestingly, she has already characterized these forms as "neoliberal." I say "interestingly" because neoliberalism is generally thought of as a "smoothening" power that levels the "striation" of sovereignty. However, I have already discussed (when engaging with Eyal Weizman's work) the reasons such an opposition cannot hold: first of all, because it was not an opposition in D+G (the smooth in D+G is really just the intensely striated); and because the IDF practises "smoothening" as part of a project of establishing sovereignty. The other thing to note, however, is that, in this passage, Lorey does not explicitly mention the smooth; that is, it is not at all clear whether she would associate the "productive" ways of dealing with precarization that she evokes here with the "smooth" rather than with the "striated." Perhaps it is more a question of *striating otherwise* – in the same way that vulnerability breaks out of the life/death binary leading into new conceptions of power.

With Lorey this still hardly puts us in the realm of sovereignty within which I have been operating. Indeed, when Lorey imagines, with Hannah Arendt, the political freedom that would become possible within precarization – the government of the precarious (subject genitive) rather than of the precarious (object genitive) – she notes that it would consist in "the virtuosity of acting together." She adds that, according to Arendt, such freedom "only functions under the condition of non-sovereignty" – and this is one of the main tensions in Butler's recent Arendt-inspired work as well.[35] The negation arrives with some doubt attached to it in a book that has otherwise been very good at escaping the sovereign either/or, for or against – the friend/enemy distinction that structures Schmitt's concept of the political. Why would such freedom be opposed to sovereignty? Couldn't other forms of sovereignty become possible through it? What about a sovereignty of the vulnerable? A sovereignty that would not be opposed to vulnerability – a *vulnerable sovereignty* – if such a thing is possible?

By partly rooting such a vulnerable sovereignty in an anthropology of the vulnerable *human being*, of *homo vulnerabilis*, I am also challenging the sovereignty of the notion of the human itself – a challenge that can be found in several of the texts that I discuss. This issue is perhaps most visible in debates about human rights politics. As opposed to the rights of citizens, which are guaranteed by nation-states, international human rights are supposed to protect the human being as such, independently of their nation-state affiliation. While, as such, human rights go beyond "national" identifiers for the people they seek to protect, it would be naïve to consider "the human" as somehow beyond identity – it would be naïve to not consider the human as itself in its turn asserting an identity. By saying this, I do not mean to create the impression that identity is "bad," though it obviously can be in some situations; I am merely drawing out the fact that "the human" is not the "universal" post-identitarian notion it claims to be. Indeed, Judith Butler, in *Frames of War*, characterizes it as a "differential norm" whose value is constantly shifting and being assigned and retracted.[36] Yet across those shifting designations, it seems the value of "the human" is kept intact – even if we can't quite put our finger on what it stands for. "The human," in other words, takes up a sovereign position of value in our societies, but when it comes to the content of that structural position, the notion appears to be strangely empty – or at least to be in constant movement. However, that is not the impression that those invested in "the human" seek to give: rather, they claim that the human resides above those shifty designations, as a universal value whose content is clear, eternal, and uncontested. In other words, it is a sovereign value – the human has, for many, a sovereign status (there is no power on earth that compares to it, as the line from Job in Hobbes's frontispiece has it). I point this out not to ditch the human altogether. But if we can recognize, with Butler, that the human is a differential norm, that as a norm it is forever shifting, it seems we should be able to recognize the contestability, temporality, and opacity even of the notion – that we should be able to see how the human is vulnerable, can be wounded and might even die – how it needs our "care and concern," to come back once more to the terms that Honig borrows from Arendt and Winnicott. The point is not to maintain it as is but to develop it as a critical concept.

To come back to human rights then: we need to recognize that the "human" that they refer to is a differential norm – that it is in question – that its assignment is by no means obvious. This means practising a critique of the way in which human rights are inscribed into a logic of sovereignty, not ditching human rights altogether but carefully considering their use and abuse. Jacques Rancière, in his critique of human rights, points out how, due to the fact that the subject of human rights is unclear, they have slipped into a discourse of humanitarianism and have become the motivator for humanitarian intervention – in other words, for the intervention by one sovereign

110 Sovereignty and Vulnerability

nation-state into the affairs of another sovereign nation-state in the name of "humanity."[37] Interestingly enough, it is Carl Schmitt who tells us that "whoever evokes humanity wants to cheat": to wage war in the name of humanity is, according to Schmitt, a fallacy because one cannot turn humanity into either a friend or an enemy – "at least not on this planet," as he puts it.[38] In other words, Schmitt assumes that we are humans and that for that reason the human cannot be turned into an enemy. Rancière's position on this count is perhaps more Schmittian than Schmitt's: indeed, Rancière considers the notion of the human to be precisely a *political* notion, where what it means to be human is continuously *contested*. The subject of human rights, for Rancière, is the one who has the rights that s/he does not have, or has not the rights that s/he has. Inscribed into the notion is a contestation – precisely the contestation that for Schmitt the notion of the human seems to deactivate.

However, Schmitt's evocation of "the planet" on this count is interesting, for the planet cannot be identified with the human, and from an ecological point of view one could argue that the human being and the planet in the age of the Anthropocene are engaged in an existential conflict that involves the real possibility of killing. In other words, in the age of the Anthropocene, the human/planet relation is turning political in Schmitt's extreme sense of the term. This is contributing to our sense of a return of sovereignty today. While the planet is obviously not a political agent in the same way that the human being is, and while the human being is a confused political agent when it comes to considering humanity's effect on the planet, it still appears to be the case that humanity, whether each individual wants it or not, is in the process of existentially negating the planet (which is, it should be noted, the human being's own living environment). In short, there is a suicidal civil war of humanity against itself that is going on and that deserves our consideration in this context – we have after all already discussed the topic of civil war or stasis earlier on in this book.

It is, perhaps, because this is a *suicidal* civil war – because waging war on the planet does equal waging war on the human being – that the notion of human rights could be (and has been) mobilized in this context as a way to fight climate change: by asserting one's right to a living environment, human beings could engage in the care of and concern for the planet. Ultimately, however, such an engagement would remain anthropocentric. It would remain an engagement that would seek to save the planet for our own sake. But another, radically

Homo Vulnerabilis

ecocentric consideration may be that humanity has to collectively off itself – to accelerate the suicidal civil war until its logical conclusion – in order to allow the planet to survive. Even such a radical path forward might still be pursued from an anthropocentric perspective, in the hope that, however many millions of years down the line, a new human species will emerge from our collective suicide. But, at its most radical, this collective act of self-annihilation wouldn't take place in the hope that humanity would return: it would be a gesture, rather, of entirely giving oneself up for the survival of the other – like a parent might for a child, or a lover for their love.

By evoking the spectre of human extinction – and not just the spectre but the real possibility of its occurrence – I am trying to go (very much against this book's inclination, which is to affirm another kind of sovereignty) to the end of the human's sovereignty, of its vulnerability, its capacity to be wounded. As an anthropological notion, *homo vulnerabilis* carries this end within it. However, at this moment it still does so in exactly Schmitt's terms, not as an actuality but as a "real possibility" from where the notion of the human can be rethought – and from where, beyond it, the notion of sovereignty can be rethought (though not exactly in Schmitt's way, obviously). To be vulnerable, then, would be to imagine one's end as a "real possibility" and to then not rage against this imagination as a possibility that needs to be kept at bay, forgotten and ignored at all costs; rather, it would mean to think and live with it, from a kind of modesty that such a real possibility produces. It would mean to care for and be concerned with humanity's, and sovereignty's, end – not in order to accomplish it but to use it as the foundation for humanity and sovereignty's alternatives. A *being-towards-death*, to reference the work of a philosopher who appears in the next chapter: but one that would counter abusive sovereignty and imagine alternative sovereignties that would prevent our suicidal end. To care for and be concerned with the planet from this point of view would lead to a radically decentred ecological thought in which the planet would solicit our attention in spite of the fact that it may survive us – in spite of the fact that, in a worst case scenario that will hopefully never come to pass, our extinction may even be necessary for its survival.

10

Democracy's Exceptions

All of politics ... is played out in the interpretation of democratic "anarchy."

Jacques Rancière, "Ten Theses on Politics"[1]

Can the discourse of vulnerability be brought together with the discourse of sovereignty in such a way that these two would not be mutually exclusive? By now, it should be clear that I am asking this question from within sovereignty. The issue is obviously different at sovereignty's borders, or outside of it, where sovereignty is rather a force that vulnerabilizes others to protect its own subjects. Such vulnerabilization goes hand in hand with the attempt to hold up a phantasm of invulnerability on *this* side of the sovereign borders.

I would now like to consider this internal question by turning to a contemporary theorist of sovereignty, Bonnie Honig. It is Honig who, while she is critical of the vulnerability perspective, nevertheless enables us to place it within a thinking about sovereignty. She does so by thinking about "exceptionalist politics" as a possibility *not only* for sovereign abuse *but also* for democratic politics. To go back to some of the discussions in part 1 and part 2: the state of exception, or more broadly speaking any emergency situation, is obviously a situation in which the vulnerability of human life (and often other forms of life as well) lies exposed. In this sense, states of exception and emergency situations are the kinds of states and situations in which we appear most visibly vulnerable – in which our usually latent ontological condition of vulnerability becomes undeniably manifest, in the way that having a minor cold or a paper cut can become reminders of the vulnerability of one's entire bodily system.

But such states or situations are not only the playing ground of Schmittian sovereignty, Honig claims. She proposes instead that we must ask "how democratic theorists and activists might go further to democratize emergency, and to do so not to resist sovereignty but to claim it."[2] In other words, Schmittian sovereignty is not the *only* sovereignty that can become meaningful in a state of exception or emergency situation. To democratize emergency, she continues, "means seeking sovereignty, not just challenging it, and insisting that sovereignty is not just a trait of executive power that must be chastened but also potentially a trait of popular power as well, one to be generated and mobilized. Rather than oppose democracy and emergency, then, we might think about democratic opportunities to claim sovereignty even in emergency settings."[3] Honig lays out different models for this: deliberative, activist, and legalist. It is through the emergency that "new forms of collective living" can come about.[4]

The deliberative model she associates with Elaine Scarry's position in *Thinking in an Emergency*, where Scarry advocates "a fully deliberative approach to emergency preparations in advance of any actual crisis" – it's an approach that has become particularly relevant during the pandemic.[5] This goes against Schmittian decisionism – what we get instead is collective deliberation and the community-building that it brings. But many other Schmittian elements remain intact: the friend/enemy distinction, for example; the threat of war, the real possibility of war, as an organizing cause. It is Honig's second, activist model, which she derives from the work of Douglas Crimp, that most obviously targets the friend/enemy distinction from a queer studies point of view, through its focus on promiscuity. In the middle of the AIDS crisis, Crimp developed promiscuity, which was under attack at the time, "as a form of life, and resisted its stigmatization by those moralists and pragmatists who treated promiscuity as an indulgence or as a sign of gay male immaturity."[6] To fight the reduction of human life to mere life in a state of emergency, Crimp (in Honig's reading) turns to "more life": to a higher, more intense form of living as opposed to its reduction to mere life. As opposed to Scarry's "devotion to deliberative processes and risk aversion," then, Crimp "sees the promises and pleasure of spontaneity."[7] For Crimp, "democracy is itself promiscuous."[8] It is, finally, in the legalist approach – associated with Louis Freeland Post – that Honig finds elements of both Scarry and Crimp combined, of deliberation and promiscuity combined. Post was a proceduralist who was weary of proceduralism, and Honig appreciates this promiscuous approach to deliberation.

Honig casts Post, whom she also discusses in *Emergency Politics*, as someone who introduces us to "the paradox of politics."[9] This refers to a touchstone in Honig's work, namely, Jean-Jacques Rousseau's problem of "how to design a good polity when, to get good law, you need good men to author it, but to get good men, you need good law to shape and socialize them?" She notes that this is a "chicken-and-egg" problem that, I would add, resonates with the problem of the state of exception itself, and whether it is the sovereign who makes the exception or the exception who makes the sovereign.[10] As Honig had already discussed in detail in *Democracy and the Foreigner*,[11] Rousseau famously brings in a "lawgiver" who comes along to give people a law that they cannot generate themselves, only to remove himself from the political scene after that. Whereas this issue is usually situated at the origin of political communities, Honig actually points out that such scenes return in political communities on a daily basis, "as new citizens are born into a regime or immigrate into it, and old ones are resocialized into its expectations and norms, and demands."[12] Honig appreciates Post because he reminds us that "the paradox of politics" is always there, that politics is always partly procedural and partly promiscuous. And both these elements, as well as their particular legalist combination, can come out of state of exception politics. In this way, state of exception politics actually revitalizes democratic politics rather than presents the fascist suspension of democracy.

Honig's argument is a major shift in the discourse about the state of exception, which, so far, we have considered largely within a Schmittian perspective, which tends to promote the state of exception's association with fascism. Here, Honig taps into a different tradition, represented through the work of Andreas Kalyvas in part 1 of this book – the reconsideration of Schmitt's work for democratic purposes. The advantage of Honig's approach is that it enables us to develop a critique of the state of exception, a consideration of its legitimate versus its illegitimate, its democratic versus its fascistic uses. Honig thus turns the state of exception into a critical concept, a concept whose politics can not in any sovereign way be decided but is perpetually under discussion. Merely by developing the democratic take on the exception, Honig challenges the sovereignty of this notion and begins to rethink it. She does not much emphasize the importance of life's vulnerability for this project, but all of her examples – the deliberative model, the activist model, and the legalist model – assume it. Moreover, by calling the democratic state of exception deliberative *and* promiscuous, Honig seems to be drawing out precisely the vulnerable sovereignty – as opposed to the sovereignty against vulnerability – that I am trying to theorize here. It becomes possible, then, to map out the difference between fascistic and democratic emergencies in relation to the vulnerability from which they both start out: the former seeks to suspend the law in an attempt at fortification that would seek to hold vulnerability at bay; the latter participates in deliberative and promiscuous legalism that would govern from the point of view of vulnerability. Importantly, I don't think these two positions can be opposed on the count of sovereignty: they are both, in my view, sovereign positions. But the latter removes from sovereignty precisely those elements that make it so problematic (and that can be found not only in Schmitt but also in other theorists of that particular power).

I want to emphasize that it is I, not Honig, who am making the connection between emergency and vulnerability. Vulnerability comes up in Honig's work as well – she engages the term in particular in *Antigone, Interrupted*.[13] But it receives a very critical treatment as a notion that has tended to lead us into the ethical rather than the political. I do not think this needs to be so. If vulnerability does mark the ethical, it is precisely as such that it can unwork some of the most problematic aspects of sovereignty – but without giving up on sovereignty and the political altogether.

*

It is worth noting, after this discussion of Honig, that fascism and democracy hardly exhaust the names for the various politics of the state of exception. In Santiago Zabala's work, for example, such a politics – or better, a politics of "the great emergency" rather than a mere politics of exception – is associated with "anarchy." In *Why Only Art Can Save Us*, Zabala takes on the contemporary talk about emergencies and states of emergencies. He argues, contrary to what one might expect, that in spite of all this emergency talk – in spite of the fact that, today, emergencies appear to be everywhere – today's real emergency is the absence of emergency. We are currently living in a state of "accomplished realism" in which the emergency is lacking.[14] By this, he doesn't mean that "the refugee crisis in Europe, ISIS terrorist attacks, and Edward Snowden's revelations of US National Security Agency surveillance" are not emergencies;[15] rather, they "mark the absence of emergency" because "they are framed within our global system."[16] "They emerge as a consequence of this frame, which is the greatest emergency."[17] Instead, Zabala is interested in what "disrupt[s]

116   Sovereignty and Vulnerability

the framing powers": "the weak, the remnants of Being, that is, every person and idea forced to the margins of this frame."[18] Those disruptive elements "inevitably [strive] for change or, better, for an alteration of the imposed representations of reality."[19] Such an alteration "is necessary," Zabala writes, "not only politically and ethically but also aesthetically. An aesthetic force is needed to shake us out of our tendency to ignore the 'social paradoxes' generated by the political, financial, and technological frames that contain us."[20] Here we discover what real emergencies he has in mind: "the 'urban discharge' of slums and plastic and electronic wastes; the 'environmental calls' caused by global warming, ocean pollution, and deforestation; and the 'historical accounts' of invisible, ignored, and denied events."[21] These emergencies are discussed in the second part of Zabala's book, which focuses on artworks. It is these kinds of emergencies that, in Zabala's view, "will disrupt not only capitalism's indefinite reproduction but also realism's metaphysical impositions." As Zabala's book title reveals, he considers artists and art to have a unique capacity to "'thrust' and 'rescue' us into the greatest emergencies."[22] Rather than saving us *from* the emergency, they save us *into* it.

Zabala's main philosophical guide for such a project is a philosopher whose work has mostly been missing in this book so far: Martin Heidegger. It is from Heidegger that Zabala takes the problem that is central to his own book, the absence of emergency, which is the consequence of what Heidegger calls "framing." More precisely, Zabala takes from Heidegger the problem that all of today's emergency talk in fact *conceals* the greatest emergency. Whereas the former concerns "aspects of law, politics, and society, which belong to the ontic realm of knowledge,"[23] the latter "involves senses and feelings, that is, 'existence,' which, Heidegger says, is never an 'object' but instead is 'Being' – it is *there* only insofar as in each case a living 'is' it."[24] In today's world picture and its "frame," Heidegger argues, "Being is marginalized, ignored, and abandoned; it becomes a remnant."[25] To look for the greatest emergency, then, means to look for "the remains of Being."[26] However, these "are not something we see or contemplate; they instead constitute everything that is beyond the logical, ethical, and 'aesthetic state' [or frame] that Heidegger defined as 'the lucidity through which we constantly see.'"[27] Thus, "the remains of Being emerge as an alteration, an event, or an emergency of the world picture, that is, an interruption of the [framed] reality we've become accustomed to."[28] The emergency is lacking "when we realize that everything is lucid and functioning correctly."[29] Heidegger believes the emergency is the greatest "where everything is held to be calculable, justifiable, and predictable, reducing the world to objective measures"[30] – where the frame has become victorious. According to Heidegger, Zabala writes, art is the "extraordinary and unimaginable" something that "discloses itself through the remains of Being. Works of art, as remnants beyond measurable contemplation, instead of being the focus of aesthetics have become its emergency, that is, what will 'help' retrieve, appropriate, and disclose Being."[31] Art thus saves us from aesthetics. More strongly even: it has a unique capacity to save Being and, by consequence, us human beings from our enframing.

Heidegger was, of course, not the only one to develop a philosophy of the emergency and the state of emergency; indeed, the emergency was (as part 1 evidences through its discussions of Schmitt and Benjamin) a central concern of "Weimar thought," the thought developed between the First and the Second World Wars. Zabala mentions early on in his book the "popular 'state of emergency' (*Ausnahmezustand*) of Benjamin, Schmitt, and Agamben,"[32] which has been central to this book. But that "popular" state of emergency is quickly left aside as a "consequence" of the abandonment of Being with which Heidegger is concerned.[33] The abandonment of Being "includes," Zabala writes, "the decision of the sovereign,"[34] which is central to the works of Benjamin, Schmitt, and Agamben: it is the abandonment of Being that in part explains the rise of the sovereign decision on the state of exception in our contemporary moment. At this point, Zabala adds a long footnote that focuses on the different ways in which "Ausnahme" has been translated in Benjamin, Schmitt, Agamben, and Heidegger;[35] however, it also focuses on Heidegger and, unfortunately, does not map out his relation to the Benjamin-Schmitt-Agamben grouping in any detail.

One feels, in fact, that such a detailed mapping is missing in Zabala's book, which, in order to truly have been convincing in its adoption of the Heideggerian point of view, should likely have spent some more time explaining how that point of view differs from the "popular 'state of emergency'" that is all too quickly dismissed here. For one, while Benjamin, Schmitt, and Agamben can certainly be discussed together when it comes to understanding the place of the state of exception in their work, it would be difficult to maintain, as I show in part 1, that they have all treated the state of exception in the same way. And it is in part a careful mapping of those differences and their politics that may have led to a more precise assessment of the ideas of the emergency and the state of emergency in Heidegger as well. Zabala's book may be about art, but it attempts to make a decidedly political point, one that hinges on a controversial reading of a decidedly controversial thinker. Like Schmitt, Heidegger is a politically dubious figure, something that the recent publication of Heidegger's *Black Notebooks* (on which Zabala relies) has only made more clear. It is unfortunate that, in a book dealing with contemporary states of exception, Zabala does not address Heidegger's association with anti-democratic, fascist politics – even if *Why Only Art Can Save Us* proposes to leave ontic emergencies having to do with law, politics, and society aside for the supposedly more ontological considerations of art. To have kept those ontic emergencies within his book's scope could have complicated Zabala's thought and helped us to assess the distinction between fascist and democratic (if we want to call them that) states of exception.

As I explain in part 1, Schmitt's *Political Theology* and its definition of the sovereign as the one who decides on the state of exception can be read as a conservative response to Benjamin's "Critique of Violence," which ultimately theorizes a "divine violence" that is outside of the sphere of the law. Schmitt could not tolerate such an outside and folded it back within through his theory of sovereignty as the peculiar position of a power that is both inside and outside the law. He thus also defined sovereignty not as democratic law-making (as Honig would have it) but as the fascistic suspension of the law. It is through such a comparative discussion (of Schmitt and Benjamin, as well as Honig) that one can understand how Schmitt's theory can be read within Zabala's Heideggerian point of view as an emergency that is "framed" within the dominant political and legal systems of the world order. Schmitt's project was indeed to frame, through the notion of sovereignty, a violence that Benjamin crucially posited outside of the law. Zabala, following Heidegger, is not interested in emergencies that are framed in this way. Instead, he is after "the greatest emergency" that pertains to Being. He wants to lay bare the remains of Being that interrupt the frame – an exception or emergency that is greater than the conservative one that Schmitt offers us. But does that turn him into a Benjaminian?

While this explains Zabala's rejection of Schmitt for Heidegger, it leaves his relation to Benjamin unaddressed. Benjamin's "Critique of Violence" isn't engaged at any point in Zabala's book, even if it seems

Democracy's Exceptions 119

indispensable for addressing Schmitt's relation to Benjamin. Given also that Zabala derives his book title by substituting "art" for "a God" in Heidegger's infamous statement that "only a God can still save us,"[36] this seems to propel us into a discussion of art's "divine" violence in Heidegger.

Zabala does turn to another text of Benjamin's that is also part of this discussion, namely, Benjamin's much later "Theses on the Philosophy of History." One understands why Zabala would engage with this text, which explicitly uses the term "state of emergency" to refer to a situation in which oppression has become the rule, but which also calls for a "real state of emergency" that "will improve our struggle against Fascism."[37] In other words, exceptionality seems to go two ways here: both in the direction of oppression and fascism, and then in the direction of something else that might defeat fascism (one imagines that Benjamin's conversation with Schmitt is continuing here). What is this something else? Is this what Honig calls "democratic"? Going back to "Critique of Violence," one might also surmise (as I indicate earlier) that Benjamin had already theorized this "real state of exception" in 1921 as "divine violence" – the "sovereign" violence beyond the sphere of legal/mythical violence that writes contracts in blood. In other words, Benjamin may be theorizing a state of exception here against Schmitt's state of exception that would be able to end the fascist state of exception with which Schmitt had become associated. The political stakes though are clear: we are dealing with fascism (and the struggle against it) throughout.

Fascism, however, does not come up – at least not by name – in Zabala's book, perhaps because it is not the kind of emergency in which he is interested. Still, given that his main philosophical guide is Heidegger, one might have expected something more than the quick dismissal of the issue in his first paragraph, in which he alludes to it as Heidegger's "political adventure of 1933 as rector of the University of Freiburg, in other words, after the failure and error implied by this political involvement, which inevitably caused him so many academic, public, and psychological difficulties, as the recent publication of his *Black Notebooks* (once again) confirmed."[38] Art, Zabala goes on, took Heidegger out of these "ontic" troubles, directing his thinking towards the lack of emergency and the greatest emergency of Being's abandonment. The art to which Zabala draws our attention in the engaging second part of his book manages to present the remains of Being in such a situation of emergency lack.

Yet we *do* learn that "democracy" does not get a good rap in Heidegger's thinking about how art rescues us into the emergency: "As it turns out, democracy, which is the political stance currently supposed to liberate the public, does not need to impose pleasantness because it is already resigned to its indifference. Words, sounds, and images, as Heidegger explains, have become means to govern the masses."[39] If art thrusts us into the greatest emergency, this is a thrusting that appears to go against democracy and its governing of the masses. So we are *not* in Honig's democratic exception either.

Just what *are* the politics of Heidegger's rescue mission here, then? What are the politics of the "greatest emergency" that are being proposed here? To answer this question, the third and final part of Zabala's book, titled "Emergency Aesthetics," is the most useful. In a short section on interpretation, Zabala traces the notion of hermeneutics back to "the messenger god Hermes, whose name points back to his winged feet." I quote at length:

> This messenger was renowned for his speed, athleticism, and swiftness; he exercised the practical activity of delivering the announcements, warnings, and prophecies of the gods of Olympus. In the *Cratylus* (407e), *Ion* (534e), and *Symposium* (202e), Plato connects the term "*hermenea*" etymologically to the name of the god Hermes and presents hermeneutics both as a theory of reception and "as a practice for transmission and mediation": Hermes must transmit what is beyond human understanding in a form that human intelligence can grasp. However, in this transmission, Hermes was often accused of thievery, treachery, and even anarchy because the messages were never accurate; in other words, his interpretations always altered the original meanings. Hermes, as Gerald L. Bruns put it, was "the many-sided, uncontainable, nocturnal transgressor."[40]

In Zabala's rephrasing, interpretation (contrary to description) "adds new vitality."[41] Presumably this is a different "vitality" than the one that Schmitt finds in the state of exception, when he writes that "the power of real life breaks through the crust of a mechanism that has become torpid by repetition." Based on what we know about the Heideggerian position by now, the vitality that would be referred to here should be what one might want to call "the greatest vitality," a vitality that exceeds the one residing within the frame of Schmitt's thought. Zabala (a representative of the exceedingly rare position of left-Heideggerianism) ends up labelling it – working through Gianni Vattimo and Bruns on the topic – as "'anarchic' in Rainer Schürmann's sense of this word; [hermeneutics] does not try to assault its *Sache* but rather tries to grant what is singular and unrepeatable an open field."[42]

At this point, though, further complications arise. Zabala seems to be adding here to the difference between Schmitt and Heidegger because Schmitt in *Political Theology* leaves "anarchy and chaos" aside as a realm where law and the exception do not apply. The exception, for Schmitt, is *not* anarchy and chaos. This is crucial to his thought. Also relevant here is the Benjamin text that Zabala ignores, "Critique of Violence." In it, Benjamin characterizes the proletarian general strike as "anarchistic": even though it destroys state power, it is non-violent because it leads to a "wholly transformed work." If Schmitt once again appears to be an opponent here, a possible positive connection with Benjamin is also once again brought to light.

Zabala wants his state of exception to be anarchic, not fascistic. But why turn to Heidegger for this? It is worth pointing out, as Zabala does, that "Heidegger never refers to 'anarchic interpretations,"[43] even if he was very interested in hermeneutics and made it a crucial part of his method. But this is the closest we come in Zabala's book to a name for Heidegger's politics, and that name is neither fascism nor democracy but anarchy – in Schürmann's sense of the word, as a politics that would "try to grant what is singular and unrepeatable an open field." At this point, we should likely tie this back to Being's abandonment and the way in which art, according to Heidegger, thrusts us into the remains of Being, those singular and unrepeatable elements that reside in the margin – to grant them an open field rather than a closed frame.

As I have already indicated, Zabala refers to this frame that he wants to break down throughout his book as "realism." When he talks about the "accomplished realism" of the frame early on, he puts some of the blame for this on the French philosopher Quentin Meillassoux who "demands a return to 'the Great Outdoors' ('le Grand Dehors')."[44] Meillassoux is quickly mentioned, one assumes, due to his criticism of correlationism, or the philosophical position that considers there is no reality outside of human observation. With the notion of the great outdoors, however, Meillassoux seeks to assert a human-independent reality – a position that Zabala labels "accomplished realism." Strange, then, at least at the superficial level of terminology, to see the project of "granting things an open field" return here as the "anarchic" gesture that exposing the greatest emergency requires. Strange also, at least to those who have read Meillassoux, that his work is not so much associated with an "accomplished realism" as with a "speculative materialism" and "speculative realism" that, for example in its investigation of the literary genre/philosophical modality of science-fiction, calls precisely for another philosophical modality, perhaps not quite a literary genre, of what Meillassoux calls "extro-science fiction." Extro-science fiction hails as its key literary expression "stories of uncertain reality, those in which the real crumbles gradually, from one day to the next ceasing to be familiar to us."[45] Such stories would capture the extro-science fiction world in which the irregularity of events "is sufficient to abolish science but not [human] consciousness."[46] I wonder how Zabala might combine what Meillassoux writes here with Heidegger and his criticism of science, which frames, and through its framing abandons, Being. It seems to me Meillassoux is anything but a representative of "accomplished realism." Zabala also mentions Graham Harman on this count as another representative of "accomplished realism." Given that Harman is in part also a scholar of Heidegger, it would be good to see this worked out in detail. One certainly wonders how the claim can be squared with the "weird realism" that Harman, in a book on Lovecraft, puts forward.[47]

Leaving these smaller points aside though, the main issue is clearly what to make of the (somewhat unlikely) "Heideggerian anarchism" with which Zabala concludes his book. How are we to conceive of it? Zabala's answer to this question brings to light new problems. For Heidegger, a work of art "is not an implement equipped with some aesthetic quality but rather the disclosure of a new origin, world, and truth," a truth that is "a *Streit*, strife or conflict, between two opposed inclinations: '*lichtung*,' clearing, and '*verborgen*,' concealing."[48] It is within this conflict – which, again, one could be reading in Schmittian terms, as a Heideggerian version of the friend/enemy distinction that, according to Schmitt, constitutes "the political" – that art institutes itself through what Heidegger calls a "Stoss," "a shock": "art happens, whenever, that is, there is a beginning, a shock enters history and history either begins or resumes."[49] But, Heidegger continues (and Zabala helpfully quotes this as well):

> there is nothing violent about this multidirectional shock, for the more purely is the work itself transported into the openness of beings it itself opens up, then the more simply does it carry

us into this openness and, at the same time, out of the realm of the usual. To submit to this displacement means: to transform all familiar relations to world and to earth, and henceforth to restrain all usual doing and prizing, knowing and looking, in order to dwell within the truth that is happening in the work. The restraint of this dwelling allows what is created to become, for the first time, the work that it is.[50]

The shock that we find here then is not the kind of "shock" that has also been associated with en-framing: the kind of shock that Naomi Klein (whose book on the climate Zabala quotes) analyzes as a technique of government in *The Shock Doctrine* (Klein's book on disaster capitalism, which Zabala does not reference).[51] Art delivers a different kind of shock: non-violent, transformative, restraining so that we are able "to dwell within the truth that has happening in the work." To my ears, especially when Heidegger associates this with history beginning or resuming, this sounds like Benjamin: not only the Benjamin of the "Theses," who writes about the "continuum of history" being "blasted open" and a new sense of history, a new calendar being established, but also the Benjamin of "Critique of Violence," who characterizes the proletarian general strike as non-violent and leading to a "wholly transformed kind of work." In both cases, Benjamin uses the verb "aufheben" – to destroy and to preserve – to characterize the transformation that he has in mind. It is not clear from Zabala's book whether there is any engagement with or even simply allusion to Hegel in Heidegger on this count. Looking more closely at Benjamin may have provoked this question.

Zabala does end up distinguishing between the shock of "Erlebnis," which Gadamer associates with "the appeal to immediacy, to the instantaneous flash of genius, to the significance of 'experiences'" and that of "Erfahrung," which refers to "the binding quality of the experience," which has to do with "the claim of human existence to continuity and unity of self-understanding."[52] It appears to be on the latter side that Heidegger's shock of art, its thrusting us into Being's emergency, comes down. It is thus along the latter lines that one must read the particular "anarchy" that is proposed in the closing pages of Zabala's book. It is not the anarchy or chaos, the kind of vitality that is immediate and instantaneous. It does not flash, like genius. Instead, it is associated with continuity and the unity of self-understanding. The language here seems to necessitate a modification of the relation to Benjamin, who famously writes of history "flashing up" at a moment of danger in his "Theses"; if there is a shock here, it is one that is ultimately folded back within continuity and self-understanding, even if it marks the instant when "history either begins or resumes." We find here something like a conservative use of the idea of anarchism. The occasion to engage with Benjamin occurs in Zabala's afterword, when Benjamin's "real state of exception" is explicitly mentioned.[53] But the reference is not explored further.

We have, then, two names for the non-fascist politics of exception that I have been pursuing: democracy (in Honig's work) and anarchy (in Zabala's). How might the two relate? When Benjamin, Schmitt, and Agamben return in Zabala's "Afterword," he writes that "the goal of this afterword is not to confront these thinkers," even if he also notes that their contributions are "central in the development of aesthetics and the problem of emergency." Instead, Zabala sets out to show "how other radical contemporary aesthetic theories in the twenty-first century have also developed in relation to current social, political, and environmental emergencies."[54] He mentions in particular the work of Arthur Danto, Jacques Rancière, and Gianni Vattimo (who, in addition to Heidegger, is another major reference in Zabala's book; Vattimo was Zabala's teacher and they have co-authored a book). I want to consider, given the framework that I set up above, Rancière's role as a contemporary representative of democratic thought (Rancière's oeuvre is interesting in the French theory scene within which he is situated, in part due to its pronounced commitment to a democratic politics that many criticize or even reject). It is because of Rancière's notion of "the distribution of the sensible" that Zabala mentions Rancière early on his book as well as in the "Afterword." This notion refers to what Rancière characterizes as the "police" order of what can be seen, heard, felt, et cetera. Art, according to Rancière, is political in the challenge it poses to this police order: in how it thrusts us (to use Zabala's Heideggerian language) into what *cannot* be seen, heard, felt, et cetera. In the quote from Rancière's *Dissensus* that – along with quotes from Danto and Vattimo – opens Zabala's book, this means that art (or at least what Rancière calls "critical art") "aims to produce a new perception of the world, and therefore to create a commitment to its transformation."

Interestingly, when in his "Ten Theses on Politics" Rancière seeks to characterize "democracy," he mentions Cleisthenes's famous democratic experiment, wherein "democracy is characterized by the drawing

Democracy's Exceptions 125

of lots, or the complete absence of any entitlement to govern. It is the state of exception in which no oppositions can function, in which there is no principle for the dividing up of roles ... Democracy is the specific situation in which it is the absence of entitlement that entitles one to exercise the *archè*."[55] Rancière takes this understanding of democracy from Plato's *Laws*, in which Plato "undertakes a systematic inventory of the qualifications (axiomata) required for governing and the correlative qualifications for being ruled."[56] Plato retains seven, four of which (Rancière notes) are based on "natural difference, that is, the difference of birth."[57] "The fifth qualification ... is the power of those with a superior nature, of the strong over the weak."[58] The sixth, which Plato considers most worthy, is that of "the power of those who know over those who do not"[59] – hence, his preference for philosopher-kings. But, Rancière notes, Plato adds a seventh qualification that produces what he considers a "break in the logic of the arkhè."[60] Plato calls this seventh qualification "the choice of God" or "the drawing of lots."[61] In a strange resonance with Heidegger, Rancière turns this into an understanding of democracy as the regime that "only a god could save."[62] It is in this way that Rancière arrives at his understanding of democracy as "the state of exception." If such a democratic state is "anarchic," this is not because of its total absence of archè but because it produces a break in the *logic* of archè in that *it turns the absence of the entitlement to rule into the entitlement to rule* – into a "commencement without commencement, a form of rule (commandement) that does not command."[63] In other words, there is rule – but not as before. This is a state of exception, as Rancière sees it – but one "that more generally makes politics in its specificity possible."[64] This is why democracy for Rancière is not so much a political regime as it is the name of politics as such. Democracy, like politics, is what produces a break within the logic of ruling as such. This has something to do with the particular anarchy, if I can use this term, that it brings. Anarchy, then, does not so much refer to the absence of all rule as it does to the democratic break in the logic of a rule that is exercised by one "determinate superiority" over "an equally determinate inferiority."[65] It refers to the rule of equality.[66]

In other words, Rancière claims democracy as anarchic and, in that sense, as politics due to its rule of equality – its rule that is based on the absence of any entitlement to rule. While such a position obviously marks a kind of shock, and an exception in this sense – it does, after all, accomplish a break in the logic of the *arkhè* – it is worth noting

126   Sovereignty and Vulnerability

that such a shock or exception does not do away with all rule. Indeed, it is folded back within the rule – but into a wholly transformed rule. This means that there is also something "conservative" about Rancière's position that ties it back to Heidegger (and Rancière's characterization of democracy as the regime that only a god can save appears to accomplish as much). However, we would have to note here that the particular "conservatism" that both Rancière's and Heidegger's positions bring is a "radical" one, one that operates through extensive transformation, transformation of the kind that Benjamin describes when he imagines the effect of the strike to a "wholly transformed work." To go back to Heidegger's issue of framing, then, the point would be not so much to have done entirely with the frame as it would be to frame otherwise – that would be the project of "the greatest emergency" and the careful attention it pays to the remnants of Being. Heidegger may not want to call this "democratic," but that is perhaps because he has a flawed understanding of democracy as the indifferent rule of the masses through aesthetics. Rancière, on the other hand, shows us that aesthetics, the politics of aesthetics, can also accomplish something else, something like the "anarchism" that Heidegger appears attached to and that Rancière defines as democracy and, by extension, as politics. It is Rancière's emphasis on a "rule" without rule in this context that puts him in line with Honig, who is interested in pursuing the democratic, deliberative/legislative side of exceptional politics – but not without, of course, the promiscuity of anarchy mixed in. Honig is a proponent of democratic politics, and anarchy is not a major term in her project – but we can begin to see here that it would be a meaningful notion for her to consider, especially as part of the "activist" interest in her work. That Heidegger, through Zabala, appears to be an unlikely ally in this project is something that remains to be negotiated in the work of several of the thinkers I have discussed.

The risk of this entire conversation may be clear and was already brought up in part 1: How does one distinguish the democratic state of exception that can be found in Rancière, and can also – via anarchy – be associated with Heidegger, from the other state of exception that can be found in Schmitt? It seems that politically Rancière and Schmitt are very much opposed. Yet how can it be that in their work on politics – one associated with democracy, the other with fascism – they sound remarkably similar? I ask this question about Schmitt and Rancière, but this concern can be expanded to art theory at large, which

Democracy's Exceptions

often characterizes art's politics in exceptionalist terms.[67] Since we are talking philosophy here, I am thinking, for example, of someone like Alain Badiou, who considers the role of art to be to force "a thinking to declare, in its area of concern, a state of exception."[68] Can one really ignore the echoes of Schmitt here, as Jean-François Lyotard already asked in an early response to Badiou's *Being and Event*?[69]

I am not saying, of course, that Badiou or Rancière are fascists. But it seems worth asking the question about echoes of Schmitt in their thought, especially given how pervasive exceptionalist discourses about art are in philosophy, art theory, and culture. To be sure, there are plenty of exceptions, and it just will not do to call all of them Schmittian. But if one wants to hold on to an exceptionalist theory of art, as Zabala (following Heidegger) seems to want to do, then it seems important – especially given the importance of Heidegger in Zabala's argument – to do so with some care for the troubling political complications that such an exceptionalism of art may bring. Rancière, perhaps recognizing the potential problems of Badiou's thinking on this count, has in an interview insisted that if there is an exception in his theory, it is different from Badiou's theory of the event: for him (Rancière) the exception is always ordinary, he insists, coming "not out of a decision or out of a radical rupture" but out of a "multiplicity of small displacements."[70] This resonates more with Heidegger than with Schmitt. But the issue remains to be pursued – and it feels like it *should* have been pursued in *Why Only Art Can Save Us*.

The project of *Why Only Art Can Save Us* appears to be to oppose art's exceptionalism, its greatest emergency, to the "aesthetic exceptionalism" that (in Zabala's Heideggerian view) in truth marks the absence of the exception. There is no doubt that this is an important point: it targets the ways in which art's critical edge has been blunted. Plato is not usually considered the artist's best friend, but the least that can be said about him is that he took art seriously. At least he still considered artists dangerous, enough so to ban them from his ideal polis. But which artist still risks incurring this charge today in liberal democratic states? Even the artists who, in Zabala's elaborate readings, thrust us into the emergency rarely do so at the risk of being banned. Many of them are supported by art councils and international grants and fellowships. Art sells. Zabala quotes Mark C. Taylor's analysis of how the financialization of art has softened its critical bite.[71] This is true even for the art that Zabala embraces. Even the exceptional art that Zabala brings to our attention fits fairly easily within the overall frame within which we live today. I understand why its exception is greater than the "aesthetic exceptionalism" that Zabala targets. But I also wonder about the extent of the challenge that such art really poses to the frame.

One might ask, more specifically, if insisting on another, greater exceptionalism in response to aesthetic exceptionalism – as Zabala, following Heidegger (and Benjamin) would have us do – is the proper solution to the political problem of exceptionalism.[72] From another point of view, and this is the one I develop here, one should surely also wonder if exceptionalism captures the politics of art correctly. Is art really all about the exception, about the suspension of the norm, the innovation and extraordinariness that is almost as a matter of fact associated with it? For many, art surely seems to suspend the law. Some would likely confuse such a suspension with art's law-breaking capacity (Schmitt of course does no such thing). But one might also look at it from the other side and focus on art's law-making or law-transforming capacities. This means moving towards, rather than away from, the frame, of which Heidegger is so critical. I bring up this idea in light of Benjamin's use of the verb "aufheben" to characterize the effect of divine violence or what he calls "the real state of exception." I do so also with reference to Rancière insistence (contra Badiou) on an exceptionalism that would consist in "the multiplicity of small displacements." I do so with respect to Gadamer's insistence on "Erfahrung" versus "Erlebnis," which Zabala embraces. Finally, I do so in view of Heidegger's "conservative" anarchism, Honig's insistence on the exception's democratic possibilities, and the particular understanding of anarchism that I derive here from Rancière. Perhaps it is time to start insisting on these particular exceptionalisms against the kind that we find in Schmitt and build new sovereignties from it.

And one might even go further: theorizing the notion of democracy, Stathis Gourgouris uses in this context Emily Apter's notion of "unexceptional politics" to capture a political regime that "does not make exceptions, if we are to take seriously Aristotle's dictum of a politics where the ruler learns by being ruled, making thus the ruled simultaneously the rulers, in a determinant affirmation of an archè that has no precedent and no uniqueness but is shared by all. No exceptions."[73] Gourgouris's mention of an archè indicates that he understands by this an anarchic politics in which "nothing is miraculous, where indeed nothing is sacred, where there is no Homo Sacer." "Anarchy as a mode of rule," he concludes this part of his article, "raises a major challenge to the inherited tradition of sovereignty in modernity." Whether this can be expanded into a challenge to the notion of sovereignty at large, and specifically into a rejection of sovereignty, remains unclear since, two paragraphs later, Gourgouris states that "sovereignty needs to be located in unexceptional collective action" – so it seems that one might still be able to hold on to it on the condition that it is located within this context. The notion Gourgouris adopts, however, to capture his own political position is "Left governmentality," a concept that Daniel Zamora recently gives some relief in his work on the late Foucault.[74] Left governmentality would "move the Left from an oppositional imaginary into a ruling imaginary." In Left governmentality, "local self-organization must disrupt hierarchical institutions of power," and for this "conditions of a new pedagogy must be fostered." Left governmentality should seek "governance against anomie [or lawlessness]." "What does it mean for the Left to create and uphold the law, in contrast to opposing and transgressing the law?" "This is a crucial question," Gourgouris concludes – and it is the question of unexceptional politics rather than of a politics of the exception, and perhaps especially a politics of the greatest exception.

11

Engage the Institution

In the first part of this book I critically consider Chantal Mouffe's turn to Carl Schmitt to revitalize – repoliticize – liberalism. The question I raise can be summarized as: Who has the privilege to think of liberalism as unpolitical? The very idea that liberalism could be separated from sovereignty seems weak in view of some of the political and economic conflict that I highlight: police violence against bodies of colour, drone wars, economic exploitation, and so on and so forth. It's not so much that one should turn to Schmitt to repoliticize liberalism, inject some sovereign energy back into it; it is, rather, that Schmitt, however problematic his thinking, can provide us with a useful framework to analyze the sovereign frictions *that are liberalism's counter-history*. Schmitt, of course, promoted a concept of the political that would be rooted in the friend/enemy distinction; and while such a concept is useful for analyzing power-relations even under liberalism, this does not mean that one should promote such a concept uncritically, without acknowledging, for example, the particular politics – on the right – with which it became associated in Schmitt. However, the left too can make use of such a concept to criticize contemporary power-relations and as part of a project to root out such a war-like politics, whether it is operative in the building of camps or walls or the use of police or drones to govern our lives and deaths. Having developed this position in both parts 1 and 2, I now return to Mouffe to reconsider what role Schmitt actually plays in her repoliticization of liberalism.

Although sovereignty has been a key term of analysis for me here, Mouffe in fact does not use it in this context – I don't think it appears a single time in the two texts she devotes to Schmitt in *The Challenge of Carl Schmitt*. Still, her political thought is obviously influenced by Schmitt, a thinker of sovereignty. In fact, when Mouffe seeks to think a truly political liberalism, a left liberalism as she calls it, she has in mind a liberalism that would incorporate Schmitt's *Concept of the Political*, which is structured by the friend/enemy distinction. It is true that by turning to Schmitt's text from 1933 she avoids having to address the notion of sovereignty, which is associated with the text from 1922, *Political Theology*. At the same time, it is hard to avoid the connection between the two texts because *Concept* begs the question of who is to decide on the determination of someone as friend or enemy. Such a decision, which is arguably ultimately a decision on the state of exception (for the enemy is the one who poses the threat of existential negation and thus may necessitate the suspension of the law), is made in Schmitt's thought by the sovereign. It is therefore the sovereign who lurks behind the friend/enemy distinction that is most visible in war.

While Mouffe does not want war, she does want the tension of Schmitt's concept of the political – she wants to rethink liberalism from there. And so she transforms the antagonism of the friend/enemy distinction into the serious but more playful agonism of adversaries who seek to convince each other through a debate. There is no cultural relativism here. Also, she insists that the debate need not have only one rational solution: to think that such a solution can be found puts unnecessary pressure on the debate. What she has in mind instead is an "agonistic pluralism" where "the political" – "the dimension of antagonism that is inherent in human relations, antagonism that can take many forms and emerge in different types of social relation"[1] – is never plastered over by "politics" – "the ensemble of practices, discourses, and institutions which seek to establish a certain order and organize human coexistence."[2] The latter operates under conditions that are always "potentially conflictual, because they are affected by the dimension of 'the political.'"[3] Politics in Mouffe's view "domesticat[es] hostility and ... [tries] to defuse the potential antagonism that exists in human relations."[4] Democracy's central question becomes then not "how to arrive at a consensus without exclusion" – a question whose answer she considers impossible from an *ontological* point of view (see, for example, "Agonistic Politics and Artistic Practices"[5]) – but "the different way" in which the us/them opposition is established, "in a way that is compatible with pluralist democracy."[6] The other is no longer the Schmittian enemy who must be existentially negated but "somebody whose ideas we combat but whose right to defend those ideas we do not put into question."[7] What this position aims for, then, is a position of "conflictual consensus."[8]

In Mouffe's view, it is the fact that this agonism always has a taint of the antagonistic to it that distinguishes her position from that of Bonnie Honig, who, she claims, "leaves open the possibility that the political could under certain conditions be made absolutely congruent with the ethical."[9] She does not explain the latter – "the ethical" – in the footnote in which she hints at the difference between her own position and Honig's; however, in the introduction to *The Challenge of Carl Schmitt*, she associates "ethics" with post-political Western liberalism, which imagines "that antagonisms have been eradicated" and has reached the state of "reflexive modernity" in which "ethics can now replace politics."[10] Mouffe's focus here appears to be on "'deliberative' or 'dialogic' forms of democracy" of the kind she attacks elsewhere – in the work of John Rawls and Jürgen Habermas, for example. But it seems that Honig can hardly be associated with this position – at least not the Honig I discuss here (and, to be fair, the works of Honig that I look at all date from after Mouffe's *The Democratic Paradox*, in which the footnote about Honig can be found).[11] When Honig discusses the deliberative model in her work on emergency politics, a model she associates with Elaine Scarry, she balances it out with Douglas Crimp's promiscuous politics in order to ultimately arrive at a legalist emergency politics that combines proceduralism with the transformation of procedure. This is perhaps not articulated in terms of antagonism, but it is definitely not the deliberation's replacement of politics by ethics either. Certainly, when Honig aligns her position with "sovereignty," which after all is a term that is closer to Carl Schmitt than "liberalism" (which Mouffe claims), it seems that it is Honig (rather than Mouffe) who may be closer to Schmitt's antagonism. Neither of them, of course, is in any way Schmittian, not even left Schmittian. One might say that they approach the same issues from different sides: Mouffe wants to "politicize" liberalism, whereas Honig wants to liberalize "sovereignty." Both are important, but my position is that, because of how our times are developing, it is Honig's position that resonates more with the contemporary moment, which is one of sovereignty rather than of liberalism.

I turn to Mouffe's work, however, because she has been trying to consider art and aesthetics in this context – to think "agonistic politics" and "artistic practices" together. This is a project that resonates with my consideration of "art" and "exceptionalism" in the previous chapter. "Art has been subsumed by the aesthetics of biopolitical capitalism," Mouffe writes, "and autonomous production is no longer possible."[12] But the new system of labour – so-called post-Fordism – that (according to some) art has helped produce and into which art has been subsumed, also "opens the way for novel forms of social relations in which art and work exist in new configurations."[13] "The objective of artistic practices should be to foster the development of those social relations," she continues, "that are made possible by the transformation of the work process."[14] Art's task, then, is "the production of new subjectivities and the elaboration of new worlds."[15] She imagines art as a "space of resistance," and artistic resistance as "agonistic interventions within the context of counter-hegemonic struggles"[16] – struggles against power-politics that claim to exhaust the social field. Instead, something is always left over, and that excluded something asserts itself counter-hegemonically against hegemonic power. Against neoliberalism's "there is no alternative" mantra, art asserts that *there is* an alternative – the alternative of what is excluded from any power formation. She associates this elsewhere with "the precarious" and "the vulnerable" – power formations are precarious and vulnerable because of this. *No hegemony is total.*

As Mouffe explains, she does "not see the relation between art and politics in terms of two separately constituted fields, art on one side and politics on the other, between which a relation needs to be established. There is an aesthetic dimension in the political and there is a political dimension in art."[17] She doesn't distinguish between political and non-political art but she thinks about possible forms of "critical art."[18] The state of things today is not "the kind of dispersion envisaged by some post-modernist thinkers. Nor are we faced with the kind of 'smooth' space envisaged by Deleuze and his followers. Public spaces are always striated and hegemonically structured."[19] This pretty much guarantees that there is an exclusion from within which a counter-hegemonic struggle can be engaged. What Mouffe calls "critical practices" cannot only deconstruct, de-identify, smoothen, et cetera. In addition, they must "bring about something positive" – and this is where her position is clearly beyond "postmodernism."

In this same text and elsewhere she articulates this position in specifically institutional terms. A leftist strategy that seeks to "ignore institutions and to occupy other spaces outside the institutional field" is, in Mouffe's view, "profoundly mistaken and clearly disempowering because it prevents us from recognizing the multiplicity of avenues that are open for political engagement."[20] Here we see, of course, her left liberalism in action. "To believe that existing institutions cannot become the terrain of contestation is to ignore the tensions that always exist within a given configuration of forces and the possibility of acting in a way that subverts their form of articulation."[21] "We should discard the essentialist idea that some institutions are by essence destined to fulfill one immutable function."[22] In short, Mouffe is telling us to engage our institutions rather than withdraw from them. To require a "total break with the existing state of affairs" is, in her view, not political. She calls it a mistake. Artists today can no longer afford to take up this position, which elsewhere she understands to be a position of "exodus."[23]

Here is how she summarizes this strategy:

> The traditional structures of power organized around the Nation State and representative democracy have today become irrelevant, and ... they could eventually disappear. Hence the belief that the multitude can ignore the existing power structures and concentrate its efforts in constructing alternative social forms outside the State power network. Any collaboration with the traditional channels of politics like parties and trade unions are to be avoided. The majoritarian model of society, organized around the State, needs to be abandoned in favor of another model of organization presented as more universal ... [P]olitical action should aim at withdrawing from existing institutions and freeing ourselves from all forms of belonging. Institutional attachments as [are?] deemed to constitute obstacles to the new non-representative forms of "absolute democracy" suitable for the self-organization of the multitude.[24]

This forecloses, Mouffe correctly notes, "an immanent critique of institutions, whose objective would be to transform them into a terrain of contestation of the hegemonic order."[25] "Such a perspective," she writes with reference to the long quote above, "is, in my view, profoundly mistaken and clearly disempowering because it impedes us from recognizing the multiplicity of avenues that are opened for political engagement."[26] Instead, she wants to advocate "a strategy of 'engagement' with institutions."[27] This comes from the conviction that "things could always have been otherwise and every order is predicated on the

Engage the Institution

exclusion of other possibilities" – the conviction of hegemony and the counter-hegemonic struggle.

When critical practices "[desert] the institutional terrain" rather than "[engage] with it," they "do not contribute to the counter-hegemonic struggle."[28] The latter "[fosters] dissent and [creates] a multiplicity of agonistic spaces where the dominant consensus is challenged and where new modes of identification are made available."[29] This seems particularly important in a time when many identities have been levelled by postmodernism or turned into mere sites for value extraction by neoliberalism. Rather than withdraw from the museum, then, critical artistic practice should engage with the museum and turn it into an agonistic space.

But to think in this way also has political parallels: "think for instance," Mouffe writes, "of the change of attitude of a part of the European left with respect to the institution of the welfare state."[30] "Similar considerations could be made towards the rule of the State which, after years of demonization, has been re-evaluated during the 2008 financial crisis," presumably as a political agent that may be able to keep economic agents in check.[31] Unfortunately, things went the other way and the State ended up bailing out the banks, realizing the fictitious capital that they had created (to put it in Anna Kornbluh's terms[32]). But, Mouffe notes, "things could have taken another direction" had "the power relations been different."[33] It seems the counter-hegemonic struggle failed in this case. The conclusion is clear: "instead of celebrating the destruction of all institutions as a move towards liberation, the task for radical politics is to engage with them, developing their progressive potential and converting them into sites of opposition to the neoliberal market hegemony."[34] This goes for the art museum just as much as it goes for the welfare state or the State tout court.

At this point, I do not think we are too far removed from Honig's position or from certain aspects of the work of Naomi Klein as well as of the work of Wendy Brown and Judith Butler. Mouffe's focus, of course, is on agonism (which has its roots in antagonism and, therefore, in Schmitt); but this is an agonism that revitalizes liberalism, makes it political again. Honig doesn't name the engagement that Mouffe calls for "counter-hegemonic," but she makes it part of a discourse on "popular sovereignty" (Mouffe doesn't use the latter term) and calls it (in her book on Antigone) "counter-sovereignty."[35] The latter she characterizes as bringing a break or interruption to "many theorists' fascination with rupture over the everyday, powerlessness over sovereignty, and heroic martyrdom over the seemingly dull work of maintenance, repair, and planning for possible futures."[36] This characterization further helps us understand the particular politics of exceptionalism in which she is interested. She is defining an exceptionalism here – she is talking about a break or interruption with the notion of counter-sovereignty – but it is an exceptionalism of the everyday, maintenance, repair, planning (as in Elaine Scarry, for example). Honig puts the point very explicitly: "I go on to ask," she writes, "whether feminist and democratic theorists might rethink the rejection of sovereignty and consider devoting themselves instead to its cultivation."[37] Reading this position back into Mouffe, this would mean pushing Mouffe so far as to have her devote herself to the cultivation of new hegemonies through counter-hegemonic politics.

Regardless of their differences, both are thinkers of a contemporary moment where liberalism has become post-political and is becoming eclipsed by sovereignty, mostly sovereignty on the right. Both are also committed to countering this situation – either by repoliticizing liberalism or by claiming sovereignty on the left. This doesn't turn either of them into a left Schmittian. But it does reveal them to be political theorists who, in the age of biopolitical liberalism, have learned a thing or two from Schmitt.

✳

While Mouffe and Honig both engage with Schmitt in this context, Judith Butler leaves Schmitt aside in their work on popular sovereignty (although they do discuss his work elsewhere). I would like to show, however, that this silence is deceiving – in other words, that Butler is in many ways closer to the Benjamin-Schmitt-Agamben side of the debate than may, at first sight, appear. In *Notes Toward a Performative Theory of Assembly*, Butler is thinking through assemblies of bodies in the street as part of political protests – and as distinct from political speech, as they repeatedly put it – and their focus is on "the people" and the institutions that claim to represent it. Specifically, they are interested in the notion of "popular sovereignty" and its claim to represent (and enact) the power of the people.

In a chapter titled "'We the People,'" they make a claim that reminds one of Mouffe's work – namely, that "no one popular assembly comes to represent the entirety of the people, but each positing of the people

Engage the Institution 137

through assembly risks or invites a set of conflicts that, in turn, prompt a growing set of doubts about who the people really are."[38] This is Mouffe's issue of hegemony and the exclusions through which it operates – which trigger what Mouffe calls counter-hegemony. There is, Butler suggests, "no assembly" that can truly claim to represent the people. Instead, there is always this "conflictual process" of constitution that raises the "epistemological" issue of who the people really are.[39] As I have shown, Mouffe *also* articulates this as an *ontological* issue in the sense that, for her, the people are never united in the way that deliberative theories of democracy like those of Rawls or Habermas would want them to be. If Butler is also interested in the speech act that constitutes the people, they are more interested in this context in the fact that assemblies already constitute themselves bodily, in the streets, before any words are uttered. So this is really much more the Arendtian position of bodies collectively appearing in space and making politics in this way. "Freedom of assembly" thus becomes, in their view, "a precondition of politics itself."[40]

It is in this way that we arrive at the notion of "popular sovereignty" as distinct from state sovereignty in Butler's text.[41] Reflecting some of what has already been rehearsed in this book, Butler writes: "I know that some people have come to consider 'sovereignty' a bad word, one that associates politics with a singular subject and a form of executive power with territorial claims. Sometimes it is used as synonymous with mastery, and other times with subordination. Perhaps it carries other connotations, though, that we would not want to lose altogether."[42]

What are those connotations? They write: "One only needs to consider debates about native sovereignty in Canada or read the important work of J. Kēhaulani Kauanui on the paradoxes of Hawaiian sovereignty to see how crucial this notion can be for popular mobilizations. Sovereignty can be one way of describing acts of political self-determination, which is why popular movements of indigenous people struggling for sovereignty have become important ways to lay claim to space, to move freely, to express one's views, and to seek reparation and justice."[43]

Voting certainly does not exhaust the meaning of popular sovereignty – there is more to it. In fact, Butler uses the reference to voting to make the claim that what is called popular sovereignty "always remains nontransferable, marking the outside of the electoral process."[44] Popular sovereignty translates into electoral power, "but that is never a full or adequate translation": "Something of popular sovereignty remains untranslatable, nontransferable, and even unsubstitutable, which is why it can both elect and dissolve regimes. As much as popular sovereignty legitimates parliamentary forms of power, it also retains the power to withdraw its support from those same forms when they prove to be illegitimate."[45] There are echoes here of Agamben's "dissolved multitude," which he considers to be the true state of politics (as opposed to the optical illusion of "sovereignty"; recall that the people-king only exists in the moment of their institution – it crumbles into the dissolved multitude immediately afterwards, a state of dissolution that might intensify into civil war, which may lead [if the rebellious side is victorious] into a disunited multitude, which might elect a people-king again, and so on).

However, given the fact that Butler is not a thinker of the multitude[46] – they in fact explicitly present themself as a thinker of "the people" and, therefore, as a thinker of sovereignty – it may be more correct to say that there are echoes here of Schmitt. In a discussion of Schmitt's book *Constitutional Theory*, Panu Minkkinen points out that, for Schmitt,

> constituent power ... can never exhaust itself into the institutions it has constituted. ... Or, in Schmitt's terms, a people "anterior to and above" the constitution, that is, the presupposed people behind every democracy, can never quite reduce itself into a people "within" the constitution, that is, into the people that the constitution identifies and recognizes as an institution. A constituent residue will, namely, always remains dormant in the institutions that the people may have constituted, and will re-emerge and activate itself if its political existence becomes threatened.[47]

For those who might object to the association with Schmitt, Minkkinen associates this position with the work of Bruce Ackerman and Jason Frank – both scholars whose works are clearly in the background of Butler's own thinking.[48]

Interestingly for us, Butler suggests that we may want to call the (Schmittian? Agambenian?) gap between popular sovereignty and electoral power "an 'anarchist' interval or a permanent principle of revolution that resides within democratic orders, one that shows up more or less both at moments of founding and moments of dissolution, but is also operative in the freedom of assembly itself."[49] This is an element that we find in Santiago Zabala's work, where it appears through a discussion of Heidegger; I discuss it here in relation to Honig's theory of a democratic emergency politics. Civil war (Agamben), anarchy (Zabala/Heidegger, Rancière), counter-hegemony (Mouffe), democracy (Rancière, Honig), popular sovereignty (Honig, Butler): these are all terms that name more or less the same thing – politics or the way in which something of politics *does not* translate into political institutions. Mouffe, openly channelling Schmitt, calls it the political, which can never be fully plastered over by politics. Butler writes that when "the sovereignty of the people is fully transferred" (as in their view, it never can be), "then what is lost are those powers we call critical, those actions we call resistance, and that lived possibility we call revolution."[50] They associate such a state of full transfer with fascism, with the troubling phantasm of the people truly speaking as one. It would have to be recognized, however, that if *this* is fascism, Schmitt appears to have been at least in part a fascist of another kind.

It is this "anarchist," untranslatable, non-exhaustive element that, in the view of all of the above theorists, reveals those institutions to be precarious and vulnerable, less stable than they perhaps claim to be. There are many differences between the above theorists, but on this they would, it seems, all agree. Some, like Agamben, seem mostly to use this position to move away from institutions; Rancière uses it to take it up for democracy; Mouffe, Honig, and Butler use it to move towards institutions and to engage them. Butler's work appears to show traces of all of the above even if, especially on the count of anarchy, it does not quite develop the notion as I do in my earlier discussion of Rancière.[51] Certainly, some of their work on the notion of "the people" relates back to the work they published immediately before this, which deals with photography, framing, and war. "Perhaps," they write, "'the people' is that designation that exceeds any and every visual frame that seeks to capture the people, and the more democratic frames are those that are able to orchestrate their porous character, where the frame does not immediately reproduce the strategy of containment, where the frame partially wrecks itself."[52] From *framing war*, then, Butler moves here to what we could call its democratic counterpart – *framing the people*. On this count they pick up the language of the "differential" that they also develop in *Frames of War* in relation to the notion of the human:[53] now the people becomes that differential notion (like the human, it is a notion that perpetually differs from itself; it's a term that "may be allocated and retracted, aggrandized, personified, degraded and disavowed, elevated and affirmed"[54]) and popular sovereignty a differential form of power.

Popular sovereignty is to be *separated* from state sovereignty within Butler's perspective, and here we see perhaps a slight tear in their association with Mouffe, who argues for an engagement *with* the state. Mouffe's language is always about hegemony *and* counter-hegemony, state *and* counter-state, if you will. But the counter always *engages* what it counters – even if it always comes about through an exclusion within the hegemonic that Mouffe understands to be "ontological." From a Mouffian perspective, I hesitate over Butler's language of separation because it risks producing the "withdrawal" that Mouffe warns against. Butler themself seems to share some of that hesitation as they move from "separate" to "distinct" to "intermittently distinguishes" to characterize the relation between popular sovereignty and state sovereignty. There is, in other words, a kind of *progressive weakening* of the language of separation that takes place in their book that is worth considering. Soon after, they recapitulate – and I add square brackets from Mouffe's point of view to highlight my reservations about Butler's insistence on separation:

> 1/ Popular sovereignty is thus a form of reflexive self-making that is separate from [but engaged with?] the very representative regime it legitimates; 2/ it arises in the course of that very separation [and through that engagement?]; 3/ it cannot legitimate any particular regime without being separate from it [and engaged with it?], that is, partially uncontrolled by a regime and not operationalized as its instrument, and yet [and here is where we get to the engagement part of this third point] it is the basis from which legitimate government is formed through fair and inclusive elections; and 4/ its act of self-making is actually a series of spatially distributed acts, ones that do not always operate in the same way and for the same purposes [the latter point does not include the language of separation and could just as well be about engagement].[55]

They add a fifth component a little later: "Further, the enactment of 'we the people' may or may not take linguistic form; speech and silence, movement and immobility, are all political enactments; the hunger strike is precisely the inverse of the fed body standing freely in the public domain and speaking – it marks and resists the deprivation of that right, and it enacts and exposes the deprivation that prison populations undergo."[56]

The example they land on – the hunger strike as the inverse of public engagement – is interesting because it foregrounds, once again, separation: the body that is deprived from, separated from, public engagement. One might be forgiven for assuming that the inverse of this body, the fed body, would be associated with "the state" and that the opposition we get here would therefore operate within the "popular sovereignty" versus "state sovereignty" conversation that the chapter develops. But such is not the case: the fed body seems to stand for popular sovereignty *as well*, at least if we accept that silence and speech, immobility and movement, all stand for enactments of popular sovereignty, as Butler suggests here.

I engage in this discussion because it seems to me that Butler is perhaps too focused on withdrawal rather than on engagement. This is, I think, the Agambenian trace in their work, the hint of civil war. They also articulate this as the "nonrepresentational and nonrepresentative"; "popular sovereignty makes sense *only* in this perpetual act of *separating* from state sovereignty."[57] *Only*? Really? From Mouffe and Honig's perspectives, they are overstating the case. What about *engaging* the state? What about *counter-sovereign acts*? As such, this "separatist" trace marks the rather uneasy negotiation of Agamben with articulations of popular sovereignty that can be found, for example, in Honig's work. And this uneasiness is crucial to the problems of sovereignty that we are pursuing here, in particular to a thinking about the politics of exceptionalism. It is, indeed, a deep engagement with the notion of the exception and its fascist, democratic, and anarchic articulations that could enable one to address how "the outside" of politics is negotiated in relation to its "within."

I am not sure about this negotiation in Butler's work. On the one hand, they appear to come down firmly on the side of the democratic "within," or on what they might describe as the side of the "anarchic" democratic (though theirs is a weak understanding of the anarchic that is not in line with the strong conceptualization of the anarchic as the rule by those who have no entitlement to rule). On the other, when they insist on the separation between popular sovereignty and state sovereignty, Butler reinforces the split of a civil war that can be found in Agamben and that, in my view, needs to be traced back to the divine violence that Benjamin theorizes (and calls "sovereign" – at least in the English translation). This is the divine violence of an *outside*. (I am not sure what to call its politics, although, like Benjamin, Butler intimates that it has a trace of the anarchic to it.) By separating so starkly between popular sovereignty and state sovereignty, Butler risks overemphasizing the divine violence of *the outside* – over and against the democratic *within* that Honig emphasizes. Like Honig, Mouffe too insists more on engagement (versus the withdrawal that Butler risks promoting) even though there is another issue here – namely, that she draws some of the inspiration for her concept of the political from Schmitt and the friend/enemy-distinction (which Honig resists). While Schmitt is ultimately also about a "within," it is a fascistic "within" (the law includes the sovereign possibility of its own suspension) rather than a democratic one.

I think we see this very negotiation between inside and outside and its different politics in Butler's text, where Butler begins by characterizing the popular sovereignty they are theorizing as an "extraparliamentary power,"[58] but one "without which no parliament can function legitimately, and that threatens every parliament with dysfunction or even dissolution."[59] They call this an "anarchic" element within "democratic orders," but I have a hard time seeing how this is different from Schmitt. "Extraparliamentary power" – now *that's* Benjamin's divine violence.[60] Folded back within the parliament, this becomes Schmitt's legal order with sovereign power included as the power to decide on the state of exception. Butler seems to be aware of this when, further down on the same page, they warn of a situation in which popular sovereignty is produced as the bare life of state sovereignty, in state sovereignty's "anarchic" state of exception. I find this difficult to square: the language here evokes Schmitt and Agamben; but Schmitt is very clear that the state of exception is *not* anarchy. So why use the word? The point appears to be to distinguish between (on the one hand) popular sovereignty as a break with state sovereignty and (on the other) the break within popular sovereignty – popular sovereignty *as* that very break. *If* the former, popular sovereignty can be produced as the bare life of state sovereignty, which they dislike. But *if* the latter, popular sovereignty is always the break with state sovereignty – and it is from this position that Butler seems to rethink democratic power. However, this is again the Agambenian civil war position, which is difficult to reconcile with Butler's argument that this kind of break should be folded back within, for example, parliamentary order, at least with reference to Agamben and Schmitt. Agamben

Engage the Institution 143

would most likely resist this. Schmitt accomplishes this folding through his problematic notion of sovereignty.

What we have here, then, in various states of tension with Schmitt, are three forms of left liberalism: Mouffe seeks to *repoliticize liberalism via Schmitt*, with all the risks that this entails; Honig seeks to *liberalize sovereignty through democratic theory* (against Schmitt – for this reason, Mouffe thinks Honig replaces politics with ethics); Butler seeks to be on Honig's side but their position is marked by *a trace of Benjamin's divine violence* (which they get from Agamben and Schmitt). The latter is ultimately incompatible with either Honig or Mouffe, even if it shares more with Mouffe, I think, than with Honig. But based on references alone, it seems Butler wants to be closer to Honig than to Mouffe.

Finally, and perhaps most important in this context, it should be noted that Butler develops their position largely through a consideration of vulnerability and its politics – again, this goes back to the fact that the starting point for their thought is the gathering of bodies for political protest in the streets. What seems striking about their theorization of vulnerability, however, is that it is not first and foremost situated on the side of the institutions themselves, that they do not talk much about instituted sovereignty as precarious or vulnerable. The focus is on the vulnerability of bodies, on the constitution of that vulnerability in relation to given infrastructure, on the use of vulnerability by power, et cetera. But what about seeking to situate vulnerability on the side of sovereignty or seeking to rethink sovereignty from the point of view of vulnerability? Indeed, when vulnerability as the "condition of resistance" is brought up, it is striking to see them write that when this vulnerability is "rendered as precarity" it "has to be opposed."[61] Such opposition does not happen through victimization or embracing weakness but instead through "mobilizing vulnerability as a deliberate and active form of political resistance, an exposure of the body to power in the plural action of resistance."[62] So vulnerability rendered as precarity has to be opposed but opposed through the mobilization of vulnerability as political resistance (against precarity, I guess?) ... This is a little tortured, and the problem is in part the use of the term "oppose," which can be tied back to the notion of "separation" earlier on.

It is in part due to these issues that the separation between popular sovereignty and state sovereignty comes across as very stark in Butler's book. Both are presented as invulnerable blocks facing each other, even if we know, of course, that the popular sovereignty block is constituted by vulnerable bodies assembling in the streets and even if we know that state sovereignty is not eternal – this is, at least, what the assembly of protesting bodies in the streets shows. But we do not revisit *sovereignty itself* in this framework as the power of (subject genitive) the vulnerable, as vulnerable power. As a result, and while popular sovereignty is proposed as a useful contemporary political category here, "state sovereignty" keeps an old notion of sovereignty intact – whereas the task would be, precisely, to dismantle that. In other words, I would have liked to have seen a connection established between the fourth and fifth chapters of Butler's book on assembly, between the chapter on bodily vulnerability and the one on popular sovereignty, one that would have articulated the vulnerability of the sovereign body itself. With the notion of a government of the precarious (subject genitive), Isabell Lorey moves in this direction – but the issue in her case is that she calls her position "non-sovereign," as I have discussed. For Lorey, the solution is not simply to "de-precarize" as to do so would risk swinging back to Hobbes and a sovereignty that is conceived against vulnerability.

Ida Danewid's critical reading of Butler draws out other political consequences of this problem – namely, that a discourse of vulnerability that focuses on the other (even if it starts by also taking into account the self) but ultimately refrains from thinking through the consequences of vulnerability for Western liberal institutions risks helping to motivate a "white, innocent" politics of care in the "black Mediterranean" that seeks to help and save the vulnerable other without transforming the Western liberal institutions that are at the root of the violence that the others traversing the Mediterranean are suffering (think of colonialism, for example).[63] As a critical reading of Butler, however, Danewid's article is only partly convincing. What it shows, which is in itself valuable, is how discourses such as Butler's can be used by certain liberal, multicultural, and far-right politics to motivate a white, innocent politics of care for the vulnerable other of the Black Mediterranean. But this is not, as far as I can tell, a charge that can be levelled against Butler themself, and the article does not at any point show that it can be. The article is worthwhile in that it points out this risk; but it does not show that Butler themself falls prey to it. In other words, the author does not provide any evidence that Butler themself is the kind of liberal, multicultural subject that the article attacks – or even that all liberalism and multiculturalism is of the kind that the author attacks. The author attacks, instead, "the

Engage the Institution

particular kind of politics [that Butler's thought] serves to legitimize," as she writes.[64] But this is hardly the same as saying that Butler themself is guilty of this politics.

In fact, and this is in line with the criticism that I here develop of Butler, I think the author focuses too much on "the other" in Butler's work. In other words, the discourse of vulnerability is articulated almost entirely with respect to the other in Danewid's article. And one can understand why this is so: because Butler, too, focuses on this. But if one looks at the beginning of the argument, Danewid makes it clear that Butler starts with a sense of vulnerability *of self*.[65] The author mentions the origins of Butler's work on vulnerability in *Precarious Life*. It's worth noting that this book was written in the aftermath of 9/11, so it comes from an experience of American (US) vulnerability – that is, of Butler's own vulnerability. To extend the argument even further back, as does Butler's *Notes toward a Performative Theory of Assembly*, one has to also see how this goes back to Butler's work on gender, which was of course to a large extent a kind of Foucauldian project on the self. It was about Butler's own vulnerability as a gendered subject, and the violence of gender; it was not about the playful assignation of gender, as many after Butler made it out to be. (This is why Kafka's story "Before the Law" is evoked as the parable that sums up *Gender Trouble* in the introduction to the book's ten-year anniversary edition.) However, when Butler works out their argument on vulnerability, they become very focused on the vulnerability of the other – and they do not articulate a concept of politics that would be rooted in vulnerability *of the self*.

So if Danewid is right that the focus on "ontological" vulnerability risks erasing history, it is also worth drawing out – and holding Butler accountable to, as I try to do here – what the focus on such vulnerability enables, which is a certain universalism of vulnerability – on *all* sides, not just on the side of the stranger.[66]

It is not inconceivable, finally, that Butler developed their work on public assembly in part in response to Bonnie Honig's criticism that they had allowed politics to collapse into the ethical. Honig makes this claim with respect to what she characterizes as Butler's Antigone-books: *Antigone's Claim*, *Precarious Life*, and *Frames of War*. Whereas in *Antigone's Claim* Antigone still emerges as an agonistic, political subject, in *Precarious Life* she becomes a figure of ethical mourning, and mortality – finitude, vulnerability – become the focus of Butler's theory of individuality and, especially, of collectivity. It is all about

Antigone versus her uncle Creon, the representative of sovereignty. As the title of the earliest Antigone book suggests, however, what is at stake is Antigone's *claim*, her claim *to* sovereignty – *against* the sovereign of her uncle. This focus on what Honig calls Antigone's counter-sovereign claim redirects attention from Antigone as the lamenting figure of ethical femininity (as which she has been construed) to Antigone as a figure seeking sovereignty. Honig holds it against Butler that they allow this political Antigone to slip out of focus. In the public assembly book, politics arguably re-enters.

12

Indigenous Sovereignties

At the end of all this, one should surely ask why one would hold on to the notion of sovereignty. Why not just chuck it out and propose another term?

Here, it can be useful to return to some of the reasons insisting on sovereignty today may be useful. When Wendy Brown uses the notion of sovereignty in her book *Undoing the Demos*, she does so in response to neoliberalism's destruction of organized popular power. "Neoliberalism," Brown writes, is "a peculiar form of reason that configures all aspects of existence in economic terms."[1] As such, "it is quietly undoing basic elements of democracy," in which she includes "vocabularies, principles of justice, political cultures, habits of citizenship, practices of rule, and above all, democratic imaginaries."[2] Her point is not only that everything is becoming economized; it is, rather, that "the distinctly political character, meaning, and operation of democracy's constituent elements" are being "converted" into "economic ones."[3] It is the end of liberal democracy, and possibly of more radical forms of democracy as well.

Of course, what such a "conversion" argument sets up is an era when said political sphere was still "noneconomic" – and critics of Brown have taken her to task for this suggestion.[4] Also, Brown acknowledges that it is not as if "liberalism," for example, is without its problems. However, can it be reduced to its problems alone? What about liberalism's emphasis on "freedom and equality universally shared and political rule by and for the people"?[5] And if liberalism is not a promising democratic project, what other such projects can we imagine that would survive the neoliberal onslaught?

148 Sovereignty and Vulnerability

My focus here is not on Brown's analysis of neoliberalism but, rather, on what she opposes to that – on what she determines, or projects, as being destroyed by neoliberalism. This is, obviously, "politics." But what names does she reserve for this politics? Democracy is one of them; liberalism is another; finally, she also mentions "popular sovereignty" to describe neoliberalism's specifically *political* target.[6] Especially in the final part of Brown's chapter "Undoing Democracy" this becomes her focus. It appears as "collective political sovereignty" on page 39 and "aspirational sovereignty" a little further down on the same page.[7]

It is Bonnie Honig who, in dialogue with Brown, articulates this turn to sovereignty most strongly – much more strongly than Brown, who remains hesitant to take it on. I have already indicated Honig's turn to sovereignty in *Emergency Politics* as well as her next book, *Antigone, Interrupted*; I'd now like to turn to the first lecture in her book *Public Things*. There she explicitly takes it up for the public things, the *res publicae* that hold together the democratic republic: "public things gather people together, materially and symbolically," she writes, "and in relation to them diverse peoples may come to see and experience themselves – even if just momentarily – as a common in relation to a commons, a collective if not a collective."[8] It is a kind of object-turn in democratic theory that she seeks to enact – a political theory of objectivation rather than subjectivation.

Part of the inspiration for Honig's project is the work of D.W. Winnicott: the child ultimately learns about "cohesion and unitariness from the object world" in Winnicott's theory, from the "transitional object" that the baby needs, the object that survives its destruction by the baby. "What if the same is true – analogously – for democratic citizens," Honig asks? "What if democratic forms of life depend partly upon objects to help collect diverse citizens into self-governing publics divested ... of fantasies of omnipotence and invested with a sense of integrated subjectivity, responsibility, agency, and concern?"[9] What if, in other words – and these are my own words now – a *vulnerable sovereignty* were possible? It is such an object-relations theory of sovereignty enabled by public things that Honig seeks to develop.

I am far from certain that "vulnerable" is the correct term for Honig's "sovereignty" that is not omnipotent; perhaps the term slips too much into omnipotence's opposite, gives away too much in the direction of mortalism, of finitude – in short, of the ethical (which was, remember, what Mouffe oddly charges Honig with). In her book on Antigone, Honig starts out by saying that, while a vulnerable humanism seeks to "bypass the intractable divisions of politics," she considers it "no adequate replacement for a (post)humanist politics with agonistic intent."[10] It's not entirely clear, however, how the term "vulnerability" relates to the latter. From what Honig writes later on, the two certainly do not seem to be opposed: "Thus, we might draw from Antigone inspiration for an agonistic humanism that sees in mortality, suffering, sound, and vulnerability resources for some form of enacted if contestable universality, while also recognizing these resources are various and opaque in their significations, just like language."[11] She adds, however: "In quest of a politics that is not reducible to an ethics nor founded on finitude, agonistic humanists draw not only nor even primarily on mortality and suffering, but also on natality and pleasure, power (not just powerlessness), desire (not just principle), and thumos (not just penthos)."[12] So her position is not just about "shared human finitude"; it "also has something to do with vengeance, politics, and the quest for sovereignty."[13] She notes in this context that, while Jacques Rancière "roundly rejects" efforts to "develop a new humanism based on finitude and vulnerability," he nevertheless also endorses it "when he approves of artistic practices of commemoration that focus on naming the dead."[14] So clearly, the notion of vulnerability itself has a contested position in her thought that deserves negotiation.

Unlike Brown, Honig is not shy about calling the democratic forms of life she evokes "sovereign." Brown laments, she writes, that sovereignty is nowhere to be found on the left. But perhaps "the left" is the wrong place to look.[15] Honig focuses on food sovereignty – also briefly discussed by Brown[16] – to draw out one contemporary politics of sovereignty. She also turns to Indigenous politics to make her case. "Resistance to neoliberal rationality" happens on both counts,[17] but Brown does not analyze such examples in any depth. Honig concludes:

> Sovereignty seems to be not so much lost as dispersed and relocated, growing like a weed in places where it has not been planted before (food sovereignty) or not permitted to grow for a long time (tribal sovereignty). Neoliberalism may "wholly" abandon "the project of individual or collective mastery of existence," deferring instead to markets, but there are other instances of action in concert on the ground, some of them practicing precisely what Brown describes as lost.[18]

With this turn towards Indigenous sovereignties, Honig also recalls Butler's mention of tribal sovereignty in Canada and the paradoxes of Hawaiian sovereignty in their own work on "popular sovereignty." If Indigenous politics emerges here as a particularly fruitful site for Honig or Butler to insist on democratic realizations of sovereignty today, this is no doubt also because the status of Indigenous peoples, as the internally excluded of settler colonial politics, works well with Agamben's theorization – after Schmitt – of bare life's state of exception.[19]

As Joan Cocks notes, the Israel/Palestine case as well as Indigenous politics are two examples that have frequently been used in defence of sovereignty today. Cocks observes this critically, as part of a project to expose sovereignty as a "delusion": she considers sovereignty as a "promising loss" – "a conceptual loss that at first glance is unthinkable and at second glance is regrettable [but that] may in fact be an opening to a more promising way of imagining and acting in the world."[20] This opening is, on the final page of the introduction to her book, described as a "transcendence" – it takes the form of a "sympathetic warning to the strugglers [for sovereignty] that they are likely to re-create for others the political injuries they are trying to escape for themselves unless they find a way to transcend the sovereign power ideal."[21] While Cocks notes that she may sound pessimistic on this count, she nevertheless expresses "hope for the future"[22] – for a future without sovereignty. Cocks's book, which was initially recommended to me by Judith Butler, is excellent and lays out an engaged and insightful criticism of sovereignty. But as will be clear from what has preceded, I do not agree with its conclusion – with the end of sovereignty that it calls for. I am one of those "strugglers" she refers to, and I do not agree with her conclusion from a politically realist and pragmatic point of view. This is also, however, an aesthetic point of view that seeks to unexceptionalize sovereignty into a political form that we make, even if we may not make it entirely as we please (to recall Marx's famous phrase).[23] Cocks notes this in her first chapter – all truly political concepts are, as she puts it, "intellectual puzzles without definitive solutions"[24] – but nevertheless proposes to leave sovereignty behind.

Focused on the formation of sovereignty in the present, I want to highlight here Cocks's language of "transcendence" and "hope for the future": both are phrases that, to me, resonate with the very core of a certain kind of sovereign thinking, specifically the theologico-political thinking of sovereignty that much of this book seeks to break down. This book is not interested in "transcending" or in "hoping for

Indigenous Sovereignties

the future": it is interested in an immanent critique that seeks to accomplish change in the present. This is a point of view that I associate with vulnerability, which demands a realist and pragmatic focus on the present – not transcendence or hope for the future. There is nothing like a wound to make you arrive in the now.

Now, let's return to Cocks's actual phrasing, which is not so much about "transcending sovereignty" as it is about "transcending the sovereign power *ideal.*" On this count – "transcending the sovereign power ideal" – we may actually be in agreement. I would still use a different verb to describe this process – something more unexceptionalizing, suggesting a move downwards rather than upwards – but I agree with the focus on "ideal." The thing is, though, that to transcend the sovereign power ideal is not to transcend sovereignty: it is to rearticulate sovereignty *outside of that ideal* in a more politically realist and pragmatic way. Not as a delusion but as a potentially emancipatory political concept. This is, as I see it, what scholars like Brown (one of Cocks's major interlocutors), Honig (who writes a blurb for Cocks's book), and Butler – as well as many others – are trying to accomplish. "Vulnerability" can be a key notion in such a project. We see here then a slippage – is Cocks targeting "the dream of sovereign power" or "sovereign power"?[25] – that is common in the literature on sovereignty, namely, a gradual substitution of a negative "aspect" of sovereignty for sovereignty *as a whole,*[26] eventually leading to a complete rejection of a concept of which really only an aspect was being targeted. Monarchical sovereignty thus comes to eclipse popular sovereignty; sovereignty's exceptionalism à la Carl Schmitt comes to eclipse, for example, multiple forms of emergency politics or popular sovereignty's deliberative aspects; sovereignty's tie to life and death leads to the centrality of vulnerability to its theorization being ignored; and before we know it the part comes to stand in for the whole and, rather than perform local surgery on the body politic, the patient is declared terminal. This very slippage is, I suggest, a sovereign one: it operates within the realm of the either/or and, as such, it does not adequately acknowledge the aesthetic dimension of sovereignty as a political form.

I am well aware that sovereignty itself, in its delusional projection of unicity, prevents such an aesthetic, plural articulation of its formations – but I also argue that the way to undo that sovereign spell is to secularize the notion and unexceptionalize it into its ongoing aesthetico-political production. We are the agents of such production.

152 Sovereignty and Vulnerability

If the Israel/Palestine case and the case of Indigenous politics, which I intend to consider now, are commonplaces in this conversation, it is because they remind us of this fact.

✳

It's worth comparing historical narratives as they are presented in different disciplines: in political theory, studies of sovereignty usually tell the story of sovereignty's decline after the Second World War due to transnational political developments such as European integration or human rights politics. In Indigenous studies, however, scholars tend to note that "following World War II, sovereignty emerged not as a new but as a particularly valued term within indigenous discourses to signify a multiplicity of legal and social rights to political, economic, and cultural self-determination."[27] Precisely when the term is waning in the West, where it was born, it is on the rise as an emancipatory tool, for example, for those communities "within" the West that seek to contest their subjection to another sovereign power. Those communities turned towards the term "sovereignty," as Joanne Barker explains, in part to refuse the label "minority group": "Instead, sovereignty defined indigenous peoples with concrete rights to self-determination, territorial integrity, and cultural autonomy under international customary law."[28] Of course, while refusing the label "minority group," the communities instead adopt the term "sovereignty," which was born and shaped in Europe. There may be a deeper problem here, as scholars like Elizabeth Povinelli have noted,[29] with the (Hegelian) politics of "recognition" ("Anerkennung," in Hegel's celebrated master/slave dialectic) and how it tends to confirm the master's terms.[30]

In *Red Skin, White Masks*, which is titled after Frantz Fanon, who plays a central role in the book's project of "Rejecting the Colonial Politics of Recognition," Glen Sean Coulthard criticizes the "liberalized appropriation" of Hegel that he considers to be active in the politics of recognition that sovereign nation-states have pursued in their relation to Indigenous communities.[31] Coulthard takes the politics of recognition "to refer to the now expansive range of recognition-based models of liberal pluralism that seek to 'reconcile' Indigenous assertions of nationhood with settler-state sovereignty via the accommodation of Indigenous identity claims in some form of renewed legal and political relationship" with the settler-state sovereignty (Coulthard focuses specifically on Canada).[32] One interesting aspect of such a liberalized

Hegelian move – "liberalized" because it erases, through the focus on reconciliation, the life-and-death struggle that is central to Hegel's master/slave-dialectic (it places the emphasis on consensus rather than on dissensus) – is that it is supposed to be a reconciliation *between sovereignties*. In other words, it also marks – and this is something Coulthard does not note – *a liberalization of the political power called sovereignty itself.*

Coulthard does get to this in a different way when he argues that "instead of ushering in an era of peaceful coexistence grounded on the ideal of *reciprocity* or *mutual* recognition, the politics of recognition in its contemporary liberal form promises to reproduce the very configurations of colonialist, racist, patriarchal state power that Indigenous peoples' demands for recognition have historically sought to transcend."[33] One may refer to this as "liberalism's counter-history," to recall the work by Domenico Losurdo that I evoke in chapter 1. Coulthard's argument also recalls my discussion of Adom Getachew's work on self-determination in chapter 7, which shows how, even after postcolonial nation-states had been granted "sovereignty," relations of domination continued in the international sphere – that is, their integration into the international "League of Nations" was unequal and continued their colonial status. With Coulthard, one can describe such processes as transitions from "a more-or-less unconcealed structure of domination to a mode of colonial *governmentality* that works through the limited freedoms afforded by state recognition and accommodation."[34] Getachew points out the connections of such a description to work in Afropessimism, specifically Saidiya Hartman's work on freedom.[35] Coulthard ultimately finds in Fanon the argument that "recognition is not posited as a source of freedom and dignity for the colonized, but rather as the field of power through which colonial relations are produced and maintained."[36] This is not a surprising turn given my discussion of Fanon.

All of the above are arguably versions of what I present in the introduction to this book as a "Backward Foreword" thesis: they demonstrate that, in various eras of so-called biopolitical liberalism, the sovereign politics of life *and death* continues. As I see it, Coulthard criticizes a colonial politics of recognition that, in a liberalized appropriation of Hegel, only in appearance presents us with a reciprocal or mutual relationship between two sovereignties; underneath such liberal recognition, he argues, an actual politics of sovereignty continues that pitches friends against enemies in a hierarchical relation

154   Sovereignty and Vulnerability

of domination. What is presented to us not so much as the end of sovereignty as equal relations between different sovereigns is in fact a continued relation of sovereign domination – sovereignty is in fact unequally distributed between multiple sovereigns. It's the same game, now played at a higher level. To return to the different models of sovereignty that Foucault discusses in his lecture on Hobbes: in its seeming attempt to go back on its sovereignty-by-acquisition by granting Indigenous communities sovereignty-by-institution, the politics of recognition actually continues sovereignty-by-acquisition, and what is made to look like sovereignty-by-institution is actually an example of domination. Rather than biopolitical liberalism, what we find here is the old politics of sovereignty that I criticize.

Given that equal "sovereignty" is precisely what is supposed to be granted in the cases that Coulthard and Getachew are looking at, is there a way to use such moments to reconfigure sovereignty beyond this outdated master-narrative and the problems that it obviously entails? Moreover, is there a way of doing so – of engaging sovereignty rather than withdrawing from it or turning one's back on it, to recall both the terms of this book and those of the debate between Coulthard and Dale Turner,[37] whose *This Is Not a Peace Pipe* comes down on the side of engagement[38] – that would both "curb," as Coulthard puts it, the interpellation of Indigenous peoples by sovereignty and ensure the interpellation of sovereignty by Indigenous peoples? Finally, might the opposition between withdrawal and engagement that I initially took from Chantal Mouffe need to be deconstructed, for example, as part of an argument for *sovereign refusal* – for a claim to sovereignty in order to refuse another sovereignty (as in Audra Simpson's *Mohawk Interruptus*, which considers a situation of "nested sovereignties," of one sovereignty "nested" within another: "Refusal comes with the requirement of having one's *political* sovereignty acknowledged and upheld"[39])?

In view of the above, it might seem strange to use the term "sovereignty" for *both* the politics that I criticize in part 2 *and* for the Indigenous struggles for self-determination that I am now considering. But such strangeness marks, I would argue, what Joanne Barker characterizes as the "contingency" of sovereignty, the fact that "there is no fixed meaning for what sovereignty is – what it means by definition, what it implies in public debate, or how it has been conceptualized in international, national, or indigenous law." The passage is worth quoting in full:

Sovereignty – and its related histories, perspectives, and identities – is embedded within specific social relations in which it is invoked, and given meaning. How and when it emerges and functions are determined by the "located" political agendas and cultural perspectives of those who rearticulate it into public debate or political document to do a specific work of opposition, invitation, or accommodation. It is no more possible to stabilize what sovereignty means and how it matters to those who invoke it than it is to forget the historical and cultural embeddedness of indigenous peoples' multiple and contradictory political perspectives and agendas for empowerment, decolonization, and social justice.[40]

Sovereignty is, as I indicate elsewhere,[41] plastic, and it is this plasticity that any *critique* of sovereignty needs to assess. This is also to say that *sovereignty is not sovereign.* In such an aesthetic reconceptualization of sovereignty, there lie possibilities amidst what I call its contemporary *resurgence.* In *Red Skin, White Masks,* Coulthard in fact understands resurgence in this "critical" way, even if he hardly applies it to sovereignty (why not?): as a notion that "draws critically on the past with an eye to radically transform the colonial power relations that have come to dominate our present."[42]

If Indigenous sovereignty thus emerges here as an experimental site for thinking through new democratic possibilities today, it is precisely because it enables an *immanent critique* of sovereignty, as a politics of sovereignty that can only be critical.[43] This is so, as Barker points out in *Critically Sovereign,* for two reasons: on the one hand, because native sovereignty relates critically to the sovereignty of the nation-state, as a sovereignty that contests the power of another; second, because native sovereignty itself suffers from many of the same problems as does the sovereignty of the nation-state, and therefore some of the criticisms that have been levelled against the sovereignty of the nation-state also apply to native sovereignty.

In essence, this criticality revolves around the fact that when it comes to the Indigenous politics of sovereignty, one can distinguish between two kinds: that which takes place "in relation to the state" and that which takes place "within the state."[44] Whereas the former relates to native sovereignty's relation to the sovereignty of the nation-state, the latter operates within the sovereignty of the nation-state, and to participate in the latter can be – and has been – perceived as participating in the imperial and colonial politics of oppression of the sovereign nation-state. This is why what Barker refers to as "Civil Rights politics" does not cover the relation between Indigeneity and sovereignty: it only covers the politics "within the state" part of the relation. In addition, one should also consider Indigenous sovereignty's relation to the sovereignty of the nation-state and the tensions it lays bare.

Barker articulates this (as well as other key parts of the critical sovereignty she develops) through a focus on "gender, sexuality, feminism" within her exploration of native sovereignty.[45] She points out, for example, how the call for "women's and gay's liberation and civil rights equality ... has been narrated as racializing and classing gender and sexuality in such a way as to further a liberal humanist normalization of 'compulsory heterosexuality,' male dominance, and white privilege."[46] In other words, there is a subject-formation that is operative in such liberation struggles, and while this does not cover the full story of those struggles, this is an important aspect of them that should be drawn out. Any hegemonic formation, in Mouffe's terms, will produce a counter-hegemonic formation; any rendering legible produces illegibility as Barker (via Judith Butler) puts it – there are always traces of internal exclusion or exception. It is from these traces that politics develops. Indigenous approaches to, for example, gender and sexuality can be interesting in this context because they can "defy binary logics and analyses"[47] – and these include, it should be pointed out, discourses of a "third" (which ultimately, in their very attempt to posit a third, appear to confirm a pre-existing binary).

The point of Barker's approach appears to be to "defamiliarize gender, sexuality, and feminist studies to unpack the constructedness of gender and sexuality and problematize feminist theory and method within Indigenous contexts."[48] Indigenous politics are interesting in this context as well because when, for example, Indigenous women seek to pursue a feminist politics to redress their own status in their communities, they run into resistance because their tribe members perceive them to be sleeping with the enemy – to be "non- or anti-Indigenous sovereignty within their communities."[49] "They accused the women of being complicit with a long history of colonization and racism that imposed, often violently, non-Indian principles and institutions on Indigenous people."[50] So gender, sexuality, and feminism have a difficult place within native sovereignties, and it is precisely around the notion of sovereignty that this difficulty gets played out.

Barker's introduction also contains hope for the future, though. Such hope articulates itself around a poetic project of remaking – of remaking masculinity, for example; but also of remaking the world. This is about asserting a sovereignty that would not fall into the old traps of sovereignty – that would not reify, for example, "heterosexist ideologies that serve conditions of imperial-colonial oppression."[51] It would be a remaking that might confront "the social realities of heterosexism and homophobia" within Indigenous communities.[52] In other words, "Indigenous manhood and masculinity [need to be redefined] in a society predicated on the violent oppression and exploitation of Indigenous women and girls and the racially motivated dispossession and genocide of Indigenous peoples."[53] It is precisely here, in the project of not opposing the violent sovereignty of the oppressor with a call for a violent sovereignty of the oppressed – with the Fanonian attempt to go beyond such a dialectical opposition – that the possibility of an Indigenous future opens up, *an Indigenous futurism (of sovereignty)*. It is because of the very particular position that Indigenous sovereignty is in that this becomes possible. And this is the reason, I think, so many contemporary theorists of sovereignty turn to this example to pursue a redefined politics of sovereignty today. The turn towards Indigenous sovereignty enables what Barker labels a "critical" sovereignty. It enables what one could, more precisely, call a "critique" of sovereignty, where the power we call sovereign is not abandoned, not transgressed, but transformed from within in view of the abuses it has enabled and the possibilities for emancipation it has opened up.

*

I begin this book by observing that Carl Schmitt's *Concept of the Political* has descriptive value when considering our contemporary "sovereign" (rather than liberal and biopolitical) situation. I suggest more specifically that Schmitt's concept can be helpful when trying to theorize the situation of black lives in the US today. While he may be a dubious legal and political theorist, Schmitt does call our attention, as other scholars ranging from political philosophers to general audience writers have noted, to the fact that politics has always been a matter of life *and death*. To "liberalism's counter-history" (Domenico Losurdo), if you will.

After Andreas Kalyvas and others, I go on to consider the democratic possibilities of Schmitt's work at large, specifically his distinction between three moments of democracy (instituting; everyday procedural; and spontaneous mobilization and direct participation – spatially, they correspond to positions prior to and above, within, and next to the constitution). I highlight in particular the radical politics that is captured by Schmitt's third, para-constitutional moment: it's what, with Dimitris Vardoulakis, one might enlarge – in a critical relationship to Schmitt – into a theory of the democratic unworking of sovereignty.

Later, I show that such a Schmittian political and democratic moment can be found in Michel Foucault's mid-1970s lectures on Thomas Hobbes and sovereignty, precisely where scholars have speculated that Foucault's thought may have been influenced by Black Panther politics. This reveals the connections between Schmitt's *Concept of the Political* and the concept of the political of the Black Panthers, however unlikely such an alliance may otherwise seem. Such a connection to Schmitt in Foucault's work is arguably in tension with Foucault's late interest in liberalism and neoliberalism – inseparable from his work on biopolitics – but I show (going back to my initial discussion of the differences between sovereignty and liberalism/ neoliberalism) that it is certainly not opposed to it: contrary to what is often assumed, Schmitt's work is in fact central to neoliberal thought, raising the need for an analysis of "authoritarian liberalism" (Chamayou) and neoliberalism today.

I then show how Giorgio Agamben escalates what Kalyvas identifies as the radical part of Schmitt's thought – his consideration of "the people" *next to* the constitution – into an *unpolitical* theory of generalized civil war in Thomas Hobbes. This is a problematic development, as Vardoulakis has shown, that comes out of Agamben's forgetting of democracy and cannot but result in a wholesale rejection of sovereignty. Such a rejection became painfully evident in Agamben's considerations of the pandemic, which Agamben considers a situation of civil war. I demonstrate how Agamben's position is inspired not so much by the conservative Schmitt as by the radicalism of Walter Benjamin, whose work has had a major influence on the contemporary political left. My conclusion is, however, that under the conditions of today's resurgence of sovereignty, it may not so much be Agamben's Benjamin-inspired rejection of sovereignty that is the more interesting to pursue but, rather, a position more like Schmitt's, which would mark the democratic possibilities for politics *within* the concept of sovereignty rather than *without it.*

Indeed, and as others like Benjamin Bratton have shown, Agamben's position – generalized civil war, the call for destituent power – was proven untenable during the pandemic. In part 2, I show how Agamben's notion of the camp, and the inflationary critical value it accrues in his work, is incapable of accounting for what I called *the sovereign politics of care* that was needed during the pandemic, a situation of heightened vulnerability. For Agamben, all sovereignty appears to amount to a camp – all forms of sovereign care can ultimately be traced back to Nazi eugenics. But this is not a critical consideration of sovereignty. I go on to pursue a similar critical analysis of the sovereign paradigm of "the wall," showing how both the building of walls and their destruction can mark the violence of sovereign power. To consider the wall critically, as scholars like Wendy Brown or Eyal Weizman do in their work, would mean to recognize that not all destructions of walls are good and that walls, in addition to confining, may also provide a comfort that we need.

Two further paradigms of sovereignty – the police and the drone – put additional pressure on my attempt to embrace the political, democratic possibilities of sovereignty amidst its often troubling resurgence today. In discussing the police, I focus on the long-standing tradition of excluding the black body from the sovereign body politic, and even destroying it as part of this process. Considering this issue through a coherent set of interventions in Black studies ranging from postcolonial nationalism (Frantz Fanon) to today (Achille Mbembe, Ta-Nehisi Coates, BlackLivesMatter), and in relation to various visual representations of a black body politic (e.g., in the work of Kadir Nelson), I consider whether there can be an Afrofuturism of sovereignty in spite of the central, and negative, role that sovereignty has played in Afropessimist scholarship. Part 2 ends with a meditation on the drone as a fully technicized sovereignty-without-a-people: if we can agree with Grégoire Chamayou that such a sovereignty ought to end up on the junkyard, can we still imagine a popular sovereignty that would constitute itself through its disidentification from the drone *into* the people – a disidentification that may bring new life to a power rooted in a non-exclusivist instantiation of the people?

In part 3, I eventually pursue a coherent set of feminist left-liberal reconsiderations of popular sovereignty (in works by Butler, Brown, Honig, and others) starting from the vulnerable human being, *homo vulnerabilis.* Here I arrive at my main contention, which is that if there is a future of sovereignty, it will require the concept to be rethought using vulnerability as a touchstone. Part 3 shows how vulnerability is quickly becoming an important condition for rethinking sovereignty today as an emancipatory notion for a left that seeks to be politically effective. Ontological vulnerability (we are all vulnerable) needs to give way in such a project to a critical consideration of political vulnerabilization – historically distributed processes of political vulnerabilization and the role of privilege in the distribution of vulnerability today; it's the difference between "All Lives Matter" and "Black Lives Matter" that I discuss. Whereas sovereignty is typically defined against vulnerability, as a power that protects us from our vulnerability and needs us to protect it against its vulnerability, such a definition feeds a phantasy of invulnerability, a sovereign ideal that cannot but become haunted by the negativity of the wound and of death – by the fear of vulnerability returning.

Against such a vicious dialectic in which sovereignty both saves us from our ontological vulnerability and becomes the agent of the historical processes of our vulnerabilization, I propose a sovereignty that would be defined through vulnerability. Acknowledging Jasbir Puar's important work on sovereign strategies of maiming that deconstruct the life/death opposition that is central to theories of both sovereignty and biopolitics, I practise caution in not countering such maiming strategies with a simple call for life/death; instead, the strategies of maiming that Puar analyzes expose a more fundamental connection of sovereignty to vulnerability, the zone of undecidability between life and death – a zone of intensified present-ness that becomes the site for sovereignty's immanent critique. If Puar's work highlights the incomplete death and vulnerability that sovereignty wields, I ask whether another kind of sovereignty is possible, starting from the reality of an incomplete life – of our ontological and historically differentiated vulnerabilities.

Pursuing an anarchic democratic thought that turns Schmitt inside-out by proposing a rule by the people that would not tolerate exceptions – an *unexceptional sovereignty*, as I call it – I suggest as part of such a project a shift away from the verb "withdraw" towards the verb "engage" when it comes to the power called sovereign. "Refuse" begins to operate, in this final chapter, in a project to deconstruct the opposition of those verbs by presenting us with a project of refusal that establishes political sovereignty – that engages by withdrawing. I find such deconstruction in the Indigenous struggles for sovereignty that demonstrate, in line with other paradigms and theories that I discuss, the need for a critical, plastic concept of sovereignty – an aesthetic reconceptualization and pluralization of the notion that would acknowledge the various forms it has taken and recognize that, even if we may not make sovereignty entirely as we please, we still make it – and can make it better.

In the end, sovereignty – small "s" – is a just a verb of which we are the subjects. We are its democratic life.

Notes

EPIGRAPH

Athena Athanasiou and Judith Butler, *Dispossession: The Performative in the Political* (Cambridge: Polity, 2013), 163.

PREFACE

By writing this, I do not mean that sovereignty was ever absent, or even that these two different understandings of politics can ever truly be separated in reality. Analytically, however, they seem to me distinct, and their distinction as well as relation can be used to characterize different political moments, their dynamics, and political history.
Michel Foucault, *The History of Sexuality*, vol. 1, *An Introduction*, trans. Robert Hurley (New York: Vintage, 1990).
Judith Butler, *Precarious Life: The Power of Mourning and Violence* (New York: Verso, 2004).
See Brown qtd in Butler, *Precarious Life*, 59. Foucault's lecture courses, published much more recently than *The History of Sexuality*, are crucial for this reassessment of Foucault's position.
Roberto Esposito, *Bíos: Biopolitics and Philosophy*, trans. Timothy Campbell (Minneapolis: University of Minnesota Press, 2008).
Arne De Boever, *Plastic Sovereignties: Agamben and the Politics of Aesthetics* (Edinburgh: Edinburgh University Press, 2016).
Bernard E. Harcourt, *The Counterrevolution: How Our Government Went to War against its Own Citizens* (New York: Basic Books, 2018).
Joshua Clover, *Riot. Strike. Riot: The New Era of Uprisings* (New York: Verso, 2016).

164 Notes to pages xii–xv

9 Édouard Louis, *Qui a tué mon père* (Paris: Seuil, 2018).

10 Ibid., 11.

11 Ibid., 76, 79, 81.

12 Ibid., 84.

13 Elizabeth Zerofsky, "I Always Write with a Sense of Shame," *New York Times Magazine*, 5 April 2020, 67.

14 Byung-Chul Han, *Topology of Violence*, trans. Amanda DeMarco (Cambridge: MIT Press, 2018), 126, emphasis in original.

15 This not-quite-pastness of sovereignty also reveals itself in Han's work in a more dubious way, due to his peculiar reliance on the work of the theorist of sovereignty Carl Schmitt. There is a way in which Han, in his analysis of the society of achievement as having overcome the society of sovereignty, in fact returns to some aspects of the latter to combat the former. In *The Burnout Society* (trans. Erik Butler [Stanford: Stanford University Press, 2015]), for example, Han follows Schmitt's *Theory of the Partisan* to criticize Facebook (40). In *The Transparency Society* (trans. Erik Butler [Stanford: Stanford University Press, 2015]), Schmitt becomes an ally in Han's criticism of transparency – and this time it's Schmitt's more problematic *The Crisis of Parliamentary Democracy* that is quoted (6–7). In *Topology of Violence*, which includes Han's longest engagement with Schmitt so far, the discussion is definitely more critical, with Han writing skeptically about Schmitt's criticism of parliamentary democracy, for example, and characterizing Schmitt (again, critically) as "a true land creature" who "has no concept of the floating or indistinguishable" (Han, *Topology*, 43). But while Han criticizes the violence that in Schmitt's theory is spent outwards (more on this in my chapter 1), the discussion also takes a turn when Han praises the inwardly stabilizing effect of this outward violence: Schmitt's attachment to character is at odds with the lack of character in today's achievement society, which Han sharply criticizes. Thus, and in tension with the quote about water from *Topology*, in *Saving Beauty* (trans. Daniel Steuer [Cambridge: Polity, 2018]) Han can praise Schmitt's criticism of water as "lacking character" (49). Instead, Schmitt is associated with "solidity and permanence," which "are not conducive to consumption" (49). Immediately after this association, *Saving Beauty* repeats the Schmitt quote from *The Burnout Society*, once again in a positive light.

16 Jasbir Puar, *The Right to Maim: Debility, Capacity, Disability* (Durham, NC: Duke University Press, 2017). I engage Puar's work in part 3 of this book.

Benjamin Bratton, *The Revenge of the Real: Politics for a Post-Pandemic World* (New York: Verso, 2021).

Ibid., 51–9.

Ibid., 134, emphasis in original.

Ibid., 145.

Ibid., 65.

Ibid., 70.

I am thinking of Michael Hardt and Antonio Negri, *Assembly* (Oxford: Oxford University Press, 2017). My own position here is that some vertical articulation of protest is needed because one simply cannot protest perpetually. Protest needs to realize itself politically and then raise its head again when the moment is right to tackle the next injustice.

See part 2 of this book.

See, for example, Pascal Gielen, ed., *Institutional Attitudes: Instituting Art in a Flat World* (Amsterdam: Valiz, 2013).

See Lena H. Sun and Juliet Eilperin, "CDC Gets Rid of Forbidden Words: Fetus, Transgender, Diversity," 15 December 2017, *Washington Post*, https://www.washingtonpost.com/national/health-science/cdc-gets-list-of-forbidden-words-fetus-transgender-diversity/2017/12/15/f503837a-e1cf-11e7-89e8-edec16379010_story.html.

De Boever, *Plastic Sovereignties*.

Rachel Greenwald Smith, *On Compromise: Art, Politics, and the Fate of an American Ideal* (Minneapolis: Graywolf, 2021).

Frantz Fanon, *The Wretched of the Earth*, trans. Richard Philcox (New York: Grove Press, 2004), 236.

CHAPTER ONE

Richard Wolin, "Carl Schmitt: The Conservative Revolutionary Habitus and the Aesthetics of Horror," *Political Theory* 20, no. 3 (1992): 426.

Christopher Fynsk, "Foreword: Experiences of Finitude," in Jean-Luc Nancy, *The Inoperative Community*, ed. Peter Connor, trans. Peter Connor, Lisa Garbus, et al. (Minneapolis: University of Minnesota Press, 1991), x.

Ibid., emphasis in original.

Carl Schmitt, *The Concept of the Political*, trans. George Schwab (Chicago: University of Chicago Press, 1996), 25.

Ibid., 26.

Ibid., 27.

Ibid., 29.

166 Notes to pages 5–9

8 Ibid., 33.
9 Ibid.
10 Ibid., 29.
11 Ibid.
12 Ibid., 32.
13 Domenico Losurdo, *Liberalism: A Counter-History*, trans. Gregory Elliott (New York: Verso, 2014).
14 Schmitt, *Concept*, 35.
15 Ibid., 54.
16 Ibid.
17 Ibid.
18 Ibid.
19 Ibid., 55.
20 Ibid.
21 Ibid., 53.
22 Ibid., 40.
23 I am relying on the English translation of the fable as it appears in Jacques Derrida's *Rogues: Two Essays on Reason*, trans. Pascale-Anne Brault and Michael Naas (Stanford: Stanford University Press, 2005). Derrida, one of Schmitt's most insightful readers, comments on this fable extensively in his lectures in *The Beast and the Sovereign*, vol. 1, ed. Michel Lisse, Marie-Lousie Mallet, and Ginette Michaud, trans. Geoffrey Bennington (Chicago: University of Chicago Press, 2009). My own use of the fable is in part inspired by Derrida's use of it.
24 See Carl Schmitt, *The Nomos of the Earth in the International Law of the Jus Publicum Europeaum.* Trans. G.L. Ulmen (Candor: Telos, 2003).
25 Chantal Mouffe, ed. *The Challenge of Carl Schmitt* (New York: Verso, 1999), 1.
26 Ibid., 3.
27 Ibid., 4.
28 Ibid., emphasis in original.
29 Ibid.
30 Rachel Greenwald Smith does so in *On Compromise: Art, Politics, and the Fate of an American Ideal* (Minneapolis: Graywolf, 2021), chap. 5.
31 See Schmitt, *Concept*, 27.
32 Carl Schmitt, *Political Theology: Four Chapters on the Concept of Sovereignty*, trans. George Schwab (Cambridge: MIT Press, 1985), 5.
33 Carl Schmitt, *Politische Theologie: Vier Kapital Zur Lehre Von der Souveränität* (Leipzig: Duncker und Humblot, 1922), 9.
34 Schmitt, *Political Theology*, 10.

Ibid., 15.

Ibid.

Ibid.

Ibid. This has led commentators to distinguish a bio-normativism in Schmitt's work to which I return later. See Kirk Wetters, "The Rule of the Norm and the Political Theology of 'Real Life' in Carl Schmitt and Giorgio Agamben," *diacritics* 36, no. 1 (2006): 31–46. Here, in particular, 35 and further.

Schmitt, *Political Theology*, 12.

Ibid., 11.

Ibid., 12.

Ibid., 6.

Ibid., 14.

Ibid., 13–14.

Ibid., 14.

Ibid.

Ibid., 7.

Ibid., 9.

Ibid., 6.

Andreas Kalyvas, "Carl Schmitt and the Three Moments of Democracy," *Cardozo Law Review* 21, no. 1,525 (1999–2000): 1529. Kalyvas later develops this argument further and with more nuance in *Democracy and the Politics of the Extraordinary: Max Weber, Carl Schmitt, and Hannah Arendt* (Cambridge: Cambridge University Press, 2008).

Kalyvas, "Carl Schmitt," 1525.

Ibid., 1529–30, emphasis in original.

Ibid., 1530.

Ibid., 1531, emphasis in original.

Ibid., 1534.

Ibid., 1537.

Ibid.

Ibid., 1549.

Dyzenhaus qtd in ibid.

Kalyvas, "Carl Schmitt," 1549.

Ibid., 1554.

Ibid., 1559.

Ibid., 1561.

Anthony McCann, *Shadowlands: Fear and Freedom at the Oregon Standoff* (New York: Bloomsbury, 2019). I addressed the relevance of Schmitt for McCann's book in an interview I did with the author:

168 Notes to pages 14–17

"Unearthly Sovereignties and the Unsovereign Earth," *boundary 2 online*, 22 January 2020, https://www.boundary2.org/2020/01/unearthly-sovereignties-and-the-unsovereign-earth-arne-de-boever-in-conversation-with-anthony-mccann.

CHAPTER TWO

1 Michel Foucault, *"Society Must Be Defended": Lectures at the Collège de France, 1975–1976*, ed. Mauro Bertani and Alessandro Fontana, trans. David Macey (New York: Picador, 2003), 108.

2 Jacques Bidet, *Foucault with Marx*, trans. Steven Corcoran (London: Zed Books, 2016), 176.

3 Mika Ojakangas, "Sovereign and Plebs: Michel Foucault Meets Carl Schmitt," *Telos* 119 (Spring, 2001): 32–40.

4 Daniel Zamora and Michael Behrent, eds., *Foucault and Neoliberalism* (Cambridge: Polity, 2016).

5 Donna Haraway would ask us to consider to what extent this Hobbesian claim is based on the observation of how actual wolves live together. See Donna Haraway, *When Species Meet* (Minneapolis: University of Minnesota Press, 2008).

6 The king has two bodies: an earthly, biological one and a spiritual, symbolic one. This image shows the king's symbolic body. It is because of this two-body problematic that we have the acclamation, "The king is dead, long live the king!" – the biological king is dead, long live the symbolic body of the king, which is immortal. There is barely a pause between the two parts of the acclamation to ensure the continuity of power. See Ernst Kantorowicz, *The King's Two Bodies: A Study in Medieval Political Theology* (Princeton, NJ: Princeton University Press, 2016).

7 See Giorgio Agamben, *Stasis: Civil War as a Political Paradigm*, trans. Nicholas Heron (Edinburgh: Edinburgh University Press, 2015).

8 Foucault, *"Society Must Be Defended,"* 90.

9 Ibid.

10 Ibid.

11 See ibid., 91.

12 Ibid.

13 Ibid.

14 Ibid., 92.

15 Ibid., 93.

16 Ibid., 94.

Ibid., 95.

Ibid., 96.

Ibid.

Ibid., 97.

Ibid.

Ibid., 99 and after.

Melinda Cooper, "Insecure Times, Tough Decisions: The *Nomos* of Neoliberalism," *Alternatives* 29 (2004): 516, emphasis in original.

See Stuart Elden, *Foucault's Last Decade* (Cambridge: Polity, 2016).

Bidet, *Foucault with Marx*, 4.

Ibid., 127.

Ibid., 173–4.

Ibid., 174.

Ibid., 175.

Ibid., 176.

The validity of this "against" may have to be contested. This certainly appears to be Agamben's project, against Foucault, in *Stasis*, where he presents Hobbes as a thinker of the dissolved multitude of civil war rather than as a theorist of the people. So rather than being a theorist of peace, Hobbes is a theorist of civil war. Following Agamben, one would have to conclude that Foucault blames Hobbes for a position that is not his.

Brady Thomas Heiner, "Foucault and the Black Panthers," *City* 11, no. 3 (2007): 313–56.

Cooper, "Insecure Times," 515. Heiner suggests Foucault arrived at the Black Panthers via Jean Genet, even if he did not share the latter's support for Palestine.

Peter Gratton, *State of Sovereignty: Lessons from the Political Fictions of Modernity* (New York: State University of New York Press, 2012), 149.

Ibid., 156.

Ojakangas, "Sovereign and Plebs."

Canguilhem qtd in Stuart Elden, *Foucault's Last Decade* (Cambridge: Polity, 2016), 24.

Carl Schmitt, *Political Theology: Four Chapters on the Concept of Sovereignty*, trans. George Schwab (Cambridge: MIT Press, 1985), 15.

Elden, *Foucault's Last Decade*, 24.

Kirk Wetters, "The Rule of the Norm and the Political Theology of 'Real Life' in Carl Schmitt and Giorgio Agamben," *diacritics* 36, no. 1 (2006): 39.

Ibid., emphasis in original.

Ibid., 40.

170 Notes to pages 21–5

43 Michel Foucault, *The History of Sexuality*, vol. 1, *An Introduction*, trans. Robert Hurley (New York: Vintage, 1990), 137.

44 Ibid., 139.

45 Zamora and Behrent, *Foucault and Neoliberalism*, 51.

46 Ibid., 54.

47 Ibid., 98, emphasis in original.

48 Nancy Fraser, "The End of Progressive Neoliberalism," *Dissent*, 2 January 2017, https://www.dissentmagazine.org/online_articles/progressive-neoliberalism-reactionary-populism-nancy-fraser.

49 Zamora and Behrent, *Foucault and Neoliberalism*, 99.

50 Ibid., 100.

51 Benjamin Bratton helpfully highlights this reading in his *The Revenge of the Real: Politics for a Post-Pandemic World* (New York: Verso, 2021), 146. But it has started appearing in general audience works as well. See, for example, Maggie Nelson, *On Freedom: Four Songs of Care and Constraint* (Minneapolis: Graywolf, 2021), 79.

52 Polanyi qtd in Pierre Dardot and Christian Laval, *The New Way of the World: On Neoliberal Society*, trans. Gregory Elliott (New York: Verso, 2013), 45, emphasis in original.

53 Philip Mirowski, *Never Let a Serious Crisis Go to Waste: How Neoliberalism Survived the Financial Meltdown* (New York: Verso, 2014), 84.

54 Ibid.

55 Ibid., 85.

56 William Scheuerman, "The Unholy Alliance of Carl Schmitt and Friedrich A. Hayek," *Constellations* 4, no. 2 (1997): 172–88.

57 Thomas Biebricher, "Sovereignty, Norms, and Exception in Neoliberalism," *Qui Parle* 23, no. 1 (2014): 77–107.

58 Grégoire Chamayou, *The Ungovernable Society: A Genealogy of Authoritarian Liberalism,* trans. Andrew Brown (Cambridge: Polity, 2021), 212.

59 Dario Gentili, *The Age of Precarity: Endless Crisis as an Art of Government* (New York: Verso, 2021).

60 Mirowski, *Never Let a Serious Crisis Go to Waste*, 358.

61 Ibid., 98.

62 Cooper, "Insecure Times," 526.

63 Ibid., 527.

64 Ibid., 528.

65 Naomi Klein, *The Shock Doctrine: The Rise of Disaster Capitalism* (New York: Picador, 2007).

Claude Lefort, *The Political Forms of Modern Society: Bureaucracy, Democracy, Totalitarianism*, trans. (Cambridge: MIT Press, 1986). While I appreciate Sergei Prozorov's attempt in this context to characterize Agamben's "positive" politics as an "affirmative biopolitics, characterized by destituent power" that "resonates with Claude Lefort's understanding of democracy as structured around the ontological void and epistemic indeterminacy," I am not convinced that the "exceptionalist" dimension of Agamben's debt to Schmitt allows for such a characterization. See Sergei Prozorov, "Living *à la mode*: Form-of-Life and Democratic Biopolitics in Giorgio Agamben's *The Use of Bodies*," *Philosophy and Social Criticism* 43, no. 2 (2017): 144.

I take this phrase from Judith Butler, "Indefinite Detention," in Judith Butler, *Precarious Life: The Power of Mourning and Violence* (New York: Verso, 2004), 51–100.

David Harvey, *A Brief History of Neoliberalism* (Oxford: Oxford University Press, 2005).

CHAPTER THREE

Dimitris Vardoulakis, *Stasis before the State: Nine Theses on Agonistic Democracy* (New York: Fordham University Press, 2018).

Joan Cocks, *On Sovereignty and Other Political Delusions* (New York: Bloomsbury, 2014).

Giorgio Agamben, *Stasis: Civil War as a Political Paradigm*, trans. Nick Heron (Edinburgh: Edinburgh University Press, 2015), 30.

Ibid., 34–5.

Ibid., 36.

Ibid., 37.

I take this image of the Moebius strip from Giorgio Agamben, *Means without End: Notes on Politics*, trans. Vincenzo Binetti and Cesare Casarino (Minneapolis: University of Minnesota Press, 2000), 25.

Giorgio Agamben, *Homo Sacer: Sovereign Power and Bare Life*, trans. Daniel Heller-Roazen (Stanford: Stanford University Press, 1998), 24.

On this see also Arne De Boever, *Against Aesthetic Exceptionalism* (Minneapolis: University of Minnesota Press, 2019).

Agamben, *Homo Sacer*, 24–5.

Ibid., 71.

Alexander Weheliye, *Habeas Viscus: Racializing Assemblages, Biopolitics, and Black Feminist Theories of the Human* (Durham, NC: Duke University Press, 2014).

172　　　　　　　　　Notes to pages 33–40

13　Agamben, *Homo Sacer*, 65.

14　Eric Santner, "Terri Schiavo and the State of Exception," http://www.press. uchicago.edu/Misc/Chicago/05april_santner.html.

15　Brady Thomas Heiner, "Foucault and the Black Panthers," *City* 11, no. 3 (2007): 313–56.

16　Giorgio Agamben, *The Use of Bodies*, trans. Adam Kotsko (Stanford: Stanford University Press, 2015), 268.

17　The Invisible Committee, *Now*, trans. Robert Hurley (Los Angeles: Semiotext[e], 2017), 76.

18　Ibid.

19　Ibid.

20　Ibid., 79, emphasis in original.

21　Ibid., emphasis in original.

22　Ibid., 80, emphasis in original.

23　Ibid., 81.

24　Ibid., 70.

25　Vardoulakis, *Stasis before the State*, 98.

26　On this, see especially Dimitris Vardoulakis, *Sovereignty and Its Other: Toward the Dejustification of Violence* (New York: Fordham University Press, 2013).

27　Emily Apter, *Unexceptional Politics: On Obstruction, Impasse, and the Impolitic* (New York: Verso, 2018).

28　See Stathis Gourgouris, "The Question Is: Society Defended against Whom? Or What?" May 2013, *New Philosopher*, https://www. newphilosopher.com/articles/the-question-is-society-defended-against-whom-or-what-in-the-name-of-what.

CHAPTER FOUR

1　Walter Benjamin, "Critique of Violence," *Selected Writings,* vol. 1, *1913–1926*, ed. Marcus Bollock and Michael W. Jennings (Cambridge, MA: Belknap/Harvard University Press, 1996), 236–52. "Legal violence" appears throughout the text. For the German original, all page references are to Walter Benjamin, "Zur Kritik der Gewalt," https:// rechtkritisch.files.wordpress.com/2014/03/walter-benjamin-zur-kritik-der-gewalt.pdf.

2　Benjamin, "Critique," 236, 237, 238.

3　Ibid., 237.

4　Ibid., 239.

5　Ibid., 242.

Giorgio Agamben, *Homo Sacer: Sovereign Power and Bare Life*, trans.
Daniel Heller-Roazen (Stanford: Stanford University Press, 1998), 15.
Benjamin, "Critique," 243.
Ibid.
Benjamin, "Kritik," 120.
Benjamin, "Critique," 249.
Ibid., 250; Benjamin, "Kritik," 126.
Benjamin, "Kritik," 129.
Benjamin, "Critique," 252.
Immanuel Kant, "Was ist Aufklärung?," in Michel Foucault, *The Politics of Truth*, trans. Lysa Hochroth and Catherine Porter (Los Angeles: Semiotext[e], 2007), 29.
Ibid.
Ibid., 31.
This is why Schmitt can write that emergency law, for Kant, was no law at all. Note, though, that while Schmitt goes beyond Kant, he remains a conservative, for he only thinks an emergency that is folded into the law.
Foucault, *Politics*, 37.
This refers to the *epimeleia eautou* or *cura sui*, and the techniques or technologies – such as writing, for example – that were used to practise it. Foucault indeed lays out a *biotechnical* approach to writing in his final work. I have been inclined to disarticulate this late work from what others understand to be Foucault's "neoliberalism," but the verdict remains out on this.
Walter Benjamin, "Über den Begriff der Geschichte," in Walter Benjamin, *Gesammelte Schrifte, Bd. I–II* (Frankfurt: Suhrkamp, 1980), 697.
Walter Benjamin, "Theses on the Philosophy of History," in Walter Benjamin, *Illuminations: Essays and Reflections*, ed. Hannah Arendt, trans. Harry Zohn (New York: Schocken, 1968). 257.
Benjamin, "Theses," 255.
See Eduardo Cadava, *Words of Light: Theses on the Photography of History* (Princeton, NJ: Princeton University Press, 1997).
Ibid., 255.
Ibid., 257.
Ibid., 258.
Benjamin qtd in Giorgio Agamben, *The Coming Community*, trans. Michael Hardt (Minneapolis: University of Minnesota Press, 1990).
Benjamin, "Theses," 263.
Ibid., 261.
Ibid., 263.
Ibid.

174 Notes to pages 49–53

CHAPTER FIVE

1 I choose the term "paradigm" in view of Agamben's presentation of his own methodology in "What Is a Paradigm?," in Giorgio Agamben, *The Signature of All Things: On Method*, trans. Luca D'Isanto and Kevin Attell (New York: Zone Books, 2009).

2 See Giorgio Agamben, *Homo Sacer: Sovereign Power and Bare Life*, trans. Daniel Heller-Roazen (Stanford: Stanford University Press, 1998).

3 Schmitt takes on those theorists in his reading of Bodin as a classic theorist of sovereignty who was already focused on the exception.

4 Agamben, *Homo Sacer*, 15.

5 Michel Foucault, Giorgio Agamben, Jean-Luc Nancy, Roberto Esposito, Sergio Benvenuto, Divya Dwivedi, Shaj Mohan, Rocco Conchi, and Massimo De Carolis, "Coronavirus and Philosophers," *European Journal of Psychoanalysis*, https://www.journal-psychoanalysis.eu/coronavirus-and-philosophers. Agamben's various responses have since been revised and published in Giorgio Agamben, *Where Are We Now? The Epidemic as Politics*. 2nd updated ed., trans. Valeria Dani (London: Eris, 2021). It is telling how, when considering Covid numbers, Agamben counts deaths (e.g., Agamben, *Where Are We Now?*, 43–4). In other words, his considerations do not recognize the short-term or even long-term suffering that Covid also causes and that we presumably also seek to prevent.

6 Christopher Caldwell, "The Coronavirus Philosopher," *New York Times*, 23 August 2020, https://www.nytimes.com/2020/08/21/opinion/sunday/giorgio-agamben-philosophy-coronavirus.html.

7 Agamben, *Homo Sacer*, 118.

8 Michel Foucault, *The Birth of Biopolitics: Lectures at the Collège de France, 1978–1979*, trans. Graham Burchell, ed. Arnold I. Davidson (New York: Picador, 2008), 188.

9 Ibid., 187.

10 Ibid. For the French original of this passage see: Michel Foucault, *Naissance de la biopolitique: Cours au Collège de France, 1978–1979* (Paris: Gallimard/Seuil, 2004), 193.

11 Ibid., 187.

12 Caldwell, "Coronavirus Philosopher."

13 Agamben, *Where Are We Now?*, 70.

14 See Anna Kornbluh, *The Order of Forms: Realism, Formalism, and Social Space* (Chicago: University of Chicago Press, 2019).

15 Giorgio Agamben, *Means without End: Notes on Politics*, trans. Vincenzo Binetti and Cesare Casarino (Minneapolis: University of Minnesota Press, 2000), 39.

Agamben, *Homo Sacer*, 24–5.

Ibid., 24.

Ibid.

Agamben, *Where Are We Now?*, 98.

Giorgio Agamben, *The Use of Bodies*, trans. Adam Kotsko (Stanford: Stanford University Press, 2016).

Giorgio Agamben, *Stanzas: Word and Phantasm in Western* Culture, trans. Ronald L. Martinez (Minneapolis: University of Minnesota Press, 1993), 137–8.

Giorgio Agamben, *Idea of Prose*, trans. Michael Sullivan and Sam Whitsitt (Albany: SUNY Press, 1995), 82.

Giorgio Agamben, *The Coming Community*, trans. Michael Hardt (Minneapolis: University of Minnesota Press, 2003).

See Arne De Boever, *Plastic Sovereignties: Agamben and the Politics of Aesthetics* (Edinburgh: Edinburgh University Press, 2016).

Agamben, *Use of Bodies*, 274–9.

Judith Butler, "Indefinite Detention," in Judith Butler, *Precarious Life: The Power of Mourning and Violence* (New York: Verso, 2004), 67.

This is why Deleuze and Guattari (D+G) (to whom I return in the next chapter) can consider "encampment" in *A Thousand Plateaus* as a "borderline phenomenon" in which the difference between "nomad" science and "State" science becomes undone. See Gilles Deleuze and Felix Guattari, *A Thousand Plateaus: Capitalism and Schizophrenia*, trans. Brian Massumi (Minneapolis: University of Minnesota Press, 2009), 363. The same goes for the practice of "breaking through walls" or "smoothing space," which Eyal Weizman has shown to be a D+G–inspired military practice of the Israeli Defense Forces (see chapter 6).

Errol Morris, *Standard Operating Procedure* (Sony Pictures Classics, 2008).

Rumsfeld qtd in Butler, "Indefinite Detention," 50.

Butler, "Indefinite Detention," 53.

Ibid., 53–4. Mika Ojakangas captures this by writing about the "resurrection of the sovereign." See Mika Ojakangas, "Sovereign and Plebs: Michel Foucault Meets Carl Schmitt," *Telos* 119 (Spring, 2001): 32–40

Butler, "Indefinite Detention," 54.

Ibid., 56.

Ibid.

Ibid., 61.

Ibid., 62.

Ibid., 50.

Ibid., 51.

176 Notes to pages 59–67

39 Ibid., 65. Schmitt, of course, had already clarified this.

40 Butler, "Indefinite Detention," 67

41 Ibid.

42 Ibid., 78.

43 Ibid., 86.

44 Walter Benjamin, "Critique of Violence," *Selected Writings*, vol. 1, *1913–1926*, ed. Marcus Bollock and Michael W. Jennings (Cambridge, MA: Belknap/Harvard University Press, 1996), 246.

45 Catherine Malabou, *Changing Difference: The Feminine and the Question of Philosophy*, trans. Carolyn Shread (Cambridge: Polity, 63).

46 Emily Apter, *Unexceptional Politics: On Obstruction, Impasse, and the Impolitic* (New York: Verso, 2018), 34.

47 Ibid., 36.

48 Agamben, *Where Are We Now?*, 45, 80.

49 Ibid., 30, 34.

CHAPTER SIX

1 Gilles Deleuze and Felix Guattari, *A Thousand Plateaus: Capitalism and Schizophrenia*, trans. Brian Massumi (Minneapolis: University of Minnesota Press, 2009), 500.

2 Wendy Brown, *Walled States, Waning Sovereignty* (New York: Zone Books, 2010), 20.

3 Ibid., 21.

4 Ibid.

5 Ibid., 23.

6 Ibid., 22.

7 Ibid.

8 Ibid., 24.

9 Ibid.

10 Ibid.

11 Ibid.

12 Ibid., 25.

13 Ibid.

14 Ibid., 26.

15 Ibid., 30.

16 Ibid., 31.

17 See Arne De Boever, *States of Exception in the Contemporary Novel: Martel, Eugenides, Coetzee, Sebald* (New York: Continuum, 2012).

18 Brown, *Walled States*, 34.

Ibid., 38.

Ibid.

Ibid.

Ibid., 39.

Ibid., 41.

This is quite striking in its marked contrast to Agamben's position on the pandemic. When considering social distancing, and a situation in which we are confined to the home or the "bubbles" of social contact that we allow ourselves, Agamben can only see a reduction to the bare life of survival. But this is an extremely limited understanding of life at home or, indeed, with a limited, but perhaps more frequent, deeper, and more meaningful, amount of social contact.

Eyal Weizman, *Hollow Land: Israel's Architecture of Occupation* (New York: Verso, 2007), 185.

Ibid.

Ibid., 186.

Ibid., 190.

Ibid., 186.

Ibid., 199.

Ibid., 188.

Ibid., 197.

Ibid., 209.

Ibid.

Elsewhere I express my reservations about the sabotaging of foreclosed homes, which Annie McClanahan discusses in her book *Dead Pledges: Debt, Crisis, and Twenty-First-Century Culture* (Stanford, CA: Stanford University Press, 2017). See Arne De Boever, "Realist Horror," *boundary 2 online*, 29 June 2017, http://www.boundary2.org/2017/06/arne-de-boever-realist-horror-review-of-dead-pledges-debt-crisis-and-twenty-first-century-culture. Marija Cetinic, "House and Field: The Aesthetics of Saturation," *Mediations* 28, no. 1 (2014): 35–44, which discusses the work of Rachel Whiteread, is also worth considering in this context. See http://www.mediationsjournal.org/articles/house-and-field.

Guillaume Sibertin-Blanc, *State and Politics: Deleuze and Guattari on Marx*, trans. Ames Hodges (South Pasadena: Semiotext[e], 2016), 105.

Ibid., 106, emphasis in original.

Ibid., 105–6.

Ibid., 106.

Ibid., 107.

Ibid.

42 Ibid., 110.

43 Ibid., 111.

44 Ibid.

45 Ibid., 112.

46 Ibid., 116.

47 Deleuze and Guattari, *Thousand Plateaus*, 351.

48 Ibid., 360.

49 Ibid., 488.

50 Ibid., 376.

CHAPTER SEVEN

I would like to thank Sarah Brouillette and Olivia C. Harrison for their helpful feedback on earlier versions of this chapter.

1 Ta-Nehisi Coates, *Between the World and Me* (New York: Spiegel and Grau, 2015).

2 Ibid., 78.

3 Arne De Boever, "Agamben and Marx: Sovereignty, Governmentality, Economy," *Law and Critique* 20, no. 3 (2009): 259–70.

4 Coates, *Between*, 83.

5 Ibid., 81.

6 Ibid.

7 Ibid., 83.

8 Ibid., 103, emphasis in original.

9 Ibid., 79.

10 To be clear, I would not want to suggest here that the European frame of reference, in particular the reference to Auschwitz, is somehow *needed* to draw out the gravity of the situation of black lives in the US. Certainly when "camp" is used as the paradigm to capture the specific historical situation of black lives in the US, the specificity of that situation and the localization of the notion of camp that it requires would need to be acknowledged. Ava DuVernay's documentary film *13th* (Kandoo Films/Netflix, 2016) does some of that work, relying in part on Michelle Alexander, *The New Jim Crow: Mass Incarceration in the Age of Color Blindness* (New York: The New Press, 2012).

11 Chris Taylor and Adom Getachew, "The Global Plantation: An Exchange," *boundary 2 online*, 23 June 2022, https://www.boundary2.org/2020/06/the-global-plantation-an-exchange-between-adom-getachew-and-christopher-taylor.

I also want to add here that, in spite of changes in the practices of policing, for example with the rise of "big data policing," I believe these paradigms hold. See, for example, the centrality of racialized policing to Andrew Guthrie Ferguson, *The Rise of Big Data Policing: Surveillance, Race, and the Future of Law Enforcement* (New York: NYU Press, 2017).

Coates, *Between*, 106.

This something partly gets a geographical name in Coates' Paris. It is in Paris where Coates realizes that there are places where he is not other people's problem. Black people are not the problem of Paris; one should add that this dubious privilege is reserved for the Arabs, though Coates does not state this explicitly. In his turning to Paris as refuge, Coates is of course not alone: James Baldwin, Richard Wright, William Gardner Smith, and others had done the same before him.

Coates, *Between*, 76.

Ibid., 99.

I would like to thank AbouMaliq Simone for reminding me of this third path. I take the phrase "continuous unsettling" from his generous comments on an earlier version of my chapter, which drew my attention to David Marriott, "Judging Fanon," *Rhizomes* 29 (2016), http://www.rhizomes.net/issue29/marriott.html.

Adom Getachew, *Worldmaking after Empire: The Rise and Fall of Self-Determination* (Princeton, NJ: Princeton University Press, 2019), 9.

Ibid., 2.

Ibid., emphasis in original.

Ibid., 3.

As I discuss in chapter 2, it seems rather that exceptionalist sovereignty and neoliberalism need to be thought together.

Achille Mbembe, "Necropolitics," trans. Libby Meintjes, *Public Culture* 15, no. 1 (2003): 11–40.

Paul Gilroy, *Darker Than Blue: On the Moral Economies of Black Atlantic Culture* (Cambridge: Harvard University Press, 2010); Alexander Weheliye, *Habeas Viscus: Racializing Assemblages, Biopolitics, and Black Feminist Theories of the Human* (Durham, NC: Duke University Press, 2014), 56 and further. To be clear, Gilroy points to the usefulness of the camp to analyze the situation of black lives in the US, but he also emphasizes Agamben's blindness to race.

Mbembe, "Necropolitics," 12.

Ibid., 14, emphasis in original.

Ibid., 15.

Ibid.

180 Notes to pages 80–2

29 Ibid.

30 Ibid., 16.

31 Ibid.

32 Ibid.

33 Ibid., 14, emphasis in original.

34 I refer here to two English translations of Fanon's text: Frantz Fanon, "Concerning Violence," trans. Constance Farrington, in Frantz Fanon, *The Wretched of the Earth* (New York: Grove, 1968); Frantz Fanon, "On Violence," trans. Richard Philcox, in Frantz Fanon, *The Wretched of the Earth* (New York: Grove, 2004). For the French original, I refer to Frantz Fanon, "De la violence," in Frantz Fanon, *Les damnés de la terre* (Paris: La découverte, 2002).

35 There is an affiliation across colonial situations that, in view of discussions of Fanon's work such as Robert Young's (*Postcolonialism: A Historical Introduction* [Oxford: Blackwell, 2001]), needs to be acknowledged here – the "I" of the native in Fanon's text cannot straightforwardly be identified with Fanon himself, as in Algeria he was not a native or "indigène," a term that Philcox unfortunately renders as "colonial subject" (Fanon, "On Violence," 15). Fanon arrived in Algeria as a French citizen, which as a Martiniquan he had become after 1946, when Martinique became a "department" of the French state.

36 Fanon, "On Violence," 6.

37 Ibid., 30.

38 Ibid., 2.

39 This is the Farrington translation: Fanon, "Concerning Violence," 37. Fanon's original French has "violence absolue" ("Concerning Violence," 41). Philcox renders this as "out and out violence" ("On Violence," 3).

40 Fanon, "On Violence," 2. Farrington renders this as "complete disorder" (Fanon, "Concerning Violence," 36). The original French has "désordre absolu" (Fanon, "De la violence," 39).

41 Fanon, "On Violence," 1.

42 Ibid., 3.

43 Ibid., 24.

44 When Fanon offers this line, he is referencing the New Testament, which casts the decolonized community he imagines in "messianic" terms. This is so even if he compares Christianity to DDT earlier on in his text.

45 Fanon, "On Violence,: 23.

46 Ibid., 33. Farrington's rendering is more correct: "the question is not always to reply to it by greater violence, but rather to see how to relax the tension" (Fanon, "Concerning Violence," 73). Here is Fanon: "la question

Notes to pages 82–7   181

n'est pas toujours d'y répondre par une plus grande violence mais plutôt de voir comment désamorcer la crise" (Fanon, "De la violence," 72).

Achille Mbembe, *Critique of Black Reason*, trans. Laurent Dubois (Durham, NC: Duke University Press, 2017), 166.

Fanon, "On Violence," 1.

Ibid.

Nigel Gibson gets this negotiation exactly right in the context of a discussion of dialectics. See Nigel Gibson, "Relative Opacity: A New Translation of Fanon's *The Wretched of the Earth* – Mission Betrayed or Fulfilled?," *Social Identities: Journal for the Study of Race, Nation and Culture* 13, no. 1 (2007): 69–95.

Brady Thomas Heiner, "Foucault and the Black Panthers," *City* 11, no. 3 (2007): 313–56.

The cover can be seen here: https://www.newyorker.com/culture/culture-desk/cover-story-2017-01-16.

Nelson in fact did another cover for the *New Yorker* that had Malcolm X on it, but he appeared there as part of a group of African American figures at the centre of which was the (much more acceptable) figure of James Baldwin. The other cover can be seen here: https://www.newyorker.com/culture/culture-desk/cover-story-2017-01-16.

The cover can be seen here: https://www.newyorker.com/culture/cover-story/cover-story-2020-06-22.

Focusing on the sovereign figure of the police in particular, it is worth noting Spike Lee's *BlacKkKlansman* (Focus Features, 2018) as refusing to promote the narrative that all police are bad or that there is something structurally wrong with the police. Lee's film, as well as his financial support of the New York Police Department, was criticized by the radical left. If the wall as a paradigm of sovereignty opens up room for negotiation, does the police? Most would probably agree that the camp does not – it is absolute negativity. For many, but not for Spike Lee, the police is, too.

Fanon, "On Violence," 2.

Mbembe, *Critique*, 159.

Ibid.

Ibid., 167, 183.

Ibid., 162.

Daniel Zamora and Michael Behrent, eds., *Foucault and Neoliberalism* (Cambridge: Polity, 2016).

Mbembe, *Critique*, 2.

Ibid., 3.

Ibid., 4.

65 Ibid., 6, emphasis in original.

66 See Fred Moten, "Of Human Flesh: An Interview with R.A. Judy" (part 2), *boundary 2 online* 6 May 2020, https://www.boundary2.org/2020/05/of-human-flesh-an-interview-with-r-a-judy-by-fred-moten.

67 Fred Moten, "Blackness and Nothingness (Mysticism in the Flesh)," *South Atlantic Quarterly* 112, no. 4 (2013): 739.

68 Ibid., 749.

69 Ibid., 750.

70 Ibid.

71 Ibid., 751.

72 Ibid.

73 Abdelkebir Khatibi, *Maghreb Pluriel* (Paris Denoël, 1983), 12.

74 Moten, "Blackness and Nothingness," 749.

75 Ibid.

76 Mbembe, *Critique*, 170.

77 Ibid., 173.

78 Ibid., 178.

79 Ibid., 173.

80 Ibid.

81 Joan Cocks, *On Sovereignty and Other Political Delusions* (New York: Bloomsbury, 2014).

CHAPTER EIGHT

1 Dimitris Vardoulakis, *Stasis before the State: Nine Theses on Agonistic Democracy* (New York: Fordham University Press, 2018).

2 Scahill qtd in Teju Cole, *Known and Strange Things* (New York: Random House, 2016), 257.

3 It is rewarding to track the dialectical turns of the chapter "In War as in Peace," which moves through a series of theses, antitheses, and synthesis, only to ultimately have done with "dronized" sovereignty.

4 Grégoire Chamayou, *A Theory of the Drone*, trans. Janet Lloyd (New York: The New Press, 2015), 177.

5 Ibid., 179.

6 Ibid.

7 Ibid.

8 Ibid., 180.

9 Ibid., 180-1.

10 Ibid., 183.

11 Ibid., 184.

Notes to pages 93–100

Ibid.

Ibid.

One would also have to consider here the fact that, in the United States, one of the most recent moments of renewed popular sovereignty – the Obama election – coincided with a presidency that would become identified with drone war. See, for example, Jonathan Beller, "Prosthetics of Whiteness: Drone Psychosis," in Jonathan Beller, *The Message Is Murder: Substrates of Computational Capital* (New York: Pluto Press, 2018). 137–57.

Chamayou, *Theory*, 220–1.

Emily Apter, *Unexceptional Politics: On Obstruction, Impasse, and the Impolitic* (New York: Verso, 2018), 162.

Chamayou, *Theory*, 221.

Butler, *Precarious Life*, xi.

CHAPTER NINE

Franz Kafka, *The Complete Stories*, ed. Nahum N. Glatzer (New York: Schocken, 1971). 429.

Judith Butler, *Precarious Life: The Power of Mourning and Violence* (New York: Verso, 2004).

Isabell Lorey, *State of Insecurity: Government of the Precarious*, trans. Aileen Derieg (New York: Verso, 2015).

The latter's position on vulnerability needs some more nuanced discussion, as I explain later.

Wendy Brown, *Undoing the Demos: Neoliberalism's Stealth Revolution* (New York: Zone Books, 2015).

Bonnie Honig, *Public Things: Democracy in Disrepair* (New York: Fordham University Press, 2017).

There is clearly an evolution here on this count in Butler's work. In a preface to a book they co-authored with Athena Athanasiou, Butler and Athanasiou still claim to be engaged with a "non-sovereign account of agency," a phrase that I don't think applies to Butler's assembly book from just a few years later. See Athena Athanasiou and Judith Butler, *Dispossession: The Performative in the Political* (Cambridge: Polity, 2013), ix. See also Rosine Kelz, "Political Theory and Migration: Concepts of Non-Sovereignty and Solidarity," *Movements: Journal für kritische Migrations- und Grenzregimeforschung* 1, no. 2 (2015): 1–17.

Judith Butler, *Notes toward a Performative Theory of Assembly* (Cambridge: Harvard University Press, 2015).

9 See Sarah Brouillette, "Neoliberalism and the Demise of the Literary," in *Neoliberalism and Contemporary Literature*, ed. Mitchum Huehls and Rachel Greenwald Smith (Baltimore, MD: John Hopkins University Press, 2017), 277–90; Annie McClanahan, "On Becoming Non–Economic: Human Capital Theory and Wendy Brown's *Undoing the Demos*," *Theory and Event* 20, no. 2 (2017): 510–19.

10 Naomi Klein, *This Changes Everything: Capitalism vs. the Climate* (New York: Simon and Schuster, 2014), 158.

11 Ibid.

12 Ibid.

13 Bruce Robbins, *The Beneficiary* (Durham, NC: Duke University Press, 2017).

14 Honig, *Public Things*, 37 and throughout.

15 Samuel Weber, *Benjamin's -abilities* (Cambridge: Harvard University Press, 2010).

16 Jasbir Puar, "The 'Right' to Maim: Disablement and Inhumanist Biopolitics in Palestine," *borderlands* 14, no. 1 (2015), http://www.borderlands.net.au/vol14no1_2015/puar_maim.pdf.

17 Jasbir Puar, *The Right to Maim: Debility, Capacity, Disability* (Durham, NC: Duke University Press, 2017), 7.

18 Lauren Berlant, *Cruel Optimism* (Durham, NC: Duke University Press, 2011), 98.

19 Ibid.

20 Ibid., emphasis in original.

21 Puar, *Right to Maim*, 8.

22 Lorey, *State of Insecurity*, 12.

23 Ibid.

24 Ibid., 1.

25 Ibid., 2.

26 Ibid.

27 Ibid.

28 Ibid.

29 Ibid., 4.

30 Ibid., 6.

31 Ibid.

32 Ibid.

33 Ibid., 7.

34 Ibid., 14.

35 Ibid., 87.

Notes to pages 109–16

Judith Butler, *Frames of War: When Is Life Grievable?* (New York: Verso, 2009), 76.

Jacques Rancière, "Who Is the Subject of the Rights of Man?," *South Atlantic Quarterly* 10, nos. 2/3 (2004): 297–310.

Carl Schmitt, *The Concept of the Political*, trans. George Schwab (Chicago: University of Chicago Press, 1996), 54.

CHAPTER TEN

Jacques Rancière, *Dissensus: On Politics and Aesthetics*, ed. and trans. Steve Corcoran (New York: Continuum, 2010), 40–1.

Bonnie Honig, "Three Models of Emergency Politics," *boundary 2* 41, no. 2 (2014): 48.

Ibid., 48.

Ibid., 49.

Ibid., 50.

Ibid., 55.

Ibid., 57.

Ibid.

Ibid., 65.

In part 1, I uncover this particular issue in Schmitt's thinking about the state of exception. The state of exception, as we have seen, is the mechanism through which Schmitt writes sovereignty into the law, but as the power to suspend it. The question for Schmitt, then, is not so much about whether it is the law or the sovereign that comes first, but the norm or the exception. Here, he unambiguously states that the exception has priority, at least when it comes to thinking sovereignty: one must look at the exception rather than the norm to understand sovereignty.

Bonnie Honig, *Democracy and the Foreigner* (Princeton, NJ: Princeton University Press, 2001).

Honig, "Three Models," 65.

Bonnie Honig, *Antigone, Interrupted* (Cambridge: Cambridge University Press, 2013).

Santiago Zabala, *Why Only Art Can Save Us* (New York: Columbia University Press, 2017), 2.

Ibid., 3.

Ibid.

Ibid.

Ibid., 5.

Ibid.

20 Ibid.

21 Ibid.

22 Ibid.

23 Ibid., 3.

24 Ibid.

25 Ibid., 16.

26 Ibid.

27 Ibid., 17.

28 Ibid.

29 Ibid.

30 Ibid.

31 Ibid., 18.

32 Ibid., 3.

33 Ibid.

34 Ibid.

35 Ibid., 136–8n16.

36 Ibid., 1.

37 Walter Benjamin, "Theses on the Philosophy of History," in Walter Benjamin, *Illuminations: Essays and Reflections*, ed. Hannah Arendt, trans. Harry Zohn (New York: Schocken, 1968), 257.

38 Zabala, *Why Only Art*, 1.

39 Ibid., 21.

40 Ibid., 114.

41 Ibid., 115.

42 Ibid., 117.

43 Ibid.

44 Ibid., 4.

45 Quentin Meillassoux, "Science Fiction and Extro-Science Fiction," trans. Robin MacKay, Florian Hecker, *Speculative Solution* [CD] (Falmouth, UK: Urbanomic, 2010), 60.

46 Ibid., 52.

47 See Graham Harman, *Weird Realism: Lovecraft and Philosophy* (Winchester: Zero Books, 2011).

48 Zabala, *Why Only Art*, 120.

49 Ibid., 121.

50 Ibid.

51 See Naomi Klein, *The Shock Doctrine: The Rise of Disaster Capitalism* (New York: Picador, 2007).

52 Zabala, *Why Only Art*, 123.

53 Ibid., 129. There is no footnote for the quotation.

Ibid., 128.

Rancière, *Dissensus*, 31.

Ibid., 30–1.

Ibid., 31.

Ibid.

Ibid.

Ibid.

Ibid.

Ibid.

Ibid.

Ibid.

Ibid., 30.

This understanding of anarchy is clear throughout Rancière's work, from his *The Ignorant Schoolmaster: Five Lessons in Intellectual Emancipation* (trans. Kirstin Ross [Stanford: Stanford University Press, 1990]) onwards. In the first chapter of that book, for example, Rancière develops a criticism of the "archè" of "explication." This is clear from the fact that he distinguishes the following two dimensions of explication: "On the one hand, [the explicator] decrees the absolute beginning" (6) – "archè" in the sense of "beginning." "On the other," he continues, the explicator "appoints himself to the task of lifting [the veil of ignorance that s/he has cast over everything that is to be learned]" (6–7). This is "archè" in the sense of "rule" – the master rules through appointing her-/himself this task. This is what Rancière later calls the "hierarchical" set-up of explication. Of course, by making the case for an ignorant schoolmaster, Rancière seeks to intervene in this. But how exactly? He proposes a kind of an-archy, but not in the loose sense of anarchy that gets rid of the master altogether – it's an an-archy that is "not ... without a master" (12), as he points out. This is the anarchy of an emancipatory teaching situation, of an equality and democracy of intelligences, freed from the hierarchy of archè – or rather, operative after a radical transformation in the logic of archè.

I discuss this issue in particular in chapter 8 of Arne De Boever, *Plastic Sovereignties: Agamben and the Politics of Aesthetics* (Edinburgh: Edinburgh University Press, 2016). I expand upon it in: Arne De Boever, *Against Aesthetic Exceptionalism* (Minneapolis: University of Minnesota Press, 2019).

Alain Badiou, *The Century*, trans. Alberto Toscano (London: Polity, 2007), 160.

188 Notes to pages 127–32

69 Philippe Lacoue-Labarthe, Jacques Rancière, Jean-François Lyotard, and Alain Badiou, "Liminaire sur l'ouvrage d'Alain Badiou 'L'être et l'évènement," *Le Cahier* (*Collège Internationale de Philosophie*) no. 8 (1989): 201–25, 227–45, 247–68.

70 Abraham Geil, "Writing, Repetition, Displacement: An Interview with Jacques Rancière," *Novel* 47, no. 2 (2014): 301–10.

71 Zabala, *Why Only Art*, 29.

72 In my view, Frédéric Neyrat's *Échapper à l'Horreur* suffers from a similar problem – in other words, it levels one kind of exceptionalism against another and thereby risks perpetuating the problems it addresses. See Frédéric Neyrat, *Échapper à l'Horreur: Court Traité des Interruptions Merveilleuses* (Paris: Lignes, 217).

73 See Stathis Gourgouris, "The Question Is: Society Defended against Whom? Or What?" May 2013, *New Philosopher*, https://www.new philosopher.com/articles/the-question-is-society-defended-against-whom-or-what-in-the-name-of-what.

74 Daniel Zamora, "Finding a 'Left Governmentality': Foucault's Last Decade" (unpublished manuscript, sent on by the author in personal correspondence).

CHAPTER ELEVEN

1 Chantal Mouffe, *The Democratic Paradox* (New York: Verso, 2009), 101.

2 Ibid.

3 Ibid.

4 Ibid.

5 In Chantal Mouffe, *Agonistics: Thinking the World Politically* (New York: Verso, 2013), 92. It is on the count of "ontology" that Mouffe's point of view may differ from Butler's, as I discuss later on. Certainly, her theory is different from Rancière's in this respect. He insists that he tries "to keep the conceptualization of exception, wrong or excess apart from any kind of ontology." See Jacques Rancière, "The Thinking of Dissensus," in *Reading Rancière*, ed. Paul Bowman and Richard Stamp (New York: Continuum, 2011), 11–12.

6 Mouffe, *Democratic Paradox*, 101.

7 Ibid., 102.

8 Ibid., 103.

9 Ibid., 107.

10 Chantal Mouffe, "Introduction," in *The Challenge of Carl Schmitt*, ed. Chantal Mouffe (New York: Verso, 1999), 2.

In fact, given Honig's own issues with the ethical as she lays them out at length – for example, in *Antigone, Interrupted* – Mouffe's charge seems rather off the mark in retrospect.

Mouffe, *Agonistics*, 86.

Ibid., 87.

Ibid.

Ibid.

Ibid., 88.

Ibid., 91.

Ibid.

Ibid.

Ibid., 100.

Ibid.

Ibid., 101.

Chantal Mouffe, "Institutions as Sites of Agonistic Intervention," in *Institutional Attitudes: Instituting Art in a Flat World*, ed. Pascal Gielen (Amsterdam: Valiz, 2013), 65.

Ibid., 65–6.

Ibid., 66.

Ibid.

Ibid.

Ibid., 68.

Ibid.

Ibid., 72.

Ibid., 71.

Anna Kornbluh, *Realizing Capital: Financial and Psychic Economies in Victorian Form* (New York: Fordham University Press, 2014).

Mouffe, "Institutions," 71.

Ibid.

Bonnie Honig, *Antigone, Interrupted* (Cambridge: Cambridge University Press, 2013), 2, 10, and elsewhere. Honig is not the only one to use this notion. See Circe Sturm, "Reflections on the Anthropology of Sovereignty and Settler Colonialism: Lessons from Native North America," *Cultural Anthropology* 32, no. 3 (2017): 344. Sturm mentions "counterhegemony" in this context as well, though without tracing the term back to Mouffe (345).

Ibid., 2.

Ibid.

Judith Butler, *Notes toward a Performative Theory of Assembly* (Cambridge: Harvard University Press, 2015), 155. Mouffe is referenced appreciatively in Butler, *Notes*, 4.

190 Notes to pages 137–42

39 Butler, *Notes*, 156.
40 Ibid., 160.
41 Ibid., 161.
42 Ibid.
43 Ibid.
44 Ibid., 162.
45 Ibid.
46 See Ibid., 135.
47 Panu Minkkinen, "Rancière and Schmitt: Sons of Ares?," in *Rancière and Law*, ed. Lerma López Mónica and Julen Etxabe (New York: Routledge, 2018), 129–48, 136.
48 The resonance with Schmitt – and this particular text of Schmitt's – should not surprise one too much given that, as Stathis Gourgouris points out, Schmitt's *Constitutional Theory* seems at first sight "an aberrant text" in Schmitt's oeuvre. But Gourgouris points out that, while Schmitt's impetus in the text is "a democratic constitutional theory," and quotes a passage from the text to illustrate Schmitt's criticism of a democracy that would take recourse to the "undemocratic transcendence" of God's will, Schmitt's theory of democracy remains a monarchic one in the sense that it thinks of the people as monarchic. The point applies as well to theories of popular sovereignty "that see the sovereign position as extra-dimensional (exceptional) to the polity." See Stathis Gourgouris, *The Perils of the One: Lessons in Secular Criticism* (Fordham: Fordham University Press, 2019), 215n9.
49 Butler, *Notes*, 163.
50 Ibid., 162.
51 Butler appears to have a "weak" concept of anarchy, perhaps inherited from Emmanuel Levinas, that refers only to the absence of rule rather than to the transformation of it that I discuss earlier.
52 Ibid., 165.
53 Ibid., 168, 172.
54 Judith Butler, *Frames of War: When Is Life Grievable?* (New York: Verso, 2009), 76.
55 Butler, *Notes*, 171.
56 Ibid., 172.
57 Ibid., 170, emphasis added.
58 Ibid., 162.
59 Ibid., 163.
60 Indeed, in her discussion of Benjamin's "Critique of Violence" essay in *Parting Ways*, Butler had already – via Derrida – considered the

Notes to pages 143–7

association of Benjamin's divine violence with "anti-parliamentarianism" in the context of a discussion of anarchy. See Judith Butler, *Parting Ways: Jewishness and the Critique of Zionism* (New York: Columbia University Press, 2012), 76 and 86.

Butler, *Notes*, 184.

Ibid.

Ida Danewid, "White Innocence in the Black Mediterranean: Hospitality and the Erasure of History," *Third World Quarterly* 38, no. 7 (2017): 1674–89.

Ibid., 1678.

Ibid., 1676.

Apart from all of this, there are two moments in the article where I think Danewid overstates her case. On page 1,679, she writes that "colonialism, genocide, and transatlantic slavery are ... [European modernity's] very essence." This is an overstatement, even in view of what the author is saying here, which is that modernity is just as much Enlightenment as it is slavery. In other words, colonialism et cetera are *part of* modernity's essence. But modernity's essence can hardly be reduced to it. Something similar happens on page 1,682, where the author writes, "it becomes possible to see how public mourning, liberal hospitality, and calls for multiculturalism ultimately function as continuations of the key premises of the populist, far-right, anti-immigrant, xenophobic, and racist political parties they supposedly seek to challenge." This does not allow for the multiple functions of, for example, public mourning. Of course one should acknowledge that it can function as a continuation of bad politics; but there is no *need* for this to be so, or for it to "ultimately" be so *in any determined way*. One can hardly say that all public mourning, liberal hospitality, and multiculturalism are ultimately on the far right. To do so would be misguided and unjust to the history of, for example, liberal politics, something that I too have been critical of in this book.

CHAPTER TWELVE

Wendy Brown, *Undoing the Demos: Neoliberalism's Stealth Revolution* (New York: Zone Books, 2015), 17.

Ibid.

Ibid.

Was there really a time when such a non-economic political sphere existed? Certainly it wasn't the era immediately before neoliberalism started, the period immediately after the Second World War when culture was thoroughly shot through with economics (see, for example, Annie McClanahan, "On Becoming Non-Economic: Human Capital Theory and Wendy Brown's *Undoing the Demos*," *Theory and Event* 20, no. 2 [2017]: 510–19). The phrase "heretofore noneconomic spheres and activities" appears twice in the chapter from Brown upon which I focus (Brown, *Undoing*, 17, 30).

5 Brown, *Undoing*, 18

6 Ibid., 35, 42.

7 Ibid., 39.

8 Bonnie Honig, *Public Things: Democracy in Disrepair* (New York: Fordham University Press, 2017), 16

9 Ibid., 17.

10 Ibid.

11 Ibid., 19.

12 Ibid.

13 Ibid.

14 Ibid., 20.

15 Ibid., 26.

16 Brown, *Undoing*, 146.

17 Ibid., 23.

18 Ibid., 27.

19 I point this out partly in view of Agamben's blindness to the situation of Indigenous peoples. See Scott Lauria Morgensen, "The Biopolitics of Settler Colonialism: Right Here, Right Now," *Settler Colonial Studies* 1, no. 1 (2011): 52–76, in particular 69–70.

20 Joan Cocks, *On Sovereignty and Other Political Delusions* (New York: Bloomsbury, 2014), 2.

21 Ibid., 10.

22 Ibid.

23 I see both this book and my *Plastic Sovereignties* as aligned on this count with recent work on "form" in literary studies. See Caroline Levine, *Forms: Whole, Rhythm, Hierarchy, Network* (Princeton, NJ: Princeton University Press, 2015); Anna Kornbluh, *The Order of Forms: Realism, Formalism, and Social Space* (Chicago: University of Chicago Press, 2019).

24 Cocks, *On Sovereignty*, 11.

25 Ibid., 2.

26 Ibid., 3.

27 Joanne Barker, "For Whom Sovereignty Matters," in *Sovereignty Matters: Locations of Contestation and Possibility in Indigenous Struggles for*

Notes to pages 152–5

Self-Determination, ed. Joanne Barker (Lincoln: University of Nebraska Press, 2005), 1.

Ibid., 18.

Elizabeth Povinelli, *The Cunning of Recognition: Indigenous Alterities and the Making of Australian Multiculturalism* (Durham, NC: Duke University Press, 2002).

On this, see my discussion of Hegel versus Bataille in Mbembe in part 2 of this book.

Glen Sean Coulthard, *Red Skin, White Masks: Rejecting the Colonial Politics of Recognition* (Minneapolis: University of Minnesota Press, 2014), 16.

Ibid., 3.

Ibid., emphasis in original.

Ibid., 15–16, emphasis in original.

See Adom Getachew, *Worldmaking after Empire: The Rise and Fall of Self-Determination* (Princeton, NJ: Princeton University Press, 2019), 54.

Coulthard, *Red Skin, White Masks*, 17.

Ibid., 46.

Dale Turner, *This Is Not a Peace Pipe: Towards a Critical Indigenous Philosophy* (Toronto: University of Toronto Press, 2006).

Audra Simpson, *Mohawk Interruptus: Political Life across the Borders of Settler States* (Durham, NC: Duke University Press, 2014), 11, emphasis in original.

Ibid., 21.

See Arne De Boever, *Plastic Sovereignties: Agamben and the Politics of Aesthetics* (Edinburgh: Edinburgh University Press, 2016).

Coulthard, *Red Skin, White Masks*, 157.

I distinguish several other such experimental sites in this book: the situation of black lives in the US, for example, or the Israel/Palestine conflict. Of course I do not mean to suggest that the role of sovereignty in these various situations is exactly the same. Amahl Bishara draws out the differences, for example, between the Native American and Palestinian performance of sovereignty. See Amahl Bishara, "Sovereignty and Popular Sovereignty for Palestinians and Beyond," *Cultural Anthropology* 32, no. 3 (2017): 349–58, in particular 350. Along similar lines, Bishara draws out the differences between Fanon's call for national liberation, which I make much of, and Butler's plea for popular sovereignty as well (353).

Joanne Barker, ed., *Critically Sovereign: Indigenous Gender, Sexuality, and Feminist Studies* (Durham, NC: Duke University Press, 2017), 8.

45 Coulthard, too, develops this angle in *Red Skin, White Masks*, 157ff.
46 Barker, *Critically Sovereign*, 12.
47 Ibid., 13.
48 Ibid., 14.
49 Ibid., 20.
50 Ibid.
51 Ibid., 24.
52 Ibid., 25.
53 Ibid., 26.

Index

absolute expenditure, 80, 81, 83, 86, 90

absolute power of negativity, 81

absolute violence, 82–3

Abu Ghraib prison, 58

accomplished realism, 121–2

Ackerman, Bruce, 138

aesthetic exceptionalism, 127, 128

aesthetics, 126

Afro-centrism, 89

Agamben, Giorgio: on aesthetics, 53; analysis of camp, 50–1, 53–4, 159; on anarchism, 57; on biopolitics, 80; blindness to race, 179n24, 192n19; civil war theory of, xx, 36, 92, 139, 141, 158; "The Coronavirus Philosopher," 50; on Covid-19 pandemic, 50, 63–4, 174n5, 177n24; critique of Badiou, 54–5; debate about form, 52; on destituent power, 35–6, 37; early work of, 56; on exception, 31, 32, 54–5; on "form-of-life," 52–3, 55, 57; Foucault's influence on, 37; *Homo Sacer,* 31, 32–3, 54, 55; idea of

dissolved multitude, 138; *The Idea of Prose,* 56; on institutions, 139; on law, 34, 43; *Means without End,* 53; political philosophy of, 29, 33–4, 52, 171n66; on radical politics, 4; reading of Hobbes, 29–32, 44–5; on reality *outside* of sovereignty, 45; *Stasis: Civil War as a Political Paradigm,* 169n31; on state of exception, 142–3; theory of sovereignty, xiii, 37–8, 45, 49–50, 51, 53, 69, 75, 90; *The Use of Bodies,* 55, 57

agonism, 5, 8, 132, 135

agonistic politics, 131–3

alternative sovereignties, 105

anarchism, 36–7, 57

anarchitecture, 70

anarchy, 124, 128–9, 142, 187n66, 190n51

anticolonial nationalism, 79

Apter, Emily, 94, 128; *Unexceptional Politics,* 62

Arbery, Ahmaud, 84

Arendt, Hannah, 3, 81, 95, 102, 108, 109

Index

art: exceptionalist theory of, 127–8; politics and, 56, 89, 128, 132–4; primary function of, 89; rescue into the emergency, 119–20; shock of, 122–3; social relations and, 133

Athanasiou, Athena, xv, 183n7

Auschwitz, 49, 50, 53, 58; comparison to city-state, 54; situation of black lives and, 76, 77, 178n10

authoritarian liberalism, 24, 26, 158

Azoulay, Ariella, 67, 69

Bacon, Francis, xv

Badiou, Alain, 32, 54, 127

balance of power between nation-states, 65

Baldwin, James, 179n14, 181n53

Ballard, J.G., xv

bare life: definition of, 33; dehumanization of, 60; management of the pandemic and, 55; negatively valued, 56; as object of sovereign power, 80; production of, 50; rendering to, 63; vs zoe, 57

Barker, Joanne, 152, 154, 156–7

barrier, 67, 69

Bataille, George, 78, 80–1, 83, 84, 86

Becker, Oskar, 87

Behrent, Michael, 22

being-towards-death, 111

Benjamin, Walter: on capital punishment, 40; conceptualization of history, 43–4, 123, 124; "Critique of Violence" essay, xxi, 29, 39, 41, 45, 53, 118, 119, 123, 190n60; on exceptionality, 43–4;

on forms of strike, 40; on police, 40; on proletarian general strike, 121, 123; on radical politics, 4, 158; Schmitt and, 29, 119; on sovereignty, 45; on state of exception, 44–5, 57, 61; study of violence, xx, 29, 39–41, 73, 141–2, 143, 191n60; "Theses on the Philosophy of History," 43, 45, 118

Berlant, Lauren, 66, 107; *Cruel Optimism*, 104

Biden, Joe, xiv

Bidet, Jacques, *Foucault with Marx*, 14, 17

Biebricher, Thomas, 24

biopolitical governmentality, 21, 58

biopolitical liberalism, xi, xiii, 5

biopolitics: negative and positive, xvi; sovereignty and, xi–xii, xvi, xvii, 26, 34, 80, 81

bios, 34, 55, 57; vs zoe, 33, 55

Bishara, Amahl, 193n43

black bodies: exclusion from sovereign body politic, 159; violence against, 75, 76, 84–5

BlacKkKlansman (film), 181n55

black life: paradigm of camp and, 76, 77, 178n10, 179n24; sovereign power and, 75, 78; state of exception of, 76

BlackLivesMatter movement, xvii, xviii, 6, 33, 79, 85, 90, 159

blackness, 85–7; otherness and, 89–90; para-ontological understanding of, 87–8

black-on-black violence, 77

Black Panther (film), 85

Black Panthers, xvii, 34, 79, 83, 90, 158

Index

Black studies, xx, 87–8, 159
Bland, Sandra, 84
Bodin, Jean, 51, 174n3
Bratton, Benjamin, xvii; *The Revenge of the Real*, xvi
breaking through walls, practice of, 69, 70, 73
Brexit, xiv, 74
Brouillette, Sarah, 100
Brown, Michael, 84
Brown, Wendy, 135, 159; analysis of sovereignty, xi, xviii, xx, 100, 101, 147, 149, 151; discussion of walls, 65–8, 70, 71, 95; on neoliberalism, 147–8; *Undoing the Demos*, 100, 147; *Walled States, Waning Sovereignty*, 65
Bundy, Ammon, 13
Butler, Judith, xv, 135, 140, 183n7; *Antigone's Claim*, 145; on civil war, 141–2; concept of anarchy, 190n51; critique of Benjamin, 190–1n60; discussion of "precarious life," 99; extraparliamentary theory of power of, 29, 142; *Frames of War*, 109, 139, 145; on freedoms, 137; on Guantánamo Bay camp, 58, 59–60; "Indefinite Detention," 58, 59–60; on institutions, 139; *Notes Toward a Performative Theory of Assembly*, 100, 136, 145; *Precarious Life*, xix, 95, 145; on sovereignty, xi, xviii, 59, 136–7, 139–42, 193n43; on vulnerability, 143, 144–6

Caldwell, Christopher, 52
camp, 63, 178n10, 179n24; as paradigm of modernity, 51, 76–7; as paradigm of sovereignty, 53, 61, 65, 159; as state of exception, 53–4. *See also* concentration camp
Canguilhem, Georges, 19
capital punishment, 40
care: *vs* control, 63–4; sovereign practice of, 53, 159
care and concern, notion of, 102, 103, 109
Castile, Philando, 84
Césaire, Aimé, 85–6, 90
Chamayou, Grégoire: on authoritarian liberalism, 24, 26; critique of sovereignty, 92–3, 94–5, 96, 99, 102, 159; on new political collectivity, 95; theory of the drone, xix, 92, 93–4
Chandler, Nahum, 87, 88
"chicken-and-egg" problem, 114
Christi, Renato, 23
citizenship, 33, 34
civil war, 30, 36, 37, 78, 141–2, 169n31
Clark, Stephon, 84
Clover, Joshua, xii
Coates, Ta-Nehisi: *Between the World and Me*, 75, 77; Black studies of, 75–6, 77, 84, 159; criticism of the "Dreamers," xx; on exceptionalist sovereignty, 79; on history of slavery, 77–8, 81; on life in Paris, 179n14
Cocks, Joan, 29, 90, 150–1
Cole, Teju, "A Reader's War," 91
colonialism, 80, 103–4, 153, 180n35, 191n66
concentration camp, 49, 50, 51–2, 81

Concept of the Political (Schmitt), 4, 9, 11, 131, 157, 158
constituent power, theory of, 35, 36–7
constitution: people and, 11–12, 138; possibility of suspension of, 38; sovereignty and, 12
Constitutional Theory (Schmitt), 11–13, 28, 138, 190n48
control: *vs* care, 63–4; sovereign practice of, 53, 64
Coogler, Ryan, 85
Cooper, Melinda, 17, 18, 24
Coulthard, Glen Sean, 152–3, 154, 155
counter-hegemonic struggle, 133, 135, 136, 156, 189n35
counter-sovereignty, 135–6
Covid-19 pandemic: as civil war situation, 158; ethical and political values during, 63; state's response to, 50, 53, 63–4, 174n5, 177n24
Crane, Stephen, xv
Crimp, Douglas, 113, 132
"critical" sovereignty, 157
Critique of Pure Reason (Kant), 41–2
"Critique of Violence" (Benjamin), xxi, 29, 39, 41, 45, 53, 118, 119, 123, 190n60

Danewid, Ida, 144–5, 191n66
Danto, Arthur, 124
Dardot, Christian, 23
Dean, Mitchell, 22
decolonization, 78–9, 82
Deleuze, Gilles, xx, 69, 72, 133, 175n27
Deleuze and Guattari's (D + G's) thinking about state and

sovereignty, 71, 72, 73, 74, 108, 175n27
democracy: anarchic nature of, 125; criticism of, 120, 171n66, 190n48; definition of, 125; institutions and, 134; neoliberalism and, 147; promiscuous nature of, 113; sovereignty and, 29, 36, 113, 158; theory of, 11–12, 124–5, 128; three moments of, 158
Derrida, Jacques, 61, 69; *Rogues: Two Essays on Reason*, 166n23
destituent power, 35–6, 37
Dick, Philip K., 59
"différance," 61
dissolved multitude, 30–1, 44, 138
disunited multitude, 30
divine violence, xxi, 29, 41, 73, 142, 143, 191n60
drones: military use of, 91–2; negative effects of, 91; in paradigm of sovereignty, xx, 91, 92, 93–6, 159
dronized sovereignty, 94–5, 96, 99
DuVernay, Ava, 178n10
Dyzenhaus, David, 12

Eghigian, Greg, 68
Elden, Stuart, *Foucault's Last Decade*, 19
emergency: greatest, 116–17, 126; philosophy of, 116–17; popular state of, 117; preparations to, 113; real, 64, 115, 116; studies of, 115–16; vulnerability and, 112, 115
emergency law, 173n17
enemy, 5, 8
Enlightenment, 41–2

Index

epimeleia eautou (cura sui), 173n19
Esposito, Roberto, xii
ethics, 132, 143, 149
Evers, Medgar, 84
exception: legal norm and creation of, 60–1; non-fascist politics of, 124; *vs* norm, 19–20; situations of, 32, 54–5; theory of, 38. *See also* state of exception
exceptionalist politics, 112, 136
exceptionality, 43–4
excrescence, 32, 54
extraparliamentary power, 13, 29, 142

Fanon, Frantz, xx, xxii, 153, 159; on absolute violence, 78, 82; background and education of, 82, 180n35; *Black Skin, White Masks*, 85, 152, 155; call for national liberation, 78, 79, 83, 85, 86, 193n43; on colonialism, 103, 180n35; on human subject, 89; influence of, 85; on notion of "Black," 85, 86; *The Wretched of the Earth*, 82, 90, 105
fascism, 51, 52, 53, 62
Floyd, George, 84
Fontaine, Jean de la, "The Wolf and the Lamb" fable, 6–7
food sovereignty, 149
form, 52, 61
"form-of-life," 52, 55, 57; *vs* life-of-form, 62
Foucault, Michel, xi, xx–xxi; analysis of Kant's *Critique of Pure Reason*, 42; *The Birth of Biopolitics*, 51; on "care of the self," 86; on dialectical materialism, 17; discussion of the state, 51; on governmentality, 58, 59; *The History of Sexuality*, 20–1, 103; influence of, 37; on (neo)liberalism, 20, 22, 107, 158, 173n19; Marx and, 17–18; reading of Hobbes, 16–17, 18, 154, 158, 169n31; Schmitt and, 3, 14–15, 18–19, 21, 26, 27; on sexuality, 21; "*Society Must Be Defended*," 16, 21; on sovereignty, 62, 103, 154, 158; theory of the political, 3; use of the term "colonialism," 80; on war, 21
Frank, Jason, 138
Fraser, Nancy, 22
French Revolution, legacy of, 35
friend/enemy conflict, 5, 6, 95, 108, 113, 122, 131
Fynsk, Christopher, 4

Garner, Eric, 84
Genet, Jean, 105
Geneva Convention, 59
Gentili, Dario, *The Age of Precarity*, 24
Getachew, Adom, 76, 77, 78–9, 153, 154
Gibson, Nigel, 181n50
Gilmore, Ruth Wilson, xii
Gilroy, Paul, 80, 179n24
Gourgouris, Stathis, 36, 128, 129, 190n48
governmentality, 58, 129. *See also* biopolitical governmentality
Gratton, Peter, 14; *State of Sovereignty*, 18
Gray, Freddie, 84
Guantánamo Bay camp, xix, 34, 58–9
Guattari, Félix, xx, 69, 72, 175n27

200 Index

Habermas, Jürgen, 132, 137
Han, Byung-Chul, xiii, 3, 164n15
Harcourt, Bernard, xii
Harman, Graham, 122
Hartman, Saidiya, 153
Harvey, David, 27
Hayek, Friedrich, 23
Hegel, G.W.F., 78, 80, 86, 93,
 152, 153
hegemonic formation, 156
Heidegger, Martin: anarchism of,
 128, 139; *Black Notebooks,* 118,
 119; on democracy, 120; on
 friend/enemy distinction, 122;
 influence of, 118, 121; on issue
 of framing, 116, 126; on
 problem of emergency, 116–17;
 on shock of art, 122–3
Heiner, Brady Thomas, "Foucault
 and the Black Panthers," 34
Heller-Roazen, Daniel, 50
hermeneutics, 120–1
history, conceptualization of, 43–4
Hobbes, Thomas: on civil war, 30,
 92, 169n31; critique of, 29–32;
 on differences between people,
 16; on dissolved multitude, 30;
 image of artificial man, 94;
 on kingdom of god, 31;
 Leviathan, 14, 29–30, 84; on
 people/body politic, 30; social
 contract theory, 15; on
 sovereignty, 14, 16–17, 51, 95,
 103, 106, 107; on state of nature,
 16; studies of, 29–30; view of
 war, 17–18
homo munitus, 68
homo sacer, 32–3
homo vulnerabilis, xv, xix, 108,
 111, 159–60

Honig, Bonnie, xviii, xix;
 critique of the state of exception,
 114–15, 128; *Democracy
 and the Foreigner,* 114; on
 democratic politics, 126;
 Emergency Politics, 113,
 148; on food sovereignty, 149;
 on institutions, 139; on
 neoliberalism, 149; on politics,
 132; *Public Things,* 100, 148;
 theory of sovereignty, 100, 101,
 102, 112–13, 135, 139, 143,
 148–51; on vulnerability, 115,
 148–9, 151
human being, 99, 109, 139–40;
 political notion of, 110; as *a
 subject,* 80
humanitarian intervention, 109–10
human rights, critique of, 108–10

inclusion, 32
incomplete death, 105–6
indefinite detention, xix
Indigenous politics, xix, 149,
 150, 151
Indigenous sovereignty:
 emergence of, 152–3, 154, 155,
 161; feminist view of, 156–7,
 159; futurism of, 157;
 neoliberalism and, 149; popular
 sovereignty and, 150; relation
 to sovereignty of nation-state,
 155–6
institutions: critique of, 134–5;
 as obstacle to democracy, 134;
 strategy of engagement with,
 133–5; vulnerability of, 101,
 139, 144–5
"inverse geometry" warfare, 68
invulnerability, phantasm of, 112

Index

Israeli Defense Forces (IDF):
military tactics, 104, 108,
175n27; urban warfare, 68,
70, 71
Israeli-Palestinian conflict, 105,
150, 152, 193n43
Israel Security Fence, 67

Jean, Botham, 84
Jones, Prince Carmen, 75–6, 77
Judy, R.A., 87

Kafka, Franz, "Before the Law,"
145
Kalyvas, Andreas, 158, 167n50;
reading of Schmitt, 11–13, 14,
28; theory of Democratic
Leviathan, 13
Kant, Immanuel, 73, 173n17;
Critique of Pure Reason,
41–2; on Enlightenment, 41–2;
on taxation, 42
Kauanui, J. Kēhaulani, 137
Khatibi, Abdelkebir, 88
King, Martin Luther, Jr, 84
King, Rodney, 84
king, the two bodies of the, 168n6
Klein, Naomi, 25, 101, 123, 135
Kochavi, Aviv, 68, 69
Kornbluh, Anna, 135

Latour, Bruno, 62
Laval, Pierre, 23
law: sovereignty and, 49–50;
suspensions of, 10–11, 49–50
law-preserving force *vs* law-making
force, 40
Lee, Spike, 181n55
Lefort, Claude, 26, 171n66
left liberalism, 143

legal violence, 39, 40, 41
Leviathan (Hobbes), 14, 15–16,
30, 84
Levinas, Emmanuel, 190n51
liberalism: "counter-history" of, 5;
critique of, 3, 7; evolution of,
136; sovereignty and, 132.
See also neoliberalism
Libeskind, Daniel, 69; *City Edge*
project, 67
life, forms of, 55–6
life-of-form *vs* "form-of-life," 62
Locke, John, 10
Lordon, Frédéric, 35
Lorey, Isabell, 99, 100, 106–7, 108,
144; *State of Insecurity*, xix, 106
Losurdo, Domenico, 5, 153, 157
Louis, Edouard, xii–xiii
Lyotard, Jean-François, 127

maiming, politics of, 104–5,
106, 160
Malabou, Catherine, 61
Malcolm X, 84, 181n53
Malheur National Wildlife Refuge,
occupation of, 13
maritime space, 72
Marriott, David, 78
Martin, Trayvon, 84
Marx, Karl, 17–18, 150
Matta-Clark, Gordon, 70
Mbembe, Achille: on biopolitics,
80; on blackness, 85–7; on
clouding, 89–90; *Critique of
Black Reason*, xxi, 78, 82, 85;
on economy of slavery and
colonialism, 81; on exceptionalist
sovereignty, 79; on human
subject, 89; on necropolitics, 76,
78, 79–80, 104; negotiation of

Hegel and Bataille, 81; on neoliberalism, 86; on politics of art, 89; reading of Fanon, 83, 85–6, 89; on sovereignty, 81, 88, 159

McAtee, David, 84

McCann, Anthony, 167n64; *Shadowlands*, 13

McCarthy, Paul, xv

McClanahan, Annie, 100

McDade, Tony, 84

McDonald, Laquan, 84

Meillassoux, Quentin, 121–2

messianism, 44

Minkkinen, Panu, 138

miracles, 25–6

Mirowski, Philip, 23, 24, 100

modernity, 191n66

monism, xii

Morris, Erroll, 58

Moten, Fred, 87–8

Mouffe, Chantal, 4, 142, 154; on art and politics, 132–4; *The Challenge of Carl Schmitt*, 7, 130–1, 132; on critical practices, 133; *The Democratic Paradox*, 132; on ethics, 132; on exceptionalism, 136; on hegemony and counter-hegemony, xix, 135, 136, 137, 189n35; on institutions, 134–5; language of, 140; on liberalism, xx, 143; polemic with Schmitt, 139; on politics, 131–2; on states, 135

mythical violence, 41

Nancy, Jean-Luc, 4

national liberation, 78, 79, 83–4, 86, 193n43

necropolitics, 76, 78, 79–80, 81, 104

negotiation between inside and outside, 142

Nelson, Kadir, 84, 159, 181n53

neoliberal economic imperialism, 24

neoliberalism: as anarchitectural force, 70; authoritarianism and, 27; critique of, 147–8, 158; definition of, 86–7; *vs* fascism, 22, 23; as governmentalization of the state, 24; impact on democracy, 147; as instrument of violence, 24; key feature of, 24; sovereignty and, 26, 100; state of exception and, 25; studies of, 22–3

new political collectivity, 95

9/11 terrorist attack, 3, 5

nomadology, 71, 73

nomad space, 72

nomos, 50, 71–2

non-sovereignty, 78, 87–8, 90, 108, 144, 183n7

norm, 32; *vs* exception, 19–20

Obama, Barack, 91

OccupyMovement, xviii

Ojakangas, Mika, 14, 18

ontological disablement, 106

ontological vulnerability, xix, 99, 100, 160

Ophir, Adi, 67, 69

pandemic "fascism," 51–2

paradox of politics, 114

para-ontological, notion of, 87, 88

Parks, Rosa, 84

peace, concept of, 56

Philcox, Richard, 83

plantation, as paradigm of modernity, 76–7

Index 203

plasticity, theory of, 61
Plato, 120, 127; *Laws,* 125
poetry, 56
Polanyi, Karl, *The Great Transformation,* 23
police, 40, 75–6, 159, 179n12
political, the: concept of, xii, 5, 23, 95, 108, 131, 158; *vs* liberalism, 6; *vs* politics, 4, 5; as state of nature, 7; territory of, 4–5; transcendent modes of, 62
political formalism, 52–3, 62
political freedom, 108
Political Theology: Four Chapters on the Concept of Sovereignty (Schmitt), 9
political vulnerabilization, xix, 93, 102, 160
politics: art and, 56, 89, 128, 132–4; counter-hegemonic, 135; definition of, 131; ethics and, 132, 143, 149; freedoms and, 137; as matter of life and death, xii, xiii; *vs* the political, 4, 5; revitalization of, xiv; Schmitt's theory of, 27; as war, xii
politics of horizontalism, xvii–xviii
politics of recognition, 152, 153
politics of the "greatest emergency," 115, 120
popular sovereignty, 135, 136–7; civil war and, 141–2; *vs* electoral power, 138; enactments of, 140–1; feminist view on, 159–60; *vs* state sovereignty, 140, 141, 142, 143–4, 151, 190n48; studies of, xx, 139; untranslatable element of, 137–8; in the US, 183n14
Post, Louis Freeland, 113, 114

post-traumatic stress disorder (PTSD), 91
power formations, 133
power of absolute negativity, 81
practical sovereignty, 104, 105
precarization, 106–7, 108
presentation/representation, 54, 55
primitive war, 16
progress, 44
protest, 165n23
Prozorov, Sergei, 171n66
Puar, Jasbir, 103, 104, 105, 160
public enemy, 5

Quinlan, Karen, 34

Rancière, Jacques: on anarchy, 187n66; comparison to Schmitt, 126; critique of human rights, 109; on democracy, 124–6; on development of new humanism, 149; on institutions, 139; notion of the human, 110; "Ten Theses on Politics," 124
Rawls, John, 132, 137
reality, logic of sovereignty and, 45, 56
remains of Being, 116–17
Rice, Tamir, 84
right-wing politics, 74
Robbins, Bruce, 101
Rousseau, Jean-Jacques, 113
Rumsfeld, Donald, 58

Said, Edward, 105
Salvini, Matteo, 52
Sanders, Bernie, xiv
Santner, Eric, 33
Scahill, Jeremy, 91

Scarry, Elaine, 132, 136; *Thinking in an Emergency*, 113
Scheuerman, William, 23
Schiavo, Terri, 33
Schmitt, Carl: affiliation with Nazism, 3; concept of the political, 4–5, 7, 9, 11, 95, 108, 130, 131, 157, 158; conservatism of, 4, 28; on constituent power, 37; *Constitutional Theory*, 11–13, 28, 138, 190n48; *The Crisis of Parliamentary Democracy*, 164n15; critique of, 12; on democracy, 12, 190n48; on distinction between outside and inside, 31–2; on emergency situation, 113; on evocation of "the planet," 110–11; Foucault and, 14–15, 18–19; on friend/enemy conflict, 5, 95; on humans, 110, 111; influence of, 3–4, 11; on liberalism, 3, 7, 13, 20, 24–5, 26; *The Nomos of the Earth*, 4, 71, 72; on parliamentary democracy, 164n15; on people's relation to constitution, 11–12; *Political Theology*, 9, 11, 12, 28, 43, 118, 121, 131; on political universe, 6; reading of Hobbes, 31; on state of exception, 9–10, 43, 57, 142, 185n10; theory of sovereignty, xix, 9, 10, 12, 25, 27, 58, 69, 95–6, 113, 118; theory of the norm and the exception, 19–20, 38; *Theory of the Partisan*, 164n15; use of the term enemy, 7–8; view of space, xx, 72; on war, 6, 8, 110
Scott, James C., xvii

Scott, Walter, 84
self-transformation, 86
Selma to Montgomery March, 84
shock, 25, 125–6
Sibertin-Blanc, Guillaume, xx, 71, 72, 73, 74, 95–6; *State and Politics: Deleuze and Guattari on Marx*, 71
Simone, AbouMaliq, 179n17
Simpson, Audra, *Mohawk Interruptus*, 154
singularity, 32, 54
slavery, 76, 77–8, 81, 191n66
"slow death", notion of, 104–5
Smith, Rachel Greenwald, xx
Smith, William Gardner, 179n14
Smith, Yvette, 84
smooth space, xx, 71, 72–3, 74, 108, 175n27
social contract theory, 15
society of sovereignty, 3
sovereign: definition of, 37; in relation to people, 92, 93
sovereign of itself, xiii
sovereign power, xix, 10, 51
sovereign refusal, 154
sovereignty: as anachronism, 159; of autonomous regions, xiv; biopolitics and, xi–xii, xv, xvi, xvii, 3, 20–1, 26, 80; black life and, 78; comparative study of, 193n43; constitution-making capacity of, 12; contemporary return to, xvi, xviii, 59, 79, 155, 157–8; contingency of, 154–5; criticism of, 29, 89, 100; decline of, 58, 151–2; definition of, 9, 66, 103, 118, 152, 153, 155; democracy and, 28–9, 36, 158; establishment of, 65–6;

Index

exceptionalist dimension of, 26, 49, 56–7; extraparliamentary, 13; feminist approach to, 156–7; French Revolution and, 26; future of, 150–1, 157, 160; governance as alternative to, xvi; as guarantor of law, 58; legitimate and illegitimate uses of, 101; liberalism and, 132; models of, 16–17, 62, 154; of the monarch, xviii, 151; neoliberalism and, 100; paradigms of, 159; paradox of, 49–50, 90; phantasm of, 104; plasticity of, 62, 155, 161; *vs* poetry and art, 56; as political self-determination, 137; politics of, xviii, xxii, 53, 149, 159; postmodern deconstruction of, 69; scholarship on, xii–xxii, 49, 152; state of exception and, 9–11, 33–4, 185n10; technicized realization of, 93–4; tension in, 92, 93; theories of, xviii, xx, 164n15; in unexceptional collective action, 129; as violation of all prohibitions, 81; vulnerability and, xv, xxi, 95, 96, 99, 102–3, 106, 108, 112, 143–4, 148, 160; war and protection of, 92–4. *See also* Indigenous sovereignty; popular sovereignty

sovereignty by acquisition, 17

sovereignty by institution, 16

sovereign violence, xiv, 41, 42–3, 157

space. *See* smooth space; striated space

spectral sovereignty, 59

speculative realism, 122

Stanley-Jones, Aiyana, 84

state, forms of, 51–2

state of exception: anarchy as, 142; as bare life, 33; biopolitical dimension of, 26; critique of, 114–15; "messianic" form of, 57; neoliberalism and, 25; notion of "good," 61; sovereignty and, 9–11, 33–4, 185n10; state of nature and, 50; suspension of law in, 10; in theology, 25; theory of, 56–7, 185n10; vulnerability of human life in, 112

state of nature, 7, 16, 50

state sovereignty, 66, 144

Sterling, Alton, 84

stories of uncertain reality, 122

striated space, xx, 71, 72

striation, notion of, 108

strike, forms of, 40

Sturm, Circe, 189n35

subject formation, 86

suicidal civil war, 110–11

suspended political solutions, 67

swarming, 68–9

Taylor, Breonna, 84

Taylor, Chris, 76, 77

Taylor, Mark C., 67, 127

Thousand Plateaus, A (Deleuze and Guattari), 73

Till, Emmett, 84

transcending sovereignty, 151

tribal sovereignty, 150

Trump, Donald J., xiv

Tschumi, Bernard, 69

Tulsa Race Massacre, 84

Turner, Dale, *This Is Not a Peace Pipe,* 154

206 Index

unexceptional sovereignty, 62, 160
United States: repoliticization in, xiv; sovereignty of, 95
universalism of the human, 6
US/Mexico Border Barrier, 67–8

Vardoulakis, Dimitris, 28, 35, 36, 158
Vattimo, Gianni, 121, 124
violence: absolute, 78; against black bodies, 84–5; black-on-black, 77; constructive context of, 83; counter-, 82; legitimate and illegitimate forms of, 39–40; national liberation and, 79, 83–4; usefulness of, 82. *See also* divine violence
"vogelfrei," notion of, 75
vulnerability: discourse of, 144, 145; emergency and, 115; as precarity, 143; privilege and distribution of, 160; scholarship on, xviii, xxi; of the self, 145; sovereignty and, xv, xvii, 103, 106, 108, 112, 148–9, 160; of Western liberal institutions, 139, 144
vulnerable power, 144

walls: in architecture, 70–1; comfort of, 73; destruction of, 68–70, 71, 175n27; paradoxical dimensions of, 65, 66–8; sovereignty and, xix–xx, 65, 66–7, 73–4; space and, 71; as suspended solution, 67
war: as analyzer of sexual and racial relations, 21; asymmetrical,

73; in the name of humanity, 110; possibility of, 6; protection of sovereignty in, 92–4
Weber, Samuel, 103, 106
Weheliye, Alexander, 80
Weizman, Eyal, 108, 159, 175n27; discussion of walls, 67, 68, 69, 70–1, 73, 74
welfare state, 51, 52, 62
Western power, transition of mode of, 20–1
Westphalia peace treaty, 65–6
Wetters, Kirk, 19
"whatever being," notion of, 56–7
Why Only Art Can Save Us (Zabala), 115, 118, 127
Winnicott, Donald, 102, 109, 148
"Wolf and the Lamb, The," as political fable, 6–7
worldmaking, 79
Wright, Richard, 179n14
"wu" ("nothing"), 87–8

Young, Robert, 180n35

Zabala, Santiago: on accomplished realism, 121–2; "Afterword," 124; Heidegger's influence of, 121; on hermeneutics, 120–1; on popular sovereignty, 139; relation to Benjamin, 118–19; on shock, 123; study of emergencies, 115–19; theory of art, 119, 127–8; *Why Only Art Can Save Us*, 115, 118, 127
Zamora, Daniel, 14, 21, 129
zoe: *vs* bios, 33, 55; as form of life, 55, 57